Sexing the City

In memory of my oma, Betty Wixon,
who first introduced me to municipal politics

Sexing the City

Lesbian and Gay Politics within the Activist State

Davina Cooper

Rivers Oram Press

London

First published in 1994 by
Rivers Oram Press
144 Hemingford Road, London N1 1DE

Published in the USA by
Paul and Company
Post Office Box 442, Concord, MA 01742

Set in 10½/12pt Garamond by EXCEPT*detail* Ltd, Southport
and printed in Great Britain
by T.J. Press (Padstow) Ltd, Padstow, Cornwall

Designed by Lesley Stewart

British Library Cataloguing in Publication Data
A catalogue record for this book is available from the British Library

ISBN 1-85489-056-5 (hb)
ISBN 1-85489-057-3 (pb)

Contents

List of Abbreviations

ALA	Association of London Authorities
CCT	Compulsory Competitive Tendering
CEO	Chief Education Officer
DES	Department of Education and Science
EOP	Equal Opportunity Policy
GLC	Greater London Council
HBA	Haringey Black Action
IAP	Inner Area Programme
ILEA	Inner London Education Authority
ISAs	Ideological State Apparatuses
LCLGR	Labour Campaign for Lesbian and Gay Rights
LGTG	London Gay Teenage Group
LGYM	Lesbian and Gay Youth Movement
MSC	Manpower Services Commission
NALGO	National Association of Local Government Officers
NEC	National Executive Committee
NUM	National Union of Mineworkers
PI	Positive Images Campaign
PRG	Parents Rights Group
PWA	People with AIDS
SWP	Socialist Workers Party

Acknowledgements

Sexing the City began life as an undergraduate project and grew into a doctoral thesis entitled 'Sexing the City: Lesbian and Gay Politics 1979–87', awarded by the University of Warwick in 1992. In the following five years in which it has been developed into this book, many people have helped and encouraged me.

Brian Webb, David Cocking, Jim Haywood, Sue Cunningham and Manchester council committee secretariat provided me with committee minutes, council reports and other useful documentation.

Lilly Brooks, Eric Liknaitzky and Graham Saggers repeatedly assisted me in the practical details of research. More generally, the doctoral funding provided by the Economic and Social Research Council enabled me to continue this project.

Haringey council, one of my case studies, afforded me excellent research facilities as well as the opportunity during my period as councillor to synthesise experience and theory. I would like to thank in particular Laura Wyles, Lynn Alderson, Rosie Chapman (who, as committee clerk to the Women's Committee, helpfully humoured my more idealistic suggestions) and the lesbian and gay unit (who soldiered on, despite the political flack, developing and trying out new initiatives).

In Appendix B, I have listed the people interviewed for this project. I am very grateful to them for their time, interest, ideas and experiences. This book could not have been written without their support. In this respect, I would also like to thank Maggie Turner of Manchester equal opportunities unit, the staff of Bristol women's unit, Lorraine Trenchard, Chris Baker of the Association of London Authorities and Tamsin Wilton.

Many other people have also assisted me through discussion and comments as this project has developed and taken shape. I would like to thank Brendan O'Leary and Patrick Dunleavy of the LSE, and Ann Stewart and Terry Lovell of Warwick University. Others who have helped me in thinking through a number of the issues include Susan Reinhold, Susan Halford and Mike Davis. In turning *Sexing the City* from a thesis into a published book, Jeffrey Weeks provided invaluable assistance in the latter stages of this project. I would also like to thank Liz Fidlon for her interest and encouragement and Linda Etchart also of Rivers Oram Press for her work on the manuscript.

I also wish to record my appreciation to Toni Williams and Mike Freeman who encouraged my early work in this area. More generally, I wish to thank UCL Law Faculty for their support and interest in my work as a councillor during the period of my studies there. Since 1991, I have lectured at Warwick University Law School. The practical support and encouragement I have received from colleagues and the department, most particularly Alan Norrie, Mike McConville, Linda Luckhaus and Bob Fine has been really valued.

Throughout this project and my term as a member of Haringey council, my parents, Kitty Cooper and Charles Cooper, have helped me in ways too numerous to mention, always being ready with a smile, a hug and auspicious advice on my nightly returns tired and frustrated from council and Party meetings.

Finally, I wish to thank my partner, Didi Herman. Invariably knowing the right moment for a break and a walk, she has been an immense source of encouragement, intellectual stimulation and practical assistance. Over the past four and a half years, I have benefited from her rigorous research standards, the opportunity to share our work, and her ability to make the impossible and unattainable manageable.

1

Sexual Politics and the Activist State:
An Introduction

> *The local state has replaced the political party within civil society as the agency of regeneration.*
> Beatrix Campbell, *Marxism Today*, February 1987

Can we use the state to bring about social change? What kinds of strategies may be required? What sorts of changes are possible? Where lie the limitations? Questions such as these have plagued the left for many decades, frequently polarising positions into pro-state, anti-state stances. Traditionally, working with or within the state has been described by many socialists and radicals as reformist, a process of containment that diffuses rather than achieves fundamental change. While many still hold this view, others have developed the ideas of Gramsci, neo-Marxism, feminism and post-structuralism to complicate both the nature of the state as well as the goals and strategies of progressive change.

This book analyses one such attempt to use state apparatus to achieve social transformation: the struggle for lesbian and gay equality—the re-formation of meanings ascribed to sexuality. Highly controversial and vociferously contested, lesbian and gay politics provides a valuable prism through which to explore the current potential and limitations of working with(in) the 'modern' state, as well as the possibilities of alternative strategies. However, this dichotomy of within/without the state also needs questioning. Unless we operate with a very narrow definition of the state, it seems unclear how we can act radically without engaging with it.

Familial relations, education, health care, the environment, all are arenas in which the state plays a part. Thus, a more valid question is *how* should we engage with the state, and to what extent can we do so differently to avoid some of the problems discussed in this book.

We also need to consider further what we mean by the state. A poststructuralist paradigm based on fragmentation and contradiction will generate very different strategic possibilities to a conceptual framework of the state as a coherent entity managed and governed by a ruling class. I return to this issue of the relationship between state theory and strategy in Chapter 10. The rest of this introduction sets out the empirical, theoretical and methodological framework for *Sexing the City*.

The Activist State

By the mid-1980s, 'loony left' had become the pejorative label for a number of urban, Labour controlled councils across Britain. These were councils embarking on a wide range of new initiatives: nuclear free zones, decentralisation, alternative economic strategies and equal opportunity policies (EOPs). Anti-discriminatory and equal opportunity initiatives, which subsequently became standard for much of the country's public and private sector, precipitated hostility, antagonism and panic. Peers, MPs, church leaders, right-wing pressure groups and the tabloid press mobilised against what they perceived as municipal lunacy. Yet, few policies created as much controversy as the strategies and initiatives developed by a handful of councils for lesbians and gay men.

Municipal lesbian and gay work emerged at the intersection of several different processes: the growing size and confidence of Britain's lesbian and gay communities; the institutionalisation of the new urban left; identity politics; and the developing influence of feminism within local politics. More particularly, the policies were precipitated by the work of lesbian and gay activists in the Labour Party, in local government employment, and as elected council members. Yet, although the period researched witnessed a number of authorities formally incorporating lesbians and gays within equal opportunity statements, few took their policies much further.

Among the handful that did, the councils best known for

developing lesbian and gay work—establishing committees and in some instances employing staff with a specialist brief—include the Greater London Council (GLC), Southampton, Manchester, and Nottingham city councils, and the London boroughs of Camden, Haringey, Islington and Lambeth.[1] Lesbian and gay policies were not exclusively a London phenomenon; yet, as this list demonstrates, London councils predominated for reasons linked to the size, nature and politics of the capital's lesbian and gay communities, and of its Labour Party branches, particularly in gentrified, inner city areas.

Sexing the City explores the evolution of lesbian and gay initiatives in British local government as well as the intense conflict their development generated. What I shall call the lesbian and gay municipal project is particularly interesting for a number of reasons. First, progressive local government initiatives in this area diverge from the traditional relationship between the state and homosexuality. Until the last decade, Western governments have tended to respond coercively (when at all) towards homosexuality, deploying criminal law sanctions, social policy, and ideological mechanisms to discourage homosexual behaviour and a lesbian or gay identity. The 1980s, in contrast, witnessed a shift, not just in Britain but also in Australia, Canada, northern Europe and parts of the USA. While heterosexuality is still clearly privileged in a multitude of subtle and more explicit ways, legal, municipal and central government initiatives have begun to challenge the sexual hierarchy. British local government policies reflected this new agenda with its emphasis on anti-discrimination, formal equality, rights, citizenship and multiculturalism.

Second, the development of lesbian and gay state initiatives raises *theoretical* questions about the relationship between sexuality and the state. How does the state engage with the sexual realm? To what extent do state struggles lead to a reshaping or reinterpretation of sexual identities and politics? To what extent is the state constituted by and through sexuality? This last question I discuss more fully elsewhere.[2] *Sexing the City* focuses on the first two. In particular, I explore the impact on lesbian and gay activism of entering state processes—the power of equal opportunities as practice and ideology; and the ways in which state policy development is bounded and limited by dominant sexual ideologies.

Third, municipal lesbian and gay policies—perceived as extreme and unusual—generate important general questions about the state, and, in particular, the progressive potential of local government. To what extent, for example, could the local state in the 1980s have *changed* social practices, meanings and institutional behaviour? What constraints were placed upon its work? From where did these emerge? And to what extent could they have been overcome? Implicit in these questions is the issue of inevitability: could it have happened differently? And what can we learn from the experiences of municipal lesbian and gay work in order to be more effective in the future? Without denying the possibility of other outcomes if developments had been different, I suggest in this book that certain political 'logics' were evident in what occurred. While these can be, and were, resisted, unless social and political circumstances radically alter, simply ignoring their processes will not bring the changes sought. This is a contentious point in an era of poststructuralist theorising. However, the experiences of a range of progressive state struggles not just in Britain but elsewhere too—for example, the emergence of Australian 'femocracy'[3]—suggest that the fate of lesbian and gay local policies in Britain was, unfortunately, not by any means unique.

Sexing the City focuses on the period 1979 to 1987—the key years of a modern, progressive, municipal sexual politics in Britain. The period also coincides with the first two terms of the Thatcher government, a key protagonist in the struggle over municipal radicalism. In the case of lesbian and gay policies, conflict culminated in the introduction of the Local Government Act 1988, S.28, which formally prohibited local authorities from promoting homosexuality. More generally, the period covered by these two terms in office represents a particular historical juncture within the trajectory of local government politics: one of idealism, resistance, vanguardism and brinkmanship.

Before going on to outline the theoretical framework of this work, I wish first to identify the ground it does not cover. Because of my focus on municipal activity, I do not discuss the broad range of lesbian and gay politics, for example, the campaigns for anti-discriminatory law reform, the intra-movement struggles over pornography and sado-masochism, and the community organising around AIDS. I also do not deal explicitly with lesbian and gay politics in rural areas. As I have suggested above, lesbian and gay local government initiatives occurred principally in London and other major cities. Thus this book deals with highly urbanised localities and my conclusions need to be read within that context. Yet, even within Britain's major cities, lesbian and gay policy development was very uneven, and largely absent in the sizeable conurbations of Leeds, Birmingham and Sheffield. Why a progressive sexual politics developed in some areas but not others is an interesting question that requires further research. Unfortunately, it is not one I have been able to explore here.

Conceptualising the Local State

Progressive analysis of local state behaviour has taken several forms. Readers familiar with the 'dual state thesis', Althusser's work on ISAs, and feminist post-structuralist state theory may wish to skip the following discussion; however, this brief overview of urban government theory may prove useful for readers new to this area.

In recent years, much local state theory has focused on the regulatory role of local government within late capitalism, examining such issues as the changing impact of central government policy and the nature of the post-fordist local state.[4] While economic theory and policy is relevant to any work on urban government, the primary focus of this book is the social, political and ideological.

Local government's relationship to these latter issues was explored by Saunders and others in the early 1980s. The 'dual state thesis' that emerged was an attempt to consider the ways in which local government differed from central government at an organisational, functional, political and ideological level.[5] Their thesis, now heavily criticised,[6] was that while the central state was primarily concerned with relations of production, local government's responsibility was to organise consumption, in particular collective consumption.

This emphasis was identified by several writers as arising out of the functional needs of capitalism—the imperative of reproducing a workforce.[7] Municipal provision therefore encompassed those personal, familial and social needs deemed by the private sector as uneconomic to provide. Such involvement by the local state in social or collective consumption had, according to several Marxist theorists, a number of serious political consequences. One was the diverting of people from realising and acting on their class identity. Instead, alternative rifts, segmentations (and presumably alliances) emerged as people fought over the allocation and form of state-provided goods and services. While some, such as Magnusson, have seen this as creating new radical fissures;[8] others consider 'consumer' identities as politically inferior to those arising from relations of production.

Yet the diversion from production to consumption is not the only way in which local government has been seen as exerting a deradicalising effect. Another is its co-option of oppressed communities. Miliband, for example, discusses how the opportunities provided for working-class people to become councillors encouraged them to identify with status quo interests, while, at the same time, legitimising local government and, thereby, the state as a whole.[9]

Yet, local government's 'contribution' to the credibility and stability of the national political system combined with its own political requirements has frequently forced it into a balancing act, trying to respond to different interests in order to win their support, yet not going so far that opposition from other more powerful groupings would be precipitated.

From the late 1970s onwards, Marxist state and local government analysis was developed by socialist feminists to encompass gender issues and a critique of patriarchy.[10] Marxist and socialist feminists argued that the state, and, in particular, local government's role, extended beyond the reproduction of a labour force to the reproduction of social relations more generally. Through the exercise of coercion, provision and ideology, dominant gender, class, sexual and racial relations were maintained. Heterosexuality, for example, was affirmed and reproduced through traditional local government policies in the area of adoption and fostering, sex education curricula, library selections and leisure activities.

At the same time, public, collective provision could provide a site of useful struggle. While welfare had disempowering elements for women, within certain contexts it could be empowering, bringing women together as service users/consumers and as producers. This emphasis on contradictory and uncertain effects has been further developed within poststructuralism. Since the state is seen (when at all) as a series of fragmented terrains within which different forces struggle, outcomes cannot be predicted. Moreover, since the state has no functional attributes, and is not controlled by a single class or structuring principle, limits to state possibility can not be conclusively anticipated. Anything is possible. It depends on the condensation of social forces at a given juncture.

While poststructuralist state theory is useful in emphasising the contingency of outcomes, the non-unitary nature of the state, and the plurality of social interests, it falls down in several ways. First, many versions lack specificity. The state is treated as a terrain of struggle without much thought being given as to how the state differs from other such terrains. Second, by downplaying cultural, economic and other 'determining' factors, poststructuralist state theory often underestimates the difficulty of achieving change compared with the relative ease of reproducing (more or less) status quo power relations. Third, the linkages between state bodies are often neglected. While these connections may be contested by state actors, as I discuss in this book, the influence that central government, for instance, exerts over local government can be substantial, as the 1980s demonstrated, and cannot be properly understood without a clear understanding of the nature of their intra-state relationship.

In *Sexing the City*, I use the prism of lesbian and gay urban politics to refract these different theoretical approaches. How can we understand the emergence of policies which appear so at odds with local government's apparent hegemonic role? Do they illustrate the local state's relative autonomy—its ability within boundaries to do as it pleases; the temporary success of oppositional social forces; the appeasement of a newly emergent social force to maintain local government's legitimacy and stability, or simply the struggle of political forces within the public sphere? To what extent does the outcome of urban sexual initiatives provide evidence for a closed or, alternatively, more open textured, postmodern reading of local government's potential?

Ideology

Lesbian and gay municipal politics incorporated a range of different, and at times competing, objectives. While discussing initiatives generally, the focus of this book is on the attempt to transform attitudes, to radically reshape the social meanings by which sexuality, and, in particular, homosexuality was understood. Ideology is therefore key. This brief discussion condenses a much longer exploration in Chapter 8.

By ideology, I refer to the various frameworks of meanings which justify, legitimise, promote and emerge out of particular networks of social relations. Since my analysis does not privilege any one social dynamic, such as, class or gender, as paramount, ideologies do not have any necessary unitary class belonging. There is no single ideology for the oppressors and another for the oppressed. Relations of power are complex, and the articulations of meaning that reflect and constitute them are equally intricate and contradictory. However, I would argue that dominant ideologies do exist, that is ideologies which are both generally accepted and which justify or promote existing unequal relations. Similarly, there are oppositional ideologies which construct new forms of common sense, justify different choices, promote pre-figurative values, and contest or deconstruct features of the status quo. In defining ideology as frameworks of meaning, it loses the pejorative connotations given to it by Marxism. Ideology is not in opposition to truth or science. It is not false consciousness or a distortion of the real; thus it plays, in many ways, the role given by foucauldians to discourse.

Two other points need to be made about ideology at this stage. First, I consider ideology to be both determined and determining. On the one hand, it is shaped by other aspects of society, and hence changes in response to a variety of social processes. For example, the increasing number of children born to lesbians through alternative insemination is likely to alter procreative and repro-ductive meanings, although the apparently oppositional nature of such a process means ideological change will probably be slow and intensely contested. At the same time, ideology can be trans-formed from within its own terrain, and such altered meanings will, in turn, affect other social relations and practices. This can be seen in the increasing readiness of state bodies to improve their provision and treatment of lesbians and gays as a result of changing attitudes towards homosexuality.

Ideology is both constituted and communicated through specific systems of meanings, the most obvious being linguistic, although most aspects of social relations and practices are involved. In this work I use 'texts' to refer to the *form* within which ideologies are being conveyed—the written, aural or visual substance, event or activity being analysed. I use 'discourse' to identify the *means* through which ideologies are experienced or read—that is the disciplinary or institutional framework—the 'grammar' by which meaning is constructed. To take an example, in analysing a meeting, the event itself becomes the text—the 'thing' to be analysed, while discourses are found in the *relationship* between the language, imagery and actions deployed within the text and particular categories of meaning. Ideology, in contrast, represents at the level of the 'imaginary', the relationship between articulations of meaning and relations of power.

I have said that one of the purposes of this book is to explore local government's ability to convey oppositional sexual meanings. To what extent, then, can local government be compared with more conventional mass communicators, such as television and the press? Does it hold its own, producing texts that are influential, widely disseminated, and which possess sufficient closure to limit readings 'against the grain', that is, opposing interpretations? Does this depend on the particular ideologies and meanings being conveyed? Is local government, for instance, currently more able to convey liberal-pluralist norms than radical interpretations or ideas?

Sexing the City draws on textual analysis to reveal the play of meaning within documentation and symbolic actions, and to draw attention to interpretive diversity, particularly between constructors and recipients of texts. Nevertheless, textual analysis can also cause difficulties. I want to make some points about this here since it has become recently a highly popular methodology within the social sciences. Traditionally used to deconstruct and examine the meaning within books, plays, films and television programmes, textual analysis is a method that works best when the phenomenon under consideration is a discrete, definable entity.

This is a controversial point. Drawing on the work of Barthes and others, a number of cultural theorists have argued that *no* mass media texts can be treated as discrete or separate works.[11] Their meaning can only be known or constructed through a process of intertextuality which recognises the interdependency of meaning between one text and another. While I fully accept that meaning does not originate, nor can be found within, a single play or book but rather depends on the context—the articulation of signifiers and signifieds with parallel elements in other works—at the same time, novels, plays, films and television programmes are easier to handle as texts than the much more diffused nature of political struggle or the policy-making process.

Council policies are fluid and ever changing. They lack consensual definition not only as to what they *mean*, but also as to what they are, that is the decisional elements they include and exclude. Local government policy-making is the result of ongoing interaction and feedback. There is rarely a finished product, despite the fact artificial boundaries can be placed on the process to delineate a particular, analysable time frame. Arguably, this is also true for plays or films, where reviews, serials and 'readers'' comments dissolve the notion of a static, unified text. However, there still tends to be a central text—or what Barthes and Ferguson describe as a work—that can be distinguished from the broader play of meaning or 'textuality'. In using textual analysis to deconstruct local government policy-making, there is a risk of losing the fluidity, struggle and interaction that comprise local government activity, fetishising instead particular moments. Freezing the operation of policy may be useful as a means of analysing what is happening, but it needs to be remembered that the process is a tactical one.

Problems also arise in analysing discursive struggles as if competing 'sides' are simply producers and consumers of 'texts'. Forces on the right and left do not wait at their collective home bases for their opponents' missives whiling away the time producing their own. Conflict is less organised, less conscious and less contained. In addition, while it is possible to use textual analysis to interpret more amorphous texts, such as demonstrations and grass-roots political activity, and indeed this is something I attempt to do, there is a danger that emphasis on discourse and meaning can marginalise the more material[12] side of the dialectic.

Sexual Politics

The third theoretical area of this book—sexual politics—is a topic generally omitted from left-wing state theory. Similarly, with one or two exceptions, such as *Councils in Conflict*, recent works on the new urban left and progressive government (local, regional and central) have also ignored initiatives in the area of sexuality. Since sexual politics is central to this project, let me briefly set out what I mean by it as well as my own approach to issues of sexual orientation.

The term sexual politics has been used in a number of ways, often as broadly coterminous with gender relations. I give it here a narrower, more specific construction to indicate the articulation of gender relations with sexuality. My focus is therefore on the political nature of sexuality, in particular, how gendered relations of power are both played out and partially constituted within its terrain.

The relationship between gender and sexuality is also mediated through other social dynamics—race, class and residency among others. Condensed, these relations of power will shape the particular conjunction of gender and sexuality. My starting point is that there is no necessary connection between biological sex, gender and sexuality. How these are in fact articulated together is a matter of cultural practice.

At the same time, *Sexing the City* takes issue with current writing which treats sexual orientation as a discrete and separate social relationship from that of gender. Current usage of the term 'heterosexism', for example, also seems to imply a distinct oppression on the basis of sexual orientation. This, I feel, is misleading. Homosexuality and heterosexuality are grounded in notions of gender and can have little meaning outside of them. Their construction and existence depend on the kinds of relations operating between men and women and on the ways in which masculinity and femininity are understood.

Linked to this tension over the relationship between sexual orientation and gender are tensions over the meaning of homosexuality and heterosexuality. Modern theorists, developing the work of Foucault, have argued that the 'homosexual' emanated from the late nineteenth century. Prior to that period, it is claimed, people were not defined by their sexual orientation, and labels such as homosexuality referred instead to specific sexual practices. While this analysis is important in affirming the social as opposed to the biological nature of sexual orientation and in stressing the importance of historical specificity, at the same time, it privileges a definition of homosexuality grounded in the modern gay men's movement. Consequently, it ignores or marginalises other inter-pretations of homosexuality and particularly of lesbianism, which deploy the term differently, for example, to refer to political, emotional and cultural solidarity or connections between women.[13]

Yet lesbian feminist definitions that marginalise the signifi-cance of self-identity or sex have been severely criticised by other lesbian writers.[14] Many of the radical feminists most closely identified with this trajectory treated sex as a minor or even irrelevant aspect of lesbianism, a practice of female resistance which emerged as a complex response to gender inequality within patriarchal society. Thus women could be defined as lesbians within different cultures and historical eras who would never have chosen the term for themselves, and quite possibly did not engage in sexual relations with other women.

Yet despite competing definitions of homosexuality within lesbian and gay politics over the past two decades, such contest-ations interestingly, did not feature as a characteristic of municipal sexual politics. Rather, the homosexual definition was deemed unproblematic. Municipal actors, focusing on identity rather than internal community politics or sexual practices, argued that 'people were what they were' and 'needed to be allowed to speak the truth about themselves'. Within this broad consensus the approach and perspective of different actors not surprisingly varied. Nevertheless, the emphasis on identity and minority group status led to an approach that prioritised multiculturalism and essentialism. This was played out most explicitly in the arguments over the Local Government Act 1988, S.28, when opponents of the government's legislative agenda argued that homosexuality neither could nor should be promoted.

In contrast, dominant right-wing perspectives on lesbian and gay municipal policies started from the claim that sexuality was not biologically determined but fluid and adaptable. Paradoxically, their argument has, in some ways, more in common with a radical sexual politics than have liberal arguments of immutability and essential sexual orientations. According to the right in the 1980s, homosexuality *was* promotable; moreover, it was actually being promoted by local authorities 'in the name of social revolution'.

The Main Argument

Sexing the City addresses a number of different issues. However, the key problematic concerns the ideological parameters of lesbian and gay work. My claim is that, for various reasons discussed later on, more radical approaches were organised out. Moreover, even the liberal pluralism that prevailed as a result of the policy-making process failed to be adequately implemented. Attempts actually to operationalise lesbian and gay initiatives faced a crisis of extraordinary magnitude.

Yet this internal, bureaucratic process of containment, while powerful, was not totalising. On several occasions it broke down or else functioned less than effectively. In such instances, when more progressive policies were publicly able to surface, however transiently, external forces intervened, led by the right, but drawing in a myriad of different organisations, groupings and individuals. Explicit conflicts therefore tended only to take place when other, more subtle mechanisms failed to work. This is an important point. Many commentators on 1980s municipal radicalism have focused on central government as the primary obstacle to local state activism. However, while government policy was influential in impacting upon the decision-making processes of local government, its more explicit forms of intervention did not prove the key impediment to a local, radical politics.

Yet why was the mobilisation against municipal lesbian and gay policies when it did occur so intense? Why did more progressive municipal approaches to sexual politics seem so inappropriate to many people? Answering these questions requires an analysis of the relationship between local government, sexual politics and ideology (see Chapter 8). Briefly, my argument is that within the dominant ideology of the 1980s, local government was discursively constructed as a provider of services. Although councils possessed some flexibility in organising their affairs, at the same time quite definite boundaries appeared to exist. While reproducing status quo views and attitudes was not deemed political, going beyond this to articulate alternative, 'counter-intuitive' forms of knowledge, or explicitly to advocate that local government contest and transform social meanings and beliefs was perceived as transgressing local government's proper role and remit.

In this book I argue that such attitudes were so deeply engrained even among progressive people that few attempted to deploy municipal apparatuses to voice views judged illegitimate. Nevertheless, when this was perceived to happen, as in the case of Haringey council's policy of 'positive images', it aroused a level of opposition not witnessed in the case of community, grass-roots campaigns advancing comparable proposals and arguments. In Chapter 8, I discuss this difference. As a result of it, local authorities such as Haringey lost some legitimacy as authoritative, hegemonic state organs. Instead they were treated by opponents as pressure groups within civil society—ironic, since if they had been, they would not have encountered the same intense, hostile response. Yet such a partial loss of legitimacy was a temporary one. With the overall balance of power within the state substantially unchanged, it did not take long for the status quo to be re-established.

Yet, even within this transient, oppositional period, the degree of success councils achieved in effectively conveying progressive meanings was limited. For they were competing against other, arguably more convincing and forceful, communicators, such as central government and the tabloid press. However, despite such limitations, as I argue in this book, local government did impact upon ideologies of homosexuality, in both positive and negative ways.

In the conclusion, I tentatively suggest ways in which a dialogue around sexual politics might have been conducted more successfully, thus enabling lesbian and gay policies to achieve a more favourable outcome. I advocate a decentred strategy which recognises the various, multiple interstices of municipal practice within which sexual politics takes place. Thus, it should not be principally a matter of conveying the 'right' attitudes from the centre, but facilitating processes of change wherever they may occur. As well as practical changes, this requires reconceptualising local government, away from the top-down, centre-periphery model, to one that recognises the different relations of power, resources and potential that exist across the terrain it occupies.

Having set out the main argument, let me briefly outline each chapter. In Chapter 2, I examine the history of lesbian and gay policies' emergence onto the local government agenda in the early 1980s. I explore the changing nature of municipal, and lesbian and gay politics, the role played by key groups of actors, and the experiences of one of the first innovators in this area: the GLC. Chapter 3 then tells the stories of four local authorities which developed lesbian and gay policies: the London Borough of Islington; Nottingham, and Manchester City Councils, and the London Borough of Camden. Focusing on the conflicts and tensions that emerged, a key theme of this chapter is the similarity in experiences, an analysis which provides the groundwork for Chapter 4.

In Chapter 4, I explore the ways in which more progressive approaches to sexual politics were organised out during the policy process. I argue that despite the ideological limitations of initial proposals, such suggestions were considerably more progressive than the policy decisions that emerged at the end of the con-sultative and scrutinising processes that proposals underwent. This was not only due to the interjections of senior bureaucrats and politicians' sexual ideologies, but also the internalisation by progressive lesbian and gay actors of the constraints within which they worked. Yet, as I discuss in Chapter 5, the watering down and limitations of the policy process were nothing compared to the obstacles faced when policies came to be implemented. In making this argument, Chapter 5 goes on to examine strategies developed to overcome obstructions, the ideological implications of this process, and the question: why were policies allowed in the first place when senior actors were so keen to block their implemen-tation? This takes us on to questions about the relationship (and difference) between policy development and implementation in the context of ideological and symbolic policies.

Chapter 6 considers what happens when the mobilisation of bias becomes temporarily fractured. Here, I examine Haringey council's educational policy of 'positive images'. My focus is the emergence and mobilisation of opposition to lesbian and gay educational work as a result of a 'freak' incident—the sending of a letter from Haringey's lesbian and gay unit to head teachers informing them of the council's equal opportunities educational policy and the need to develop appropriate work in schools. Pre-empting the formal emergence of specific policy within the education department and without the knowledge of that depart-ment, the letter was a clear contravention of municipal decision-making processes and precedents.

Chapter 7 develops this discussion by examining the role of the mass media in the discursive and political struggle that took place. Through close textual analysis, I demonstrate some of the ways in which the mass media steered perceptions of the policies in particular directions. I argue that the mass media's claims to objectivity or, in the case of the tabloid press, their use of story telling and narrative imagery facilitated the right's interpretation of events and hence their political project.

Chapter 8 brings together several strands from the preceding chapters by theorising the ideological limitations on local government. In particular, it asks: why were certain perspectives 'organised out' before even being raised, and why was the opposition so intense? Thus, it explores the prohibition and opposition to perceived state penetration of the private and the impact and nature of homophobia. Chapter 9 briefly examines what happened to lesbian and gay work between 1987 and 1993. It explores several factors that led to a falling off of interest, including the process of delegitimisation and community demoralisation. Within a changing environment of urban politics and local government power, what possibilities remained for a municipal sexual politics? This question is picked up in the last chapter which explores the possibilities for a different state strategy entailing the decentring of local government.

Acting Within the Activist State

This book was written for several reasons. In part it emerged from an ongoing political and theoretical concern with the potential of the local state to facilitate or bring about progressive social change. More specifically, it grew out of my own experiences as a member of Haringey council between 1986 and 1990. Being an actor within local government provided me with an opportunity to experience directly the contradictions, and competing pressures and tensions of working within the local state. On the one hand, I was part of an innovative, left-wing local authority; on the other, particularly as financial cutbacks started to bite, I had to come to terms with my participation in an organisation that would only go so far to introduce a radical agenda when budgetary, legislative and electoral demands were pulling in a contrary direction. The decisions I took, remaining a committee chair and thus formally part of the front bench, while refusing to implement, and indeed opposing, financial cutbacks and restrictive legislation, provide a personal context to my analysis of the choices and options facing actors in this book. I left local government in 1990, conscious of and still optimistic about the progressive possibilities it offered even during a period of retrenchment, but at the same time more bitterly aware of the limitations and immense difficulty in achieving such potential. Every step was part of an unrelenting struggle which politicised those involved in the conflict far more, probably, than anyone else. Yet, to what extent could things have been done differently?

This last enquiry provided the specific impetus for this project. For it was a question located at the heart of the tension between pluralist practice and neo-Marxist theorising. By this I mean that, on the one hand, we, as left-wing councillors, were acting as if anything were possible given sufficient support and political commitment; on the other, for many of us, our theoretical framework not only undermined such optimism but challenged the very notion that lasting, 'real' change could be brought about in this manner.

When I began *Sexing the City* in 1988, I intended positively to explore the possibilities of municipal radicalism. However, as I researched further, speaking to many of the people involved, and grew myself personally more detached from local government politics, what came to the fore were the limitations and constraints, the mistakes and lost potential. In a book aimed at those sympathetic rather than hostile to lesbian and gay equality, it is useful to explore the miscalculations, and the things that could have been done differently. But it is also important to know the limits of the possible, in part, because only then can we celebrate what was achieved. Lesbian and gay urban policies should not be dismissed as irrelevant or condemned as a gigantic error. Despite the problems faced, we need to acknowledge the tremendous effort and commitment of people developing progressive, innovative work at a time of intense political conservatism and reaction.

Sexing the City has been written for different readers with different interests. On the one hand it is a theoretical and empirical study of an attempt to use state institutions to bring about social change, and the problems in doing so. It is also intended to provide a record of lesbian and gay urban struggles in the 1980s and early 1990s for those who were involved and want to remember, as well as for those interested in finding out more about one of the most publicised and controversial political issues of the decade. Finally, this book is for activists and practitioners currently attempting to develop anti-discriminatory policies and working to bring about progressive transformations in society.

2

Agenda Politics:

The Lesbian and Gay Community and the New Urban Left

> *'Domestic life' and 'the quality of human relationships' are emerging from the silent secrecy of 'the private' to enter the public world of town hall committees.*
>
> Lynne Segal[1]

Reaching a high point in the mid-1980s, lesbian and gay policies were among the most controversial urban initiatives of the decade. Positive images of lesbians and gays within school curricula, 'pink plaques', housing succession rights for gay couples, AIDS policies, all these and many more were proposed, and in some cases put into effect, by lesbian and gay municipal actors and their supporters. The era of the lesbian and gay municipal project forms the subject matter of this book; in this chapter I focus on the process of getting gay issues onto the municipal agenda. How did it happen? Why did previously hostile Labour authorities begin to identify sexual orientation as an integral part of their commitment to equality? And why did lesbian and gay communities, with a history of political practice rooted in civil society rather than state structures, turn to local government for political solutions?

To tackle these questions, this chapter examines the emergence of lesbian and gay issues onto the local government agenda of the early 1980s. What seemed to many an abrupt, sudden development, diverting attention from the 'real' issues of local government, was in fact a complex process, intricately connected to the deep changes being wrought in urban Labour politics and within the polity more generally. Two issues provide a particular focus for this chapter. The first concerns the shifting paradigms of urban left, and lesbian and gay communities, towards a common concern with equal opportunities, rights and identity politics. The second addresses the problematic of Labour Party interest in lesbian and gay issues, and the extent of their commitment. I argue that the ambivalent nature of the party's response in conjunction with the superficial process of its policy development contributed to the cramping and precarious status of subsequent lesbian and gay work. A similar plight faced other areas of local government equality development, such as 'race' policies, where social movement ideas and practice met formal party and bureaucratic procedures.

Although it is beyond the scope of this chapter to examine how lesbian and gay issues were developed within local government up to the present time, I finish by examining the work of one of the first and, perhaps, the best known of the authorities to develop lesbian and gay policy initiatives: the Greater London Council (GLC). In so doing, I address some of the problems and tensions that characterised municipal developments in this area. It is important to stress, however, that municipal engagement with homosexuality was not new. Explicit, as well as more covert, negative policies and practices had existed for a long time as had the promotion and privileging of heterosexuality. What was novel in the 1980s was not the *emergence* of work in this area by a small number of progressive authorities, but rather the *content* of such work which treated discrimination and prejudice rather than homosexuality as the problem.

The Changing Shape of Local Government

The emergence in Britain of the new, urban left in the late 1970s and early 1980s has been well documented by Boddy and Fudge,[2] Gyford,[3] Lansley et al.[4] and others. It was a transformation crucial for the development of lesbian and gay policies within local authorities. New people with new ideas and a new approach entered municipal government. More open to lesbian and gay demands, their arrival generated a new interest among lesbians and gay men in the potential of local government.

The emergence of a new, urban left in local government was the result of several interconnected processes.[5] First, the changing composition of the Labour Party, with the entry of feminists and other radical and grass-roots activists, brought to the party a different politics, set of experiences, and concerns. Second, local government restructuring and the development of community work (despite its problems and limited nature) facilitated a shift in relations between the local state and civil society. In addition it encouraged an influx of young, progressive people into municipal employment. Third, the growth and influence of Gramscian and neo-Marxist theory moved left-wing politics towards an emphasis on counter-hegemonic practice and the exploitation of institutional contradictions. Rejecting the proletarian-led overthrow of the state as a realistic possibility, many on the left began to look more closely at the prospects state and community practice offered for a different kind of politics. Finally, the post-1979 Thatcher government shifted the political focus of many on the left from the national towards the local. With central government as the adversary rather than the aspiration, people turned to the local state as a hopeful site of resistance and prefigurative development.

In 1981, a new left-wing leadership was installed in the GLC. Local elections the following year witnessed a similar process in a number of other London authorities, such as Islington, Southwark and Camden. In Manchester, Sheffield, and elsewhere, traditional Labour leaderships were defeated. The politics of councils such as Manchester, Islington, and the GLC in the early 1980s embodied a shift away from traditional perceptions of local government's role. Emphasis was placed on community participation and consultation, particularly with sections of the community historically ignored. New structures were established to facilitate this, and stress was placed on making council information accessible. Increased openness—a focus on community involvement—played an important role in the subsequent emergence of lesbian and gay policies; so did two other initiatives: equal opportunities policies (EOPs) and cultural ventures.

EOPs have been a well-established feature of western social policy for several decades. Grounded in notions of universal citizenship, meritocracy, and formal rights, they have proven a powerful ideological framework for government as well as for 'disadvantaged' groups. Municipal EOPs in the late 1970s and early 1980s focused on gender and race discrimination. Although for many people these two issues formed a sufficient and complete basis for equality work, the ideological framework deployed negated such a closure. Citizenship and rights could not easily be constrained. If other groups such as lesbians and gays gained inclusion, municipal EOPs needed to encompass them as well.

Although EOPs provided a means of entry onto the urban political agenda for lesbian and gay issues in the mid-1980s, it was not an unequivocally beneficial discourse. On the one hand, it generated a bureaucratic structure—committees and units—and substantive policy demands that lesbians and gays could lock into; on the other, it created an equivalence between identities—Black, female, disabled and homosexual—which was frequently inappropriate, and which also had the effect of reducing social relations of power to questions of personal identity.

Alongside the focus on community development and EOPs by new urban left authorities, the expansion of cultural and artistic ventures by councils such as the GLC also held an important resonance for lesbians and gays. This was not just due to the opportunities funding provided for large gay and lesbian festivals: 'In the pink',[6] 'Lark in the park',[7] 'Strength and pride'.[8] It was also because of the links—identified by gay men in particular— between issues of sexuality and of culture, that is their shared emphasis on identity, community, the body, ideology, sexual expression and pleasure.[9]

According to Cohen and Dyer, culture was a place where one could be 'queer', an identity which brought with it an artistic sensitivity. Moreover, linked with femininity, culture held a resonance for men who did not perceive themselves as masculine. One could argue that this equation of homosexuality with culture affirms a number of social stereotypes, but that would be to miss the point. For gay men and lesbians negotiating their sexual and social identity, the arts, and culture more generally, provided both an important site of struggle and a means of expression. Consequently, local authority initiatives in this area, their funding of artifacts and performances as a means of community development and identity affirmation, drew lesbians and gays towards municipal infrastructures.

An Emerging Politics of Gay Affirmation

By the early 1980s, the lesbian and gay movement had undergone a substantial shift of emphasis. While the 1970s witnessed an emphasis on 'revolutionary' strategies: separatism, political lesbianism and sexual deconstruction, the 1980s saw a renewed interest in *affirming* gay identity, developing political alliances, particularly between men and women, and working within the state.

The movement towards identity politics occurred for a number of reasons. Among feminists it grew out of a sense of difference as lesbians challenged notions of an all-encompassing sisterhood predicated simply on a shared gender and sexuality. Other oppressions and relations of power became more firmly recognised, facilitated by the growing interest and influence of poststructuralism, and gender began to be seen as one among several determinants of social positioning. Similar developments occurred in some gay male communities. However, there the rising commercialism also played an important role. Increasingly, particularly in large cities, gay men could lead 'gay' lives. In conjunction with the growing size and strength of gay communities, identity affirmation rather than sexual deconstruction became the priority.

Alongside the new identity politics of the early 1980s emerged a renewed interest in formal political processes. What was demanded was not 'revolution' but reforms that would defend and protect social identities such as homosexuality. Thus, the focus shifted towards state provision and services including those of local government. The 1979 general election results also had an impact on political strategies, leading, paradoxically, to a greater preparedness to work within traditional political forums. Linda Bellos, community activist and leader of Lambeth council during the mid-1980s, describes how she no longer found lesbian separatism an appropriate strategy.[10] Bellos's words reflect the growing 'realism' and anti-Utopianism of many lesbian feminist communities at that time who saw separatist structures as elitist, only benefiting the minority able to participate. For the majority of lesbians and other women, it was argued, their lives were too closely bound up with state policies and provision. Hence it was important to engage with these arenas. As Linda Bellos states, 'Thatcher was having a real, very dangerous effect on working-class women's lives.'[11] For Bellos, at the time, the only vehicle that could proffer a challenge was a vibrant Labour Party. According to her, many other lesbian feminists came to similar decisions.

The renewed interest in formal politics, the willingness to work with a broad range of people, was perhaps an unexpected consequence of the identity politics that emerged in the early and mid-1980s. Within lesbian communities, in particular, identity politics was *perceived* as leading to fragmentation as groups splintered further and further along race, class and disability lines. Yet identity politics has been in many ways a contradictory process. At the same time as leading to separation, it brought forth a culture of alliances. It deconstructed lesbian and gay sexuality as too broad an identity, while at the same time affirming it. Here I want to focus on one particular alliance that emerged, an alliance central to the establishment of council policies in this area—improved working relations between gay men and lesbians.

The shift away from treating oppression as operating along a single dimension of gender increased many lesbian feminists' willingness to work with men. Still, the extent of joint political organising between lesbians and gay men in the early 1980s should not be overestimated. According to Peter Tatchell, it did not occur on any widespread scale until the mobilisation against S.28.[12] It was also an extremely uneven process geographically. Facilitated in London by GLC funding of mixed gay projects, it was barely noticeable in Leeds and Manchester. Even in London, many lesbian feminists refused to adopt the new politics.

> I find it disturbing that some women who call
> themselves lesbian feminists have joined up with gay
> men in London, particularly after the experiences of
> lesbians in the GLF who had to recognise in 1972 that
> gay male interests were as oppressive to lesbians as
> those of heterosexual men. But now lesbians are work-
> ing in the...recently launched Pink Paper, and the
> London Lesbian and Gay Centre. (Lynne Harne)[13]

The increasing willingness to acknowledge, and in some cases prioritise, a *homosexual* identity was an important factor in shaping the development of lesbian and gay municipal initiatives. One illustration of this tendency, described in the introduction, was the popularisation of the term 'heterosexism' during the

1980s to refer to the oppression of lesbians and gays *as* homosexuals. Like 'EOPs', 'heterosexism' emerged at the interface of social movement and bureaucratic politics, intended to provide an equivalence to 'sexism' and 'racism'. Like EOPS, the impact of 'heterosexism' was also equivocal, in part because of its similar foundations within liberal discourse but also because of its implicit assumptions of gender neutrality.

The deployment of a model of sexuality which encompassed men and women within a single category had several benefits for lesbian and gay communities. Policy analysts have argued that the larger a constituency, the more likely an issue will reach the political agenda. Constructing a shared identity, therefore, may well have increased the chances of homosexuality securing a place on the municipal agenda, particularly compared to lesbians organising alone. Equally important was the ability of a trans-gender approach (lesbians and gays together) to realise political congruence with existing municipal agendas. Local government generally perceived lesbians and gay men as defined by their sexuality, that is as homosexuals, just as Black men and women were defined by their race. Ostensibly, this created a balance, considered, mistakenly, by local councils to be crucial if 'hierarchies of oppression' were to be avoided.

Yet the drawback was the marginalisation of lesbian and gay specificity, ignoring gendered differences and other relations of power. In some authorities, such as the LB of Haringey, lesbian and gay initiatives prioritised affirming homosexual diversity. However, this was less apparent in those developments emerging in the early 1980s which tended to prioritise (not always intentionally) the problems facing white, middle-class men. Moreover, even when difference was recognised, the impact of identity politics combined with municipal categorisation tended to mean people were seen as arithmetical accumulations or layers of oppression, rather than as condensing a complex network of different social relations mediated through experience and a non-ontologically privileged subjectivity.

So far I have discussed the general openness of the new urban left to issues of equality; however, on its own, this articulation of multicultural citizenship was not sufficient to ensure lesbian and gay policies were adopted by municipal councils. Labour authority agendas are formed out of a complex process which encompasses community demands, financial, central government and electoral pressures, and internal, party commitments. It is with this latter that I begin this part of my story, by examining how lesbian and gay activists within the Labour Party were able to achieve the adoption of gay equality policies at a national and local level.

Struggling Within an Equivocal National Party

In the late 1970s and early 1980s, many lesbians and gays joined the Labour Party, while those who were already members 'came out' in larger numbers.[14] A key organisation during this period was the Labour Campaign for Gay Rights (later, the Labour Campaign for Lesbian and Gay Rights) which lobbied for equality policies within the party, and later pressurised Labour councils to place lesbian and gay issues on their agenda. Equally important was the pressure exerted by feminist members through formal women's sections and caucuses for greater attention to be paid to sexual relations and the domestic sphere.

Tatchell describes the dominant political approach of the Labour left to lesbian and gay issues as 'civil rights oriented' (see Chapter 4).[15] It emphasised lesbians and gays' right to equal treatment and non-discrimination rather than constructing a radical analysis of sexuality. With the exception of some early articles, for example in the Streetlife section of London Labour Briefing, the emphasis was on public gay identity rather than on personal sexual practices and relations. Thus the links between gender and sexual orientation tended to be lost. Similarly, despite the adoption in the mid-1980s of the concept 'heterosexism', little public discussion took place within the Labour Party on the nature of heterosexuality.

The left's analysis reflected the fact that most of the work was carried out by heterosexual feminists and gay men. Few radical feminists worked within the Labour Party during this period. Those who did either participated too late, chose other priorities, or were too politically marginalised to shape the direction of its sexual politics. Yet, despite such limitations, the left's position on homosexuality was far more radical than the party mainstream.

In 1979, the Labour Government left office having resolutely managed to ignore gay demands for legal equality. However in subsequent years, pressure from LCLGR, from other groups, and from individual members persuaded the party to proffer some kind of commitment. In 1981, the National Executive Committee (NEC) endorsed a policy document *The Rights of Gay Men and Women*. Publicly critical of the Labour Party's lack of activity on gay rights, the report made several recommendations including reducing the age of consent for gay male sexual activity from 21 to 18 (or possibly 16). However, it was a document firmly located within a liberal sexual politics. It argued that sexuality was fixed early, hence young people could not be 'damaged', and that what was required was 'protection' for gays as a sexual minority. In 1982, this document was followed by an NEC policy statement on homosexuality which included promises to reform the age of consent.

Despite these steps towards reform, misgivings as to the party's commitment remained.[16] The 1982 policy statement, for example, committed the NEC to advocating a gay age of consent of 18 rather than 16. According to Jeffery-Poulter, the campaign document for the 1983 general election was even more cautious: the Labour Party would only protect homosexuals from *'unfair'* discrimination.[17]

However the event which was to become a catalyst for the mobilisation of lesbians and gays in and against the Labour Party during the early 1980s, particularly in London, was the treatment of gay Labour candidate, Peter Tatchell, in the 1982 Bermondsey by-election.[18] The London constituency of Bermondsey had always been a safe Labour seat. However, in 1982, it was won for the first time by the Social Democratic Party (SDP), largely due to the media's character assassination of Tatchell, an assassination barely impeded by the national Labour Party.[19]

Tatchell's defeat had a significant effect on lesbian and gay party activists. His experiences reinforced perceptions of media homophobia, while demonstrating the unwillingness of the Labour leadership to support gay members under attack. People feared Tatchell's failure to win election in a 'safe' Labour seat would reduce the chances of other 'out' gays being selected to stand. Yet, at the same time, Tatchell's experience had an empowering effect. A number of party members 'came out' in their constituency parties as a result of his treatment.[20] Meanwhile, lesbian and gay party activists became determined to ensure that the party's explicit disregard of gay candidates could never happen again.

As a result of their work, in 1984 the London Labour Party at its annual conference resolved to promote the introduction of 'protective' legislation for lesbians and gays. At the same time, LCLGR began campaigning for lesbian and gay rights to be discussed at national conference, an important site of policy development and symbolic recognition. Throughout the 1980s, motions were sent but never considered. Finally, in 1985, sufficient motions were sent on lesbian and gay rights to force its debate at conference. Yet NEC support, with the personal exception of MP Jo Richardson, remained equivocal. But despite their calls for remittance, the composite motion was passed. The following year, a similar motion received the two-thirds of votes required for automatic inclusion within the party's national manifesto.

An important factor, identified by lesbians and gay men, in achieving these results were the alliances formed with other sections of the community. During the mid-1980s, the high profile support of gays and lesbians for the miners and Wapping printers' strikes, earned the community a degree of reciprocal (although possibly transient) respect, illustrated by the NUM contingent on the 1985 Gay Pride march.

> 1985 was a very significant year for lesbian and gay
> rights, if not a turning point. That was the year we went
> more public with our vision....The Pride march was the
> biggest ever...including contingents from mining commu-
> nities returning the solidarity and support of lesbians
> and gay men during the 1984–5 miners strike. That was
> the year we, at last, began to get on the mainstream
> political agenda. (Jan Parker)[21]

In Manchester, Shiers argues, 'visible' gays in the Labour Party working with other party activists on a whole range of issues were instrumental in achieving greater support for lesbian and gay demands.[22]

The gradual emergence of a formal Labour Party position in favour of lesbian and gay rights was an important factor in facilitating constituency struggles to have lesbian and gay issues placed on local election manifestos. After 1985, lesbians and gays 'labouring' in local parties could point to conference policies to legitimise and give weight to their demands. More than that, the debates at conference and within local parties attempting to send motions on the subject publicised and drew attention to the issues. Lesbian and gay rights *began* to be seen within the party (although clearly this was geographically uneven) as a standard component of equal opportunity policies. Indeed, as a result of the success at national conference, Larry Whitty, Labour Party general secretary, was obliged to write to all council Labour groups informing them that lesbian and gay rights was now party policy.

Yet the equivocation of the national party did not evaporate with conference triumphs. Nor did constituency opposition disappear with lesbian and gay issues' inclusion in local manifestos. The superficial nature of policy development within mainstream political parties is clearly revealed in the history of lesbian and gay initiatives. Even among supporters, little consideration was generally given to the form, history and implications of heterosexist and homophobic practices. For many, the admission of lesbian and gay 'equality' onto Labour Party agendas was something to which they had given little thought—a knee-jerk reaction of the 'right-on' left. For others, it was intended as a purely token measure—a gesture of appeasement to lesbian and gay members. The surprise was that lesbian and gay activists managed to convert this 'pseudo-agenda' into a real one. Yet despite this success, the lack of thorough debate and fully understood commitment seriously affected the development of lesbian and gay work as the experiences of the late 1980s demonstrate.

Unequal Provision and Community Activism

The involvement of grass-roots lesbian and gay communities in the beginnings of a municipal sexual politics is a complex and contradictory one. As the involvement of Labour Party activists suggests, policies did not originate in the lobbying and campaigns of community pressure groups but in a much more mediated fashion. In discussing the community-council interface, I want to explore the interactive nature of municipal developments. Lesbian and gay demands tended to be made in areas where a positive, or at least broadly sympathetic, response from local government could be anticipated. In addition, such demands increased as authorities demonstrated a willingness to take lesbian and gay issues seriously.

From the late 1970s, in common with other community groupings, lesbian and gay voluntary sector projects and organisations began to request local authority resources on an increasingly widespread scale. The GLC was the first body to respond in any significant way. Between 1981 and 1986 it granted over one million pounds to lesbian and gay groups, a fraction of the total grant aid for the period. Other councils too provided financial support. Early funders included London Borough of Islington, Manchester and the West Midlands.

Among lesbian and gay activists, decisions about whether to apply for local authority funding remained hotly contested. Many people were wary of accepting state resources, fearing it might lead to co-option, dependency and de-politicisation.[23] Femi Otitoju describes her position in the 'Should we, shouldn't we? debate' in relation to the GLC:

> I was suspicious. I had heard all sorts of tales about
> what happened to small voluntary organisations that
> were funded by bigger statutory organisations, and I
> didn't like the prospect of being co-opted in this
> way....You were accountable to the council, and they
> controlled what you could and couldn't do once you had
> their money.[24]

Although lesbian and gay groups mostly decided to take the route of municipal funding, the problems raised in these early debates of dependency, municipal state control, depoliticisation and divisions between paid and voluntary staff continued to rear their heads throughout the decade.

From the mid-1980s, a second issue which brought many gay men, in particular, into a closer working relationship with local government was AIDS. As more people either became ill or suffered harassment and discrimination as a result of the moral panic surrounding the virus, local government increasingly seemed a pertinent site for campaigning activity. Not only was it an arena in which many gay men and people with AIDS (PWAs) experienced the most severe forms of ill-treatment, it was also a provider of key needed services such as home helps and housing, and of employment. As a result, AIDS organisations alongside other groups and individuals campaigned for improved local government services and treatment of PWAs. For many gay men, AIDS changed their political priorities. According to Dennis Altman, discourses on sex shifted from libertarian imperatives to safety and education.[25] Similarly, the need for anti-discriminatory measures superseded an earlier political focus on lowering the age of consent.[26]

In the case of AIDS, it was changing circumstances that drew the lesbian and gay community towards local government. In other instances, the growing prevalence of a rights-based identity politics led lesbian and gay residents to become increasingly conscious of and frustrated by areas of council provision within which they experienced unequal treatment. One such area was adoption and fostering policies. For gay men, adoption was almost impossible, although occasionally they were given 'hard to place' children to foster. For lesbians, it was marginally easier. However, at best, they were granted parity with single women since their relationships were not recognised as an asset to their ability to parent. This contrasted with the preference given to heterosexual couples, particularly where married.

Homelessness formed another area which increasingly became a site of engagement with local government. Problems resulting from the general housing shortage were exacerbated by the hostile familial treatment accorded to growing numbers of young lesbians and gay men 'coming out'.[27] Other housing problems also related to the conjuncture of increased homosexual visibility and expectations of equal treatment. These included harassment, insensitive attitudes of housing officers, difficulties in acquiring joint tenancies, and discriminatory succession policies.

Discrimination in housing and social services provision was experienced by lesbians and gays, in the main, on an individualistic basis. Combined with the relative powerlessness of, for example, council tenants, this made community action to remedy disadvantage difficult. According to Linda Bellos, in 1983 a member of Lambeth Lesbian and Gay Working Party: 'We all complained but didn't know how to make inroads into the council.'[28] Before units and committees were established, Ken Livingstone suggests, the main option for lesbians and gays with problems was to approach individual councillors.[29] This strategy relied heavily on councillors' goodwill, according to Anne Matthews, former leader of Southwark council:

> Lesbians and gay men came to me before there was a
> formal policy to get rehoused. It was important to get
> things formally agreed, so people were not reliant on
> certain councillors and officers.[30]

Consequently, where municipal actors were unsympathetic, many lesbians and gays chose not to take problems to them. A Birmingham council women's officer makes a similar point, claiming that in Birmingham lesbians and gays did not make demands because they felt the council would not respond.

The situation was somewhat different in the field of education. There, from the early 1970s, feminist and gay teachers worked collectively to develop anti-sexist curricula and to protect homosexual staff and students from harassment. Most of this work took place at a grass-roots level within the classroom, sometimes with the support and backing of the principal, sometimes without. Until the early 1980s, it rarely involved management in the local education authority directly, although clearly councils were involved since schools formed part of the local government apparatus.

Within the youth service, early initiatives included the formation in 1976 of the predominantly male London Gay Teenage Group (LGTG). It took between two and three years' campaigning to win funding and recognition from the Inner London Education Authority (ILEA). Dixon et al. describe the relationship between the local state and gay youth provision.

> It is...important to note that it was not the Inner London
> Education Authority [ILEA] or other London education
> authority hierarchies who started to do this work, but
> lesbians and gays within these youth services who
> struggled for years to persuade them to take it on.
> ILEA's recognition was valuable in terms of mainstream
> status, money and facilities....The registration process for
> the LGTG took two years [1977-1979]. The group was
> considered highly controversial by the ILEA hierarchy,
> but the members of the group systematically set about
> putting their case forward to youth officers, committees
> and members of ILEA.[31]

Youth workers, but even more teachers, were assisted by having an institutional base that could bring gay and lesbian educational workers together, enabling them to share concerns and strategies. Unions such as the NUT provided some organisational support. Also important were the Women in Education Group and the Gay Teachers Group.

Nevertheless, despite work in fields such as education and the demands for voluntary sector funding, the formal, organisational structures established by local government for lesbian and gay work did not in general emerge out of community demands and pressure. Gays, and in particular the lesbian feminist community, remained detached from traditional forms of political power during this period. Even when activists requested municipal funding, they did so intent on achieving minimal compromises to their political autonomy. Few perceived funding requests as a route to greater involvement with local government. Robert Crossman, a leading, gay, Islington councillor, commented when interviewed on how hard it was to involve people in the policy-making process. Other interviewees made similar statements. Lesbians and gays would attend public meetings called by councillors and officers, and a minority became co-optees. However, as an organised community, with a few exceptions, they were not a primary motivating force in establishing lesbian and gay municipal structures. Linda Bellos takes this point even further: 'We were very introspective and insular. Dress codes, words used...local government took the initiative. It led to lesbians and gay men being redirected towards service provision.'[32]

The lesbian and gay community did, however, play an important and influential role in *resisting* municipal attempts to backtrack, and in opposing authorities with explicitly homophobic policies. In Rugby (1984), the Conservative council leadership's decision to strike out 'sexual orientation' from an equal opportunities clause in an employment policy was opposed by Labour councillors, trade unions and CHE,[33] leading to a march and rally on 10 November 1984, attended by over 1,000 demonstrators.[34] Subsequently, a more progressive policy statement was issued.

Similar successes were evident in other local authorities. Fitzpatrick and Love (*Lesbian and Gay Socialist*, Winter 1985) describe how Stirling District Council, which first turned down a request by the Scottish Homosexual Rights Group to include sexual orientation in their EOP, changed their minds after discussion with LCLGR. In Stockport (1985), a refusal by the council to include lesbians and gays in their equal opportunity job code led to a campaign aimed at reversing the policy.[35] After several failed attempts working within the council, a national demonstration was called for 15 March 1986. Paul Hinshaw, a gay men's officer with Manchester City Council, told *Gay Times* (March 1986, no. 90:11), 'our victory at Rugby proves that we have the power to change the attitudes of local authorities who because of prejudice, discriminate against us.' The Stockport demonstration was attended by over 600 people.[36] In July 1986, Stockport changed its EOP to include sexual orientation.[37]

Although in relation to other authorities, most noticeably Nottingham County Council, lesbian and gay community pressure was largely unsuccessful, the effectiveness of the campaigns described above demonstrates the emerging clout and legitimacy of lesbian and gay demands for equal treatment. This was particularly evident in the case of Labour authorities that espoused broad notions of equality of opportunity and human rights. To deny such opportunities and rights to lesbians and gays became increasingly hard to justify. In the case of other authorities, issues of political stability were more important in ensuring paper commitments to lesbians and gays. The size and strength of opposition to homophobic policies and the publicity engendered made it easier to offer a tokenistic commitment than to continue to say no.

Employee Organising

Earlier in this chapter, I referred to the changing workforce composition of urban authorities. As with the Labour Party, during this period more lesbians and gays came to work for local government and more began to 'come out'. From the mid-1970s, lesbian and gay council officers began to organise autonomously within their jobs. This took the form of union committees, policy working parties which examined issues of discrimination, and groups to provide lesbian and gay employees with support. Initially, employee groups tended to focus on staff concerns such as harassment, compassionate and carers leave, pensions, and recruitment policies. Later, they widened their remit to encompass service provision, and began to lobby for municipal structures comparable to those being established on gender, race and disability issues. Jane Skeates, lesbian and gay research officer in Camden, 1985–6, describes this process within her authority: 'People (officers) talked about a unit from the beginning. That was the expectation. We had absorbed municipal values to know we wanted a unit, like the women's unit.'[38]

For a number of lesbians, a key motivating factor, alongside the growing identification with gay men, was disillusionment with the response to lesbian issues by women's equality structures. In many, including the GLC women's unit, lesbians were particularly active.[39] However, councillors and senior managers tended to resist attempts by women's committees and units to engage publicly in work concerning lesbians. Gay issues were seen as marginal, diversionary, and contrary to the interests of ordinary (working-class) women. Yet, despite the constant struggles between officers, community and politicians over the degree of attention to be given to lesbian concerns, the feminist culture and relatively high concentration of lesbians within women's units and committees led them in many authorities, particularly where gay structures were not established, to be the most sympathetic environments for lesbians (and often for gay men too).

Pioneering Municipal Lesbian and Gay Work: Ken Livingstone and the GLC

The GLC was by no means the first authority to develop lesbian and gay municipal work, nor was it the most radical. However, it is probably the best known of the pre-1986 developments. GLC renown was an important factor in the development of lesbian and gay work in other authorities. Its approach to equal opportunities also helped form a blueprint for initiatives elsewhere. Thus, many of the problems and tensions encountered by the GLC were replicated in other places.

The Labour Party fought the 1981 GLC elections on a manifesto which did not include a commitment to lesbian and gay rights. Consequently, Livingstone argues, initiation of lesbian and gay work by the GLC was largely accidental.[40] It arose, according to him, out of a chance encounter with the Harrow Gay Unity Group, whom Livingstone addressed in 1981, and was the paradoxical response to the press's subsequent outcry over his comments to the group.[41]

Whether, and in what form, lesbian and gay work might otherwise have arisen is impossible to say. What is evident, however, is that Livingstone's vocalised support for lesbian and gay equality as an identified heterosexual, his comments on bisexual innateness, challenged the traditional, low key, slightly shame-faced approach towards homosexuality of many progressive activists. Livingstone takes up this point:

> Seeing 'Before Stonewall' reminded me of how in the
> 1960s I took advantage of being 'tolerant to a
> disadvantaged minority'. It wasn't 'til 1971–2 when I was
> on Lambeth Council and the first debates were sparked
> off by the GLF down Railton Road that I got my head
> round the concept of equally valid sexualities.[42]

According to Femi Otitoju, Livingstone's public support encouraged lesbians and gays working for the GLC to 'come out' and push for progressive policies.[43] Jan Parker, a former officer with the GLC states: 'He was happy to stick his foot in the door to help it open and then let others get on with it'.[44]

Yet, according to Bellos, other factors were also significant in explaining the GLC's ability to support lesbian and gay equality.[45] These included left-wing GLC councillors' willingness to respond to lesbian and gay demands (such as for funding) because of their status as *community* demands, the paucity of services the GLC had to deliver as a strategic authority with few powers, their extensive resources (compared to other authorities), and the existence of a well-developed bureaucratic infrastructure. These factors, she claims, allowed the GLC to campaign on issues like lesbian and gay equality without detrimentally affecting service provision, a situation unmatched elsewhere.[46]

Despite the praise, the GLC's approach to lesbian and gay issues also came under criticism. Otitoju states that despite proponents' wishes, because of the 'flak', the Gay Working Party never received full committee status; specialist officers were not employed; and resourcing for lesbian and gay work was extremely limited.[47] Jan Parker, when interviewed, argued that the GLC received kudos from lesbian and gay work that was carried out by committed council officers on top of regular jobs. Tobin makes similar points.[48] She claims support within the GLC for lesbian and gay issues was always equivocal. Coterminous with the launch of the GLC charter *Changing the World*, the council's housing department refused to fund a project investigating lesbian and gay housing need. There was also a lack of strategic thought which caused tensions between various aspects of equality work, particularly around sexuality and class.

> It was...a system that was ripe for guilt-tripping and denunciations. GLC equalities at times resembled a wartime bunker or a city under siege, riven by internal strife while the Tory enemy massed its forces around the city's or County Hall's walls.[49]

However, despite the national focus on the GLC, in other authorities progress was also taking place. In London, by the autumn of 1985, at least 10 of the 32 boroughs included lesbians and gays in their equal opportunity policy statements for employment and housing.[50] Elsewhere, by 1 April 1986, when the Metropolitan authorities were abolished, Manchester, Southampton and Nottingham had all developed lesbian and gay committees and many other councils across the country were taking up, in different ways, lesbian and gay work.

Conclusion

The emergence of lesbian and gay issues on the agenda of local government was a process which witnessed a change in both the Labour Party and the lesbian and gay movements. The former shifted towards formal support for equal rights, while the latter moved in the direction of demands for affirmation and anti-discriminatory initiatives, away from a politics which privileged sexuality or gender as the originary motor for 'fundamental' social change. Yet, despite this apparent consensus, beneath the surface serious differences existed: was homosexuality as valid as hetero-sexuality? How far should the Labour Party and Labour councils go in their support for lesbians and gay men when faced with growing local opposition? These questions and the divergent answers they generated were seriously to weaken and eventually undermine the development of municipal lesbian and gay policies.

3

(Dis)trust, Hope and (Dis)illusionment:

A Cycle of Structures, Symbols and Resistance

In Chapter 2, I discussed the largely accidental emergence of lesbian and gay work at the Greater London Council (GLC). Yet, despite the GLC's radical reputation, lesbian and gay developments never became fully incorporated within the council's infrastructure. In this chapter I consider four authorities which did pursue an integrationist strategy, consciously developing structures to deliver—at least ostensibly—lesbian and gay work. These authorities: Islington, Nottingham, Manchester and Camden represent different stages of development. Each offered a more sophisticated bureaucratic framework for the integration of lesbian and gay politics than the authority that preceded them. In telling their stories, my focus is the cycle of organisational and policy development within each authority from the beginnings of lesbian and gay work to its culmination in 1987. What problems and tensions did co-option produce/encounter? To what extent was the experience a positive one for lesbian and gay social forces?

In theory, the committees established to develop lesbian and gay work were no different from other departmental committees: education, housing, social services. In practice, however, the differences were substantial. Although lesbian and gay committees, too, focused on service improvements and changes, they were also concerned with using state power more broadly. In this chapter, I concentrate on what marks and differentiates lesbian and gay work: the symbolic policies, campaigns and struggles in order to explore the tensions and possibilities of state activism.

Struggling Against its Yuppie, Loony Image: The London Borough of Islington

Situated just to the north of the City of London, the London Borough of Islington has a population of about 168,000,[1] approximately two-thirds of whom come from dominant ethnic communities.[2] It possesses an older working-class community and a newer, middle-class one with a liberal, arty image. It also has an established gay community. Since the abolition of the GLC in 1986, the borough has been a single tier authority responsible for all services with the exception of education.[3] All fifty-two council seats are up for re-election every four years.

Islington council's earliest, publicised lesbian and gay initiative was the funding of London Friend, a counselling and support agency, in 1975. By 1980, responding to what it perceived as an emerging gay community, the council began to stock books of particular lesbian and gay interest. However, substantial developments did not get under way until after the 1982 local borough elections.

Striving for Success

Islington's lesbian and gay strategy, formulated at the same time as the GLC began work in this area, provided a prototype for similar work elsewhere. Based on pre-election manifesto commitments, a council committee (Gay and Lesbian Advisory Working Party) of councillors and community representatives (co-optees) was established to initiate and monitor departmental policy development. The early years of Islington's committee were taken up, as in other authorities, with an effectiveness deficit. Meetings became inquorate, the leadership cancelled others; generally, signals were given that despite electoral promises, lesbian and gay work was too hot to handle. In turn, the response of the lesbian and gay committee was to demand greater formal status, a political gesture of reassurance that the work remained a council priority. In July 1983, the working party became a sub-committee and in November 1987, five years after its formal inauguration, full committee status was bestowed.

Keeping Lesbian and Gay Work Unpaid

From 1983, a key demand of Islington's committee was for the employment of a specialist lesbian and gay officer, paralleling the officers that existed to deal with gender and race issues. Without such a post, it was argued, the initiatives which the committee was proposing could not be effectively developed or implemented because nobody would have the time, remit or status to work on them. From 1983–7, repeated attempts for officer support failed.

The committee's struggle for a lesbian and gay officer, was, like the aspiration to be a full committee, a constant striving for full and proper inclusion within the council's EOPs. By the mid-1980s, Islington council, one of the first to respond to lesbian and gay discrimination, was being rapidly overtaken by other authorities such as Camden and Haringey. Later I discuss whether this equation of organisational status with effectiveness, this emphasis on bureaucratic structures was misguided. Here I wish briefly to consider why the response of Islington's leadership was so restrained.

Clearly a major factor in the committee's inability to bid successfully for funds was the council's own shortage of resources. Yet financial hardship was equally evident in other local councils such as Haringey and Camden. Islington had a larger, more vocal gay community than other authorities, yet lesbians and gays were still unable to make their demands fully felt within the process of resource prioritisation. Moreover, electoral considerations, a factor elsewhere, were barely relevant for an authority which, after 1986, had one of the largest Labour majorities in London.

Perhaps then the principal reason for Islington's policy lag, its refusal to appoint specialist staff to develop lesbian and gay work, lay in internal Labour Party politicking, in particular the determination of the council leadership to rid themselves of any 'loony left' image that might still linger. From 1987 onwards, for electoral and ideological reasons, the national Labour Party moved further away from EOPs, dropping even its semblance of sympathy for lesbian and gay municipal policies. This realignment was closely mirrored by Islington council leader, Margaret Hodge, who, in the late 1980s, adopted a high profile political role beyond her borough boundaries.

Extending the Boundaries of Municipal Practice

Did Islington council, then, do anything to improve the quality of life for its lesbian and gay residents, and users of its services? To what extent was the lesbian and gay committee responsible for improvements, or was it no more than a 'talking shop' while the real work took place elsewhere?

Let me begin with the symbolic. While some writers use this term in an explicitly derogatory manner, I have chosen a more neutral approach. By symbolic, I refer to those initiatives that prefigure ostensibly desired meanings and norms. This is a metaphorical process where the initiative becomes the 'as if' of the desired discursive structure. For example, Islington committee's eventual decision to give lesbians precedence in their title was intended to acknowledge lesbians' greater oppression and, hence, symbolise a commitment to prioritising their needs. The notion of prefiguring thus also suggests that the representational nature of metaphorical policies will help to *achieve* the desired result, that is, go beyond the purely aspirational. In the above example, by putting lesbians first in committee titles, it was hoped that lesbian invisibility and lack of power would be reduced. Symbolic policies formed an important element of lesbian and gay committees' work; however, their status and role remained ambiguous. Not only were symbolic policies signifiers of social progress, but their 'as if' illusory status rendered them useful as practices of containment. This caused problems, as I discuss in Chapter 5. In Islington tensions over symbolic policies frequently emerged, illustrated by the committee's attempt to introduce a 'pink plaques' policy.

On 6 January 1983, Robert Crossman, committee chair, proposed that a commemorative plaque be erected in memory of the playwright Joe Orton and his partner, Kenneth Halliwell—an ironic gesture, since, in the 1960s, both were convicted for defacing Islington library books. (These books were subsequently displayed as Islington library service's contribution to Lesbian and Gay Strength and Pride.) The recommendation was referred to the libraries committee responsible, which replied that no more than one individual could be named on a single plaque and, moreover, it was unnecessary to refer to Joe Orton's sexuality. The matter was settled, but two years later the committees clashed again, this time in relation to the Old Albany Trust Meeting House, one of the first modern homophile organisations in Britain. The libraries committee refused to install a plaque, this time on the grounds of budgetary limitations. The Gay and Lesbian Sub-Committee requested they go ahead, promising to take responsibility for any costs incurred.

The struggle between the two committees illustrates the conflicting perceptions different departments and committees possessed towards combatting anti-gay discrimination. While the libraries committee strove to treat sexual orientation as an irrelevant detail, the Gay and Lesbian Sub-Committee perceived its acknowledgement as vital in circumstances where it would produce positive role models or 'images'. 'Pink plaques' were seen as a useful way of bringing to public attention the contribution lesbians and gays had made to cultural, social and political life; moreover, they symbolised the council's recognition of these achievements.

Islington lesbian and gay committee also focused on developing a campaigning role, to use its public standing and formal municipal status to object to the discriminatory behaviour of other bodies. It criticised the negative attitudes of the Independent Broadcasting Authority towards gay television advertising and condemned police harassment and lack of assistance towards lesbians and gay men. Yet despite prolific discussion on the discrimination faced, the extent of any action remained slight. The committee wrote letters but had little power to direct the council to go further. Neither did it have the resources or capacity to mobilise community protest.

In addition to using its intra-state location to criticise other public institutions, the gay and lesbian committee considered the council's responsibility for organisations and bodies which benefited from council assistance. One of its first proposals was that firms receiving financial aid should promise to comply with the council's policy of non-discrimination on grounds of sexual orientation. The committee requested that the council's economic development service monitor firms to ensure compliance. The request was ignored.

A somewhat similar issue arose over the external use of council-owned premises. Islington's Policy Committee resolved on 14 July 1983 that the council would only prohibit the hire of their buildings to the National Front. The Gay and Lesbian Advisory

Working Party argued that this was too narrow; expressing their unease that organisations which contravened manifesto commitments could nevertheless hire council properties, they proposed that the council should refuse to let its premises to all groups with declared anti-gay views. Again the committee was unsuccessful.

These attempts to use local state power to penalise discriminatory bodies, attempts made also in other authorities such as Nottingham and Southampton, demonstrate the tensions surrounding the full realisation of lesbian and gay equality. Serious implementation of Islington committee's proposals would have created uproar among officers, community groups and local firms, as well as rendering the council vulnerable to legal challenge. It would have necessitated an investment of staff time which the council leadership was unprepared to make. However, this lack of support so early on in the life of the committee highlighted the limitations within which it operated.

> The impression given was that the Sub-Committee was low down in the committee pecking order....Decisions were never acted upon and always had to go through other committees. This was very frustrating. (D. Dawson interview)

Departmental Activism?

The degree to which departments took responsibility for developing lesbian and gay policies varied enormously. Some services, such as libraries (and later arts and entertainments), initiated work in this area, occasionally reporting to the lesbian and gay committee on progress made. But departments like the library service were an exception. Most took a less pro-active role and the emergence of any policy depended on constant scrutiny by the lesbian and gay committee, asking for reports and making recommendations. Part of the problem was that officers did not really understand what they were supposed to include within lesbian and gay reports. Consequently, even when reports were produced, they tended to be defensive, limited to assuring members that discrimination did not take place in the services they provided.[4] According to Robert Crossman: 'It took three years to get a report from housing and then it said there were no issues and it wasn't a priority.'[5]

Delay made any form of dialogue impossible. Departments reporting would neglect to respond to the actual recommendations and issues raised by the lesbian and gay committee. Alongside the frequent failure of departmental officers to attend lesbian and gay committee meetings even when formally requested to do so, the ability of the committee to implement change was limited. David Dawson, co-optee, stated:

> The time factor was very hard. The fact issues couldn't
> be handled by the Gay and Lesbian Sub-Committee
> slowed down the process. By the time the issue came
> back [to committee] the impetus had gone.[6]

In conclusion, it would seem that the popular image of Islington council during this period bore little resemblance to the reality. Development and implementation of lesbian and gay policies remained minimal and those which made progress owed more to individual officers' initiatives than to the lesbian and gay committee. The committee also had little success in raising public awareness of lesbian and gay rights. Among officers, many were oblivious to the committee's existence, and awareness among the general public was undoubtedly even lower.

In his period as mayor, Robert Crossman gave lesbian and gay municipal issues a higher profile, but this had little direct impact on the work of the committee. What did have an impact, however, was the media hysteria which followed his mayoralty, 'making work in this area even more difficult...as the shutters were pulled down'.[7] The gay and lesbian committee continued to meet, but despite initiatives, such as Arts and Entertainments' involvement in the annual North London strength and pride festival, it was never to have the impact or success for which it had wished.

Us and Them: Nottingham City Council

Nottingham City Council is located in the north-east Midlands, encompassing a population of just over 268,000,[8] almost 8 per cent of whom are from minority ethnic communities.[9] The City Council, the focus of this discussion, is a second-tier authority. The first, Nottingham County Council, has responsibility for many key services. The City Council re-elects a third of its seats every year (except the year of the European elections). Recently, it has tended to be ruled by very slim majorities with, at different times, Labour, Conservative and Communist councillors holding the balance of power.

In May 1983, Labour was returned with a majority of one. Yet it was this wafer-thin majority, paradoxically, which made lesbian and gay policy development possible. Despite manifesto commitments, support for gay policies was not extensive in the party or Labour group. As a result, 'out' gay councillor, Richard McCance, was forced to use his vote as a lever, threatening resignation and defeating the leadership's budgetary proposals in order to ensure the council did not backtrack. Successful in the short term, in the long run it backfired, losing McCance the support of many colleagues in the Labour group and party.[10]

Encouraging Community Participation

From the outset, tensions existed over the scale of Nottingham's equal opportunities unit. The leadership's initial aim was for a limited, low-profile structure with just a co-ordinator and secretary. This was not to be. First a women's officer and race equality officer were appointed, raising the question whether there should be someone to deal with issues of sexual orientation. Community activists argued for several posts on the basis that lesbians and gay men were separate communities. Eventually they accepted the council's compromise of one job-share to maintain the unit's—'one oppression, one officer'—balance.

Establishing Nottingham's Gay and Lesbian Sub-Committee followed a similar path to that of lesbian and gay committees in other authorities. A series of public meetings were held, attended by local lesbians, gay men and Labour councillors to discuss the organisational structure and priorities for future work. Gay and lesbian activists agreed not to demand two separate committees and there appeared, according to Jo Fraser, then lesbian officer, a readiness among men and women in the community to try and work together. However, with the sub-committee in place, consultation meetings with lesbians and gay men tended to take place separately and the two groups developed in different directions.

Conflict and Tension

As time went on, lesbian and gay co-optees and support staff found themselves, as in Islington, increasingly at odds with the council leadership. According to Jo Fraser:

> The structures would be used by councillors to stop [us doing] things. It became a matter of 'us' and 'them'...the community also saw the councillors as them.[11]

The emerging tensions between the lesbian and gay community, and council, came to a head over a series of issues. Condensed in these is the interplay of bureaucratic politics with sex/gender struggles. The first concerned the withdrawal by a Labour councillor of a progress report on a proposed Nottingham lesbian and gay centre.

Having asked for the report to be written, the Gay and Lesbian Sub-Committee was concerned at its absence. Perceiving such action as overriding their prerogative, they passed a resolution censuring Labour councillors for unjustified interference. The minutes of 6 February 1986 refer to their 'abhorrence at an attempt by the Labour group to suppress discussion' which was 'regarded...as a flagrant breach of trust'.[12] The issue took up the entire meeting. All other matters were deferred. The dispute continued at the next Sub-Committee when the decision of the Equal Opportunities Committee neither to confirm nor adopt the Sub-Committee's censure motion was deplored.[13]

Eventually, the report on the centre was presented and addressed. However, this ruction between the Sub-Committee and council had revealed a number of problems. First, that the Sub-Committee had little formal power if the Equal Opportunities

Committee to whom it reported refused to offer support. Second, that the Sub-Committee's insecurity, its concern with status and 'insubordination', could detract from other work. In this instance, a procedural slight had been allowed to take up a disproportionate amount of time and energy.

Meanwhile, another division was intensifying, this time between lesbians and gay men on the committee. On 10 April 1986, sub-committee members heard a report from lesbian representatives about the lesbian open day, a community event, held the preceding month, at which lesbians decided they wanted a separate sub-committee. The formal reason given was that the current Sub-Committee was perceived as too large for many representatives to feel comfortable making contributions. However, a key factor was lesbians' perceptions that they had little in common with gay men and more with other groups of women. According to Jo Fraser, lesbians had also, on occasions, become irritated by the level of sexual innuendo at meetings.

Political differences came to the fore again in a disagreement between lesbian and gay sub-committees over the use of the term 'sexual orientation' within the council's equal opportunities statement. Lesbian representatives objected to the phrase on the grounds that it was an 'umbrella term' which 'lumps lesbians together with male practices with which they have nothing in common' and which 'suggests lesbianism is only about who we have sexual relationships with'.[14] Instead, they advocated the use of 'lesbian or gay' in order to make public documents as explicit as possible as to what the council's EOP actually entailed.

In contrast to other authorities where this debate was played out, the Gay Men's Sub-Committee did not accede to the lesbian representatives' request. Arguing from a pluralist position which did not engage with the women's attack on essentialism, the men claimed that removal of the term 'sexual orientation' could lead to the exclusion of equality of opportunity for other groups defined by their sexual identity, including heterosexuals. Nevertheless, they proposed what they deemed a compromise—the word 'sexuality'—and asked the Lesbian Sub-Committee for its comments.[15] The matter went backwards and forwards between the two committees, but time was running out and it was never to be resolved to their, or the council's, satisfaction before the 1987 council elections.

Aside from this incident, the Lesbian Sub-Committee lived a fairly uncontentious life. However, two actions by the Gay Men's Sub-Committee re-opened previous intra-municipal tensions, prompting a level of media interest that alarmed the Labour leadership protecting a one seat majority, with local elections imminent.

The first, and less publicly controversial event, concerned a magazine produced for Gay Pride 1986 which was sent out with the agenda for the June meeting. A Conservative councillor, on receiving the material, complained that it was offensive; in turn, he obtained an apology from the council for the magazine's distribution. Attending the committee's September meeting, the chief executive reported that, as a result of the incident, a review would be instituted on the procedure for compiling agendas to ensure a similar embarrassing incident did not reoccur. His report echoed the leadership's concerns at the behaviour of the gay men's representatives in sending out the magazine. By doing so and by condoning Conservative outrage, the chief executive affirmed the presumption that explicit gay material was distasteful. Co-optees responded with anxiety about the future censoring of material on AIDS, and began to wonder, not for the first time, what commitment the City Council truly possessed to challenging the discrimination they faced.

The second incident, which received national media attention, involved the introduction of gay men's swimming sessions. Derided by sections of the council, it was seen by the Gay Men's Sub-Committee as no different to the separate swimming provision offered to other groups in the community. However, coming as it did in the midst of the 'AIDS panic', it provided a focus for intensified anti-gay rhetoric among local opponents of the council's EOPs. The leadership, furious at the level of publicity and opposition being aroused, demanded the scheme be axed. In turn McCance threatened to resign.[16] The swimming sessions were allowed to continue, but due to the public limelight, few gay men used them. Eventually, through lack of attendance the scheme was discontinued.

In March 1987, in the midst of this uproar, Ben Benson, the gay men's officer, tendered his resignation. In a press interview shortly afterwards, he explained that although he was leaving largely for personal reasons, his decision had been influenced by the behaviour of senior officers who did not support equal opportunities and by the 'obstinacy' of some councillors.[17]

In May 1987, the local elections gave the Conservative Party control of the council and, as they had promised, the equal opportunities unit was closed down and its committees abolished. Jo Fraser, the lesbian officer, remained until the end, but, like Ben Benson, she had become increasingly unhappy with the council's treatment of lesbian and gay issues.

> It went from a positive, achieving atmosphere to the opposite—very negative and static. By the end we knew that should Labour return (after the 1987 elections) they wouldn't support the policies to the same extent. (J. Fraser interview)

Richard McCance did not stand again. His experience of trying to maintain the council's commitment to lesbian and gay issues had left him disillusioned and exhausted.

> Most of the sub-committee's energy went into surviving....Not much pro-active work was carried out...and little was achieved....The committee existed to prove a point. It was an endurance test for four years....People didn't realise how slow it was and how much hard work was needed to get something to happen....It just ground on so that even filling up an agenda became a problem. (R. McCance interview)

Campaigning for Equality

As in Islington, the development of symbolic initiatives proved a major aspect of Nottingham's lesbian and gay committees' work in an attempt to challenge conceptions of homosexuality as unacceptable and abnormal. Lesbians and gays wished to be included within the mainstream, to be acknowledged as legitimate, respectable sections of the community. Two events demonstrate the committees' approach. The first was the resolution that lesbian and gay representatives be invited to participate in Remembrance Day ceremonies since lesbians and gays were among those killed in the Second World War. The second incident concerned Nottingham council's 'twinning' activities. Initially, the Gay and

Lesbian Sub-Committee proposed that links be established with lesbians and gays in the twinned city.[18] Subsequently, this was extended to a request that the next civic delegation to Harare (one of the twinned cities) should include a lesbian representative. Later, the request was withdrawn. Its raising seemed more an attempt to provoke deep-lying homophobia into speaking—to force the council to make their position clear—than a genuine wish to visit the city.

Pushing councils to take a stand became a compelling tactic for many municipal lesbian and gay actors. That Nottingham's committees took this direction was partly, as in Islington, due to the enormous difficulty in achieving substantive change or even in developing a productive working relationship with most service departments. While the leadership tended to perceive these kinds of initiatives as harmless providing they retained a low profile, the committees' diversion from more traditional municipal issues left them vulnerable to charges of 'wasting rate-payers' money'.

Alongside attempts to create positive images, individual grievances were addressed, such as the harassment of a gay postal worker, and a law student's complaint of homophobia within his department. Support was also given to national campaigns against recalcitrant authorities, in particular Nottingham County Council, which, despite being Labour controlled, refused to include lesbians and gay men in its EOP, thereby breaching its manifesto commitments (see Chapter 2). The Gay and Lesbian Sub-Committee raised the matter of the County Council's intransigence at a number of meetings: first, with the suggestion that links be made to help establish county lesbian and gay policies; later, to demand that the council be pressurised to implement their manifesto promises.[19]

The committees also engaged in solidarity work that included, but also went beyond, specific lesbian and gay concerns. Letters of support were sent to Simon Nkholi, Chair of the Gay Association of South African Students, greetings minuted to the Asian Gay Conference in Tokyo, and backing given for an Irish delegation to address a Nottingham meeting on the treatment of prisoners in Northern Ireland. The sub-committees also assisted local solidarity groups which had sprung up within the lesbian and gay movement in response to the miners and print workers' strikes. However, a request by the joint Sub-Committee for funding for an exhibition produced by Lesbians and Gays Support the Miners was rejected by the Leisure Committee.

Funding Raised Expectations

In common with several lesbian and gay committees, Nottingham's Sub-Committee tried to assist local groups. Because the committee did not possess its own budget, support took the form of backing bids to other committees, and providing help in kind. For instance, the committee found low-cost premises, organised publicity and gave a civic reception for LGYM's (Lesbian and Gay Youth Movement) winter festival and congress—an event, McCance says, 'councillors had to be dragged to'. The main funding focus, however, was on obtaining support from central government, either through the Inner Area Programme (IAP), a scheme intended principally for capital intensive, economic projects in urban districts or through the Manpower Services Commission (MSC) which paid salaries for staff on short-term contracts in community projects.

The Nottingham Gay People's Co-operative, hoping to establish a lesbian and gay centre, was one organisation the Sub-Committee directed towards central government funding. Others, such as Lesbian Line, also applied, considering this their only hope in an environment of stringent local government financial constraints. The Sub-Committee's optimism even went so far as to pressurise the chair of the Inner Area Programme Committee to facilitate a city-wide meeting for lesbians and gays on governmental funding opportunities.[20]

Several groups made bids, but the response from central government, when it came, was predictable. The Agency manager responsible for allocating Manpower Services Commission funds informed the Nottingham Gay People's Co-operative that their submission for development workers would not be approved on the grounds that funding such a project might bring the programme into public controversy or disrepute.[21] Similarly, Department of the Environment officials made it clear that their Minister would not look favourably at gay projects.

Why, then, did officers and councillors encourage gay and lesbian groups to apply for IAP and MSC funding, knowing they would be extremely unlikely to be successful? Harry Joshua, co-ordinator of the equal opportunities unit at the time, argues it was because nobody wanted to say 'no'.[22] Perhaps, also, doing so would have placed the council under pressure to make funding available out of its own capital and revenue programme. However, raising expectations in this way wasted organisational time and resources, undermining community development. For the Gay People's Co-operative, by the time they realised central government funds would not be forthcoming, property prices had rocketed and self-financing was no longer a viable option.

Struggling to Amend Policies and Provision

Nottingham's Sub-Committees tried to engage with a range of different service departments, to evaluate and improve the pro-vision they offered for lesbians and gay men. One issue that proved central even before the committees were running was public housing and in particular succession: what would happen to the surviving partner in a gay or lesbian relationship when the person named on the tenancy agreement died? This was a growing concern within the gay male community with the rise in AIDS-related deaths. Lesbians and gay men demanded parity with married couples for whom rights of succession already existed.

In response, the director of housing argued that same sex partnerships should take out a joint tenancy. Only in this way would such relationships 'whether lesbian, gay or friend' be given legal rights of survivorship.[23] The director's response did not satisfy the committee. Rights of succession were not only of practical, but also symbolic importance, asserting equality between gay and heterosexual relationships. It was felt that underlying the director's position was the view that homosexuals were on the whole promiscuous, unlikely to have long-term stable relation-ships and that therefore succession rights were inappropriate. According to Richard McCance:

> The right to succession was a real battle. We got minor concessions leading to a wider interpretation of housing policy in its practical application. But the chair of Housing was not supportive.[24]

AIDS was another issue which frequently arose, and became
identified from 1986 as a priority area. Requests were made for
Gay Switchboard stickers in public toilets, voluntary sector funding, publicity, information and an AIDS co-ordinator. Nottingham's AIDS initiatives appear to have been more successful than
lesbian and gay work with the housing department. Also more
successful was work with the arts and leisure departments. Partly,
this was due to the more community-oriented ethos of arts
provision, but also, Richard McCance suggests, because these
departments could respond more easily to sections of the
community such as lesbians and gays without this interfering with
their mainstream work.

> Arts and entertainments is 'safe'. They can put on a
> week of films for lesbians and gay men once a year, or
> periodically. (R. McCance interview)

For lesbian and gay sub-committee members, leisure and
entertainments provision seemed achievable. It was also a *visible*
benefit to members of their communities not involved with the
Sub-Committees' work. However, even here, obstacles were
encountered, particularly in relation to requests to participate in
mainstream arts events. For instance, in the 1986 Nottingham
Festival, the committee was requested to submit proposals for
events. Having done so, it was subsequently informed that it was
too late and the programme was already finalised.

In conclusion, Nottingham City Council's Gay and Lesbian Sub-
Committee, like other similar committees, spent its life making
suggestions and proposals which for the most part never came to
fruition. In the case of initiatives which began to be developed,
time and resources were deployed with few visible results. Lesbian
and gay issues had been forced on the council by a few Labour
Party activists; more specifically, by one, openly gay, councillor,
who, because of the political balance, could use his vote to some
effect. Yet the lack of widespread support, commitment and
understanding among Labour councillors meant that the Gay and
Lesbian Sub-Committees were given little assistance in their
battles with the officer hierarchy. Rather, councillors tended to
take the side of senior officers, seeing the Sub-Committees first as
an irrelevance and then, increasingly, as a political embarrassment
that could cost them control of the council. It is a moot point

whether the defeat suffered by Nottingham Labour Party in the 1987 municipal elections was due to the Gay and Lesbian Sub-Committees and the political capital made out of them by the Conservative Party locally. However, it is likely that the Labour leadership's electoral position was not helped by their silence, neither disbanding the Sub-Committees, nor publicly supporting and justifying their existence.

Shifting Commitment: Manchester City Council

Since the abolition of the metropolitan authorities in 1986, Manchester, a large, urban conurbation in North-West England, has been governed by a number of smaller councils including Manchester City Council. The city has had a long history of radical activism. According to Paul Hinshaw, subsequently gay officer for the city council, Manchester possessed the largest and most organised lesbian and gay community in Britain outside London. Several of the early gay campaigns were based here, in particular the North-West Committee for Law Reform and its successor, the Campaign for Homosexual Equality (CHE). In addition, since the early 1970s, Manchester has possessed a gay centre, funded by the city council.

Changes in the composition of Manchester's Labour Party—an influx of non-Mancunians, graduates, and gay activists—and the mobilisation of the party left, witnessed the ousting of the old-guard right on Manchester City Council in the 1984 council elections. In their place, a new left-wing leadership was formed backed by councillors from the political centre of the Labour Party.

Participation and Representation

From the autumn of 1984, a series of meetings were held to consult local lesbians and gays on the council's new EOP's initiative of unit plus committees. For lesbians and gays this meant four officers and two separate committees. Yet, as elsewhere, despite high turnouts, local activists were sceptical. Councillors promised the commitment of both themselves and senior officers,[25] but, in attempting to assuage doubts, they opened up the prospect of further disappointment. The changes required for lesbian and gay initiatives to succeed were more substantial than they realised and the obstacles more deeply entrenched.

Early disappointment with Manchester's lesbian and gay structures arose in several quarters. First, representation on the Lesbian and Gay Sub-Committees was almost entirely white. Attempts made to widen community participation were seen by several white gays as unnecessary;[26] not surprisingly this led Black activists to feel that racism was not being treated seriously. Friction also emerged between lesbian and gay community representatives and council management over the work of the four lesbian and gay officers employed. Activists felt the officers should be accountable to them, and should focus on community development. The co-ordinator of the equal opportunities unit and senior management were emphatic, however, that the officers were not part of community structures, but local government employees whose priority should be municipal policy work. The coordinator and management won through, but criticisms remained. Gay men's officer, Paul Hinshaw, for instance, felt that the emphasis on policy formation meant enormous amounts of work for very little progress (interview).

Community development was not, however, neglected. As elsewhere, the Sub-Committees supported campaigns against homophobia, the demands of local groups, as well as the ubiquitous calls for lesbian and gay centres. In the case of Manchester, the demand was for larger accommodation to meet the existing gay centre's increased use. The eventual success of the centre in being rehoused contrasted with the failure of lesbians to win a venue for themselves. A number of factors seem to have played a part in this: the lesbian community's lack of experience in working with the council over such a project; the absence of a clear commitment from senior management and councillors; and the ambivalence among lesbians in the city over what such a centre should provide, and, even, whether they really wanted one.[27]

Action on AIDS

Despite hard work, the Lesbian Sub-Committee during this period seemed to make little headway. Lacking a clear focus and with little organisational support, it tended to be sidetracked onto matters that were either too general or else overly parochial. While it carried out some important work in education, its suggestions and recommendations to the service were stymied by departmental anxiety and backtracking. In contrast, the gay men's project appeared more successful, perhaps in part, because of the stronger political and friendship links between gay officers, council leadership, and co-optees on the Sub-Committee. The efficacy of this network was seen most clearly in the response that met the forced hospitalisation of a PWA, under the Public Health (Infectious Diseases) Regulations 1985, authorised, late one night, by a senior Labour councillor.[28]

As soon as they heard of the detention, the gay men on the Sub-Committee took action, publicly supported by the council leader, to ensure the man's release. Amidst the uproar from Manchester's gay community, representatives on the Gay Men's Sub-Committee met to demand the council apologise to the detainee's family, review council procedures, and instigate positive AIDS work. Thus, as a result of the incident and the response it evoked, progress began in developing an AIDS policy. This included the establishment of an AIDS unit, an interdepartmental working party, and funding to AIDS organisations. AIDS, an issue which had previously been treated by the council as a gay men's responsibility, now became a corporate obligation, allowing the gay men's project to concentrate on other aspects of its work.

Changing Mood

Despite the AIDS developments which emerged between 1985 and 1987, by late 1987, the mood of the council towards equal opportunities was changing. Political and managerial power had become increasingly centralised and, as a result, lesbian and gay officers within the equal opportunities unit felt that they and the Sub-Committees were rapidly losing control over the direction of their work. Concern intensified as the leadership moved to the political centre, and tensions within the unit began increasingly to dominate the work environment. According to Chris Root, lesbian officer,

> From early 1987 onwards, more pressure was placed on
> officers to be very careful about not raising
> controversial issues...and there was a rapidly developing
> fear about the press picking things up. (interview)

Yet even before this, interest in lesbian and gay policies by gay
activists had peaked, and a number withdrew from council politics.
There were also fewer left-wing councillors around. Several had
decided not to stand in the 1987 elections as a result of budget
reductions and rate increases. Of those who stood as candidates,
the combination of a large rent and rate rise meant a number of
marginal seats, held by sympathetic councillors, were lost.

A Sophisticated Start: London Borough of Camden

Situated in the capital's West End and extending north, this final
authority, Camden, has a population of approximately 183,000,[29]
one-third of whom come from minority ethnic communities.[30]
Residents in the borough reflect a range of incomes from the very
affluent districts of Hampstead and Highgate to the poorer inner
city areas. Camden also possesses a large number of politically
active communities, including well organised lesbian feminists.
During the mid 1980s, Labour held the borough council with a
sizeable majority. Most of the political struggles therefore were
played out within the Labour group.

   Since Camden's lesbian and gay structures were established later
than in Islington, Nottingham and Manchester, by the end of this
period developments were still in their early stages. My focus,
therefore, is on the ways in which Camden began its lesbian and
gay work rather than on what followed. Having learned from
experiences elsewhere, Camden's approach was arguably the most
sophisticated—ideologically and bureaucratically. Nevertheless,
many of the same problems were encountered.

Struggling for the Best Resourced, Right Framework

The initial impetus for municipal lesbian and gay initiatives came,
in Camden, from several directions. Since the early 1980s, an

informal officer group had been working on lesbian and gay issues within the council alongside an active NALGO lesbian and gay group. In addition, a lesbian centre group, disillusioned by council treatment and the opposition of local residents, were also demanding a better display of political commitment. In 1985, backed by left-wing councillor Sandra Plummer, they proposed the establishment of a lesbian and gay unit to parallel the existing women's unit.

Despite staff and community support, the local Labour Party remained reticent, unlike in other authorities, such as Haringey and Manchester, where Labour Party members played an important role. Nevertheless, it is doubtful whether much would have happened in Camden without the work of Labour Party member and councillor, Sandra Plummer. In her role as chair of Staff and Management Services she was able to bring together the disparate groups of interested lesbians and gays. She was also able to allocate funds for the employment of two temporary workers to research into the needs of lesbians and gay men in the borough.

The use of researchers prior to establishing a unit and committee was a device not utilised in the other authorities examined here although some London authorities later took it up. Perhaps because Camden already had lesbian and gay working groups within or connected to the council, it did not perceive establishing a formal committee as a first step. Also, because Camden's goal was more ambitious—to institute a full lesbian and gay unit—it was necessary fully to lay the groundwork in advance.

The two research workers began work in 1985 with the brief of identifying the 'self-perceived' needs of lesbian and gay communities in the borough, and from there to make recommendations concerning Camden's role as both service provider and employer. Careful thought had gone into making the research project as successful as possible. It reported directly to the most senior council committee—Policy and Resources—to facilitate progress and to symbolise the seriousness with which the research project's work was being taken. Monitored by a support group chaired by Sandra Plummer, the project acquired a close nexus of experienced, committed council officers as well as an influential chair to steer recommendations through the most appropriate, effective channels. Terms of reference were broad so the researchers would not be constrained, and access was formally granted to chief officers and other senior staff.

The initial plan of the research project was for a lesbian and gay unit of six staff with both a lesbian and a gay officer working in each of three areas—employment, service provision, and community development. However, this proposal was soon extended. Local lesbians, meeting separately from gay men, demanded a separate unit reporting to a lesbian sub-committee. This would then feed into a full lesbian and gay committee. Sandra Plummer gave her support to these proposals. However, when the matter came to the Labour group shortly before the 1986 borough elections, a number of Labour councillors expressed concern and suggested it would be better to have a lesbian and gay sub-committee reporting to a full equalities committee. This would be less resource intensive and minimise attention in the run-up to the elections.

No final arrangement was made, and in May 1986, the local elections took place. Camden Labour Party fought them with a 'radical' manifesto that included several specific commitments to lesbians and gay men. Yet, despite the progressive nature of the manifesto, the political balance within the local Labour Party was changing, reflected in the new council leadership and composition of the Labour group. According to Sandra Plummer:

> The Labour Co-ordinating Committee [the new
> leadership] wanted the stress on service delivery to
> white men, to allow managers to manage efficiently and
> believed that since equal opportunities had been
> achieved there was no need for committees. (interview)

However, for the lesbian and gay research project in the late spring and early summer of 1986, the new political balance was yet to make an impact as the project's report and recommendations successfully weaved their way through the council's committee structure. The report described the widespread cynicism and anger of lesbians and gay men at the level of support offered to them by the council. Taking up the demand of lesbians for two separate units, it argued this was necessary to maintain the relatively high level of women's involvement and to demonstrate recognition of the 'double oppression' lesbians faced. Each unit was to have eight workers. There should be an AIDS worker located *outside* the gay men's unit to co-ordinate AIDS work, and a full committee on lesbian and gay issues.

Policy and Resources agreed the full committee with a membership of two-thirds councillors, one-third co-optees of whom a majority were to be women, and a proportionate number Black and minority ethnic, and disabled. However, although it agreed two separate units with a target of eight workers in each by the end of the four-year term, Policy and Resources Committee resolved that due to the current financial situation for the immediate future there would be one joint unit of only four workers.

The decision satisfied neither the two project workers nor the lesbians and gay men involved. Mindful of the newly established lesbian and gay unit in Haringey with six officers, an administrator, and a support worker for one officer, the Camden project continued to argue for more posts. But Policy and Resources Committee were not prepared to agree extra monies immediately. They compromised with a commitment to fund four additional officers to be appointed within the forthcoming financial year 1987/8.

Political Tensions

The generally positive response of the council to the lesbian and gay research project gave added momentum to community participation. At open meetings, attendance levels were high and activists enthusiastic. Discussions began to sort out the co-optee structure. Both project workers and community activists argued for the most representative and accessible arrangement possible. But right in the middle of the election process, with the gay men's co-optees already chosen, a dispute erupted that was to leave the Lesbian and Gay Committee without co-optees for the entire period discussed.

> There were to be two elections—one for lesbians and one
> for gay men. The gay men could elect two men which
> they did. The lesbians could elect four women but there
> was then a row over how all lesbians and lesbian issues
> could be covered. The lesbian representative from the
> Women's Committee alerted the meeting to the fact that
> their co-optees were boycotting the [Women's] Committee

> *at present, so it was decided not to elect anyone until*
> *that problem had been resolved. Then the men decided*
> *to suspend their co-optees until lesbians had been*
> *elected. Personalities and politics combined, and*
> *carefully laid plans fell apart....Community activists*
> *realised that the co-optees could never win a vote if they*
> *were ever in conflict with the fourteen councillors on the*
> *committee. People felt alienated from the whole process*
> *and community representation via the formal committee*
> *structure ended. (J. Skeates interview)*

Meanwhile, another major blow was to hit the work of the lesbian and gay unit and committee in the summer and autumn of 1987. With the Conservative general election victory, many authorities found themselves forced to reconsider their financial position since assistance could no longer be anticipated from central government. Across London, authorities slashed their budgets.

The crisis in Camden hit the work of the Lesbian and Gay Committee in two ways. First, Sandra Plummer and other left wing councillors were removed by the chief whip from all committees as a disciplinary measure for voting against the leadership's budgetary reduction proposals. This meant Plummer was no longer chair of the Lesbian and Gay Committee, a position she did not return to until May 1989. According to Plummer:

> *No strategy was developed during that period. The*
> *workers were very disoriented, but the new chair felt the*
> *workers would know what to do.*[31]

The second major effect of the financial crisis was that it became very difficult for the lesbian and gay unit to persuade services to initiate new policies or practices. Departments, struggling to cope with budget and staff reductions, were not inclined to release resources or officer time for new and, what many considered, peripheral issues. The lesbian and gay unit was also affected by the cuts, and instructed to introduce savings of 20 per cent. This was achieved by cutting the non-salaries budget to just under 60 per cent of what it had previously been. The alternative—making one officer redundant—was considered impossible given the size of their workload.

By the end of 1987, Camden council's lesbian and gay unit and

Committee had only just begun.

> A lot of the work initiated by the end of 1987 went on to
> be implemented later, especially in social services such
> as adoption and fostering. (S. Plummer interview)

However the work was already encountering difficulties. Budgetary reductions, political strife, serious tensions within the unit, implementation difficulties and a rapid fall-off of interest within the lesbian and gay communities, all jeopardised the effectiveness of Camden's lesbian and gay policies.

Moreover, in contrast to other authorities where a move to the right within the leadership had led to a distancing from lesbian and gay work, in Camden, the leadership tried to absorb the Committee by choosing a chair (after Plummer was removed) from among its own ranks. While this safeguarded the Committee's short-term future and that of the unit, in the long-run the strategy allowed both to become ineffectual and increasingly irrelevant to the borough's lesbian and gay communities. It was to take more than three years for the Committee and unit to find their feet again; but by then the environment of Labour authorities had fundamentally changed.

Similarities, Differences and Cycles

The focus of this chapter has been the similarities between different authorities developing lesbian and gay work. However, before discussing this further, I first wish to consider some of the differences in approach between the councils studied and the impact this had on their relative success.

Between 1982 and 1987, the development of lesbian and gay initiatives grew increasingly complex as new authorities commenced work on an ever larger scale. In part this resulted from the close networks of lesbian and gay activists which enabled one authority's aspirations to become another's reality. Council developments in one district set precedents for what was realistic and reasonable to demand elsewhere. By 1986, with an increasing number of authorities commencing work in this area, the process looked as though it would expand indefinitely. Then came the

Conservative general election victory in 1987, the severe financial crises in local government that followed, and the changing mood of the national Labour Party as it moved towards a more pragmatic, electorally-obsessed politics.

Haringey's lesbian and gay unit, established immediately before these financial and political changes, was the largest in the country (see Chapter 6). By the time Camden's unit and committee came actually to be instituted, the political and economic sea change was already taking effect, and the complex structures proposed remained unactualised. Yet although Camden's lesbian and gay structure never fulfilled its expectations, the organisational and policy proposals advanced illustrate how far lesbian and gay initiatives had moved from the early work of authorities such as Islington in the early 1980s. For this reason I have described the process of establishing Camden's unit and committee in some depth. The use of a research project, the allocation of support staff to various areas (training, outreach, policy development), the emphasis on proper community representation, the initial reports on all areas of council provision and service with far-reaching recommendations, all these demonstrate how rapidly lesbian and gay work had developed in five years.

Yet the impact on lesbian and gay policy development of greater status and more formal power alone are not clear cut. Islington as a lesbian and gay committee was barely more successful than as a working party. Resources were perhaps more central. Most people interviewed emphasised the importance of having paid support staff and a proper budget. Substantial resources, controlled directly by a lesbian and gay committee, barely existed, however, in any of the authorities discussed. Yet, where committees did possess small budgets it enabled them to develop work without being entirely dependent on the goodwill of other services. The ability to fund community projects, for example, increased a committee's relevance within the voluntary sector. Yet, having an independent budget could also backfire, if other departments abdicated their responsibility, and if lesbian and gay committees and support staff ended up focusing on small, independently organised initiatives instead of struggling with departments for service provision changes.

Much stress has been placed on having paid support staff, but I would suggest stronger determinants of success existed than the size of the specialist officer core. One such factor was the extent and location of political and managerial support for lesbian and gay work. To what extent were councillors, the leadership, community activists and other council officers not only passively acquiescent, but actually prepared to initiate and help develop lesbian and gay policies? In terms of member support, several considerations seem to have been relevant: how many openly lesbian and gay councillors existed? How experienced were they? What kind of seniority did they possess? Were they allied with or against the leadership? And what was their relationship with lesbian and gay activists and committee support officers? One cannot assume this was good. Many lesbian and gay councillors were, for different reasons, at odds with community activists. The relationship between lesbian and gay committees and the council leadership also proved crucial. In neither Nottingham nor Islington was this particularly good. In other authorities, such as Manchester, leadership support was an important factor in the early development of lesbian and gay policy.

The energy and enthusiasm of community activists also proved key in keeping municipal lesbian and gay work relevant. The experience of Camden, where lesbian and gay activists did not participate in the early work of the committee, can be compared to authorities such as Nottingham. There, co-optees played a high profile role. Yet, without support from senior management and the council leadership, suggestions and initiatives raised by Nottingham's committees were continuously blocked, hindered or ignored.

Nottingham's experience also highlights the importance of involving sympathetic officers across the council in the development of lesbian and gay work. Yet, this relies on such officers being already in place, a situation more prevalent in some of the authorities studied than others. In Camden, cross-departmental officer structures were developed to ensure the lesbian and gay unit did not take on the full brunt of work. People feared otherwise that gay initiatives would be marginalised, and unit workers burnt out from the impossibility of their task. Similar strategies were adopted in Manchester and Haringey, where sympathetic, departmentally located officers were prepared to work both within and across services to develop gay policies. Although cross-departmental officer groups were not particularly successful in any of the authorities examined, I would argue that this failing contributed to the limitations of the initiatives described.

Yet, despite the superficial differences in structure and emphasis between the authorities, what is more remarkable are the similarities in experience and approach. These are evident in the use of committees and miniature, strategic departments (units) to deliver anti-discriminatory policies; the location of lesbian and gay policies within an equal opportunities discourse; the tensions and, in some cases, separation of lesbians from gay men; the stress on outreach, community participation, anti-heterosexism training, campaigning and symbolic initiatives; and the demand of nearly every lesbian and gay committee for a local centre. Moreover, the work on service provision and personnel issues within authorities picked up many similar issues: housing succession, harassment, education adoption and fostering, cultural events, improved library resources and EOP slogans on recruitment advertisements.

Another common factor was the existence of a single key figure: Robert Crossman in Islington, Richard McCance in Nottingham, and Sandra Plummer in Camden. In each case, the actor was a Labour Party councillor, committed to developing lesbian and gay policies, and with the power and knowledge to do so. Yet there are also problems in saying that lesbian and gay municipal policies resulted from the work of a few individuals.

In Chapter 2 I set out the historical changes which enabled lesbian and gay politics to reach the municipal agenda. While individual actors played a part in exerting pressure and initiating organisational processes—for example, setting up meetings or steering motions through the requisite forums—little would have happened without broader social, political and economic changes, the interest and commitment of lesbian and gay public sector employees, community activists and Labour Party members. Moreover, lesbian and gay initiatives developed most successfully in those authorities where the impetus and initiative did not come from one sole figure, such as in Haringey and Manchester where policies had a broader base of support.

But perhaps the most striking similarity within municipal lesbian and gay work was the cycle of development, repeated in all the authorities studied. Such a cycle seems to have had four key stages. First, initial enthusiasm among lesbian and gay activists in the Labour Party, NALGO and elsewhere, with the support of left-wing councillors, is followed by the establishment of a committee and, in some cases, the introduction of officer support. Second, a peak in work output and departmental responsiveness is reached as specialist officers, new councillors and community co-optees become more experienced and confident. Third, this is followed by growing disillusionment and a decline in interest among community representatives as few concrete results are evident despite a plethora of formal policies. At the same time, specialist officers begin to 'burnout', caught between community demands and council pressures. This is exacerbated by a reduction in the support offered by sympathetic (heterosexual) councillors who have found a new cause or given them up altogether. Meanwhile, the combined effects of local residents' hostility, media outrage and electoral anxieties cause the leadership to pull back. They then try to reduce the profile of lesbian and gay work by censoring agenda papers, threatening or making substantial resource reductions, or by reducing the power and authority of the specialist officers and committee. Finally, only a small core of activity remains, carried out by officers with little external support and direction.

Despite the short and rocky lifespan of lesbian and gay work during the 1980s, it should not be dismissed as a failure. The committees and units established stretched the boundaries of municipal possibility. Local government became a political resource; a form of power and authority that could be used to support some movements and campaigns, while repudiating others, that could be used to demand more of other public bodies and private firms. It was hardly surprising, then, that lesbian and gay equality work struggled to survive. Yet, in the process of struggling, not only did it make a difference for many council staff and service users, but its presence revealed both the possibilities and tensions of equality aspirations within an activist state.

4

Something Nice for the Poor People:

Watered-Down Policies and the Limits of Liberal Bureaucracy

In the previous chapter, I examined the rise and fall of municipal lesbian and gay work within four authorities between 1983 and 1987. One of the main problems experienced was the difficulty in getting departments to develop new policies. As a result of such service intransigence, where specialist lesbian and gay officers were in place they tended to initiate and develop new work. But the problem was not that easily solved. The processes to which lesbian and gay policy development was subjected facilitated the watering down and undermining of progressive proposals.

In this chapter, I follow the policy 'wheel' of lesbian and gay work. As many analysts have argued, policy is not a linear process. There is no obvious start and finish, policy development goes in waves, circles, new directions that can be picked up at any moment and then dropped. However, because lesbian and gay work started from a near-zero base, many initiatives took a fairly linear form. Thus, we can identify a series of policy stages, beginning, typically, with an equal opportunities unit proposal, followed by consultation, committee consideration and, finally, implementation by departmental officers.

The 'mobilisation of bias' described in this chapter is not unusual. Indeed, it represents, for the most part, the general organisation of policy formation. Usually unnoticed and unremarkable, the process of containment and ideological steerage tends only to be evident by its excess, the radical surplus that finds itself organised out. Yet, while this chapter explores the process of structuration—the overdetermined reproduction of particular structural forms and interests—the process lacked closure. Lesbian and gay work, like other strategic municipal initiatives, involved a range of actors: equalities officers, departmental staff, councillors, community activists. While, in some ways, this increased confusion and uncertainty, making policy development less linear, at the same time, as I describe below, it facilitated challenges to the ideological steer that operated. Community representatives, for instance—free from official accountability—could be used to target vulnerable points in the system, and collectively-run equal opportunity units shielded risk-taking individual officers from managerial wrath.

Competing Paradigms of Sexual Politics

State Actors and Sexual Strategies

Lansley et al., in *Councils in Conflict*, distinguish between two approaches to municipal lesbian and gay work.[1] The first—civil rights—focuses on the need to eradicate discrimination and prejudice: homosexual people's right not to have their homosexuality used or counted against them.

> This large minority group is still the target of
> considerable prejudice and misunderstanding...[2]

In interviews, several people, inlcuding Robert Crossman, characterised this, somewhat dismissively, as the dominant approach among heterosexual Labour councillors.

> Let's do something nice for the poor people...Give them
> something to shut them up. But not too much.

Civil rights objectives included the eradication of formal discrimination in employment policies, and condemnation of anti-gay harassment. Among advocates of this perspective which I shall define here as weak liberal-pluralism, opinions varied as to whether anti-discriminatory measures should include policies which might constitute acceptance or validation of lesbian and gay lifestyles, for example, enabling lesbians and gay men to adopt, or encouraging discussion of gay sexuality within sex education lessons. Although within this paradigm equal opportunities discourse was deployed, its meaning remained uncertain. What was apparent, according to Crossman, however, was a depiction of lesbians and gays as victims (see Chapter 6), unable to control or determine their sexual orientation. Homosexuality was depicted as a fixed and permanent characteristic, and homosexuals as a discrete section of the community defined by their sexuality. Thus, the socio-biological indigenity of homosexuality was emphasised, epitomised by the notion that the level of incidence was fixed universally at 10 per cent. Many reports in different authorities, for instance, referred to Kinsey's statistics as if what was 'true' for the USA in the 1950s must be equally applicable in 1980s Britain.

The second approach, described by Lansley et al. as 'countering heterosexism',[3] was principally articulated by lesbian and gay municipal actors and a few left-wing, heterosexual councillors and officers. However, between heterosexuals and homosexuals adopting this approach perspectives generally differed. While the former tended to advance a strong liberal-pluralism, lesbians and gays were more likely to articulate a sexual politics I shall define as radical-pluralism.

Strong liberal-pluralism acknowledged the institutionalised nature of the problems lesbians and gay men faced, thus the deployment of the term heterosexism.

> Heterosexism is the belief and practice that hetero-
> sexuality is the only natural form of sexuality....[It] also
> teaches people to regard lesbians and gay men as
> 'queer', as 'perverted'...because of the way these attitudes
> have been institutionalised, lesbians and gay men are
> subject both to serious discrimination...and harassment.[4]

Despite the fact that the obstacles were still identified as bigotry and discrimination, this approach went beyond that of weak liberal pluralists, who focused on formal equality to stamp out direct forms of discrimination, arguing instead for training and education. People needed to 'unlearn' their homophobia. It was not just a matter of how people behaved but what was going on in their heads as well. Like their civil-rights oriented colleagues, strong liberal pluralists tended also to treat lesbians and gays as a discrete community. While the former group perceived sexuality as a matter of sexual practices, the latter focused on identity. Neither, though, treated *heterosexuality* as a political structure nor perceived its norms, practices and strictures as having any bearing on the 'homosexual' experience.

Where strong liberal-pluralism primarily differed from its weaker counterpart was in the value judgment attached to homosexuality, affirming homosexuality's normative equivalence to heterosexuality. Deploying a multicultural framework, it was argued, homosexual lifestyles were as positive and rewarding as heterosexual ones. Lesbians and gays needed to be assisted to appreciate the validity of their sexual orientation with policies such as 'positive images'. Positive action and targeted provision were vital to improve the quality of life for lesbians and gays. Indirect discrimination was also to be challenged.

Although some lesbians and gay men adopted this position, others articulated a more radical sexual politics, using the language of oppression and liberation as well as of rights.

> We went in looking for high profile change....They
> [councillors] saw discrimination, individuals suffering;
> we saw oppression. (F. Otitoju interview)

While a radical-pluralist paradigm accepted those tenets of multiculturalism that refused to make value judgments between different lifestyles, at the same time it began to problematise the relationship between heterosexuality and homosexuality. Camden lesbian councillor, Sandra Plummer, for example, argued that homosexuality touches the sexual dilemma for heterosexuals in an uncomfortable way.[5]

Focusing on the institutionalised nature of oppression, lesbians and gays perceived the problem as extending beyond ignorance and bigotry to the way social institutions such as the family were organised. Yet, despite using social constructionism to explain the majority sexual orientation, the notion of sexuality as fluid and changeable remained implicit rather than explicit. Lesbian and gay municipal actors emphasised the *existence* of their communities, not their cultural contingency, hence, they argued, the need for participation and empowerment.

The final approach, lesbian feminism, while it differed from many of the tenets of early radical feminism, was, nevertheless, a framework that extended lesbianism beyond matters of personal sexual preference. For many lesbian feminist municipal actors, their sexuality entailed a prefigurative lifestyle, not equal to heterosexuality, but preferred; *chosen* for its less institutionally oppressive nature. Within this lesbian feminist paradigm, municipal actors tended to approach local government in one of two ways.

The first argued that working in local government around lesbian issues necessitated building links with gay men.

> *Before I joined the [Haringey] lesbian and gay unit, I worked in LAGER [Lesbian and Gay Employment Rights] and became more open to working with gay men. As a feminist I rethought things about gay men....Some were taking on issues of sexism. To work within the system meant making compromises.* (S. Levy interview)

Gender alliances focused on matters of common concern: institutionalised discrimination, community development, and the need for positive images (although notions of what this latter entailed undoubtedly differed). At the same time, aspects of lesbian feminist politics potentially compatible with local government practice were incorporated, for example, the recognition of 'multiple oppression' and the right of oppressed groups to speak on their own behalf.

The second strategy, adopted in the main by community activists rather than by specialist lesbian and gay officers, entailed, in contrast, lesbians distancing themselves from gay men and gay-identified issues. The aim was instead to develop initiatives which would link lesbian municipal actors directly with grass-roots lesbian politics—through, for example, funding groups and campaigns, and solidarity gestures. This approach was particularly evident in the case of co-optees in Manchester and Nottingham and to a lesser extent among lesbian feminist community activists in Camden.

Prevailing Ideas and Policy Development

As different actors became involved, liberal, radical and feminist frameworks informed policy discourse. This proved a complex process since not only were participants involved at different stages, but, in addition, certain actors' contributions became 'organised out', able to influence only the most peripheral aspects of policy development. In the main, however, an explicit 'mobilis-ation of bias' proved unnecessary. Officers, politicians, and community activists monitored and disciplined themselves, especially as they became increasingly socialised within municipal politics and culture. This process of silencing, and the operation of power which rendered some possibilities unthought, began prior to the stages of policy formation discussed here. This absence is important to remember since it lies at the heart of state activism (see Chapter 8).

My starting point in this chapter is with proposals as they moved from the relative safety of an equal opportunities unit to wider consultation and scrutiny. Proposals actually raised and considered by lesbian and gay officers and councillors tended to express a strong liberal or radical pluralist perspective that combined challenging institutionalised discrimination, opposing prejudice, and a communitarian ideology of empowerment, non-exclusion, accountability and participation. To what extent did these ideological principles remain through the second frame of the policy process? Or were they organised out and initiatives grounded instead in other discursive meanings?

Steering Policies Through Bureaucratic Turbulence

Censorship, Scrutiny and Organised Consent

The initial decision whether to 'work up' a proposal tended to be a 'private' one, taken by lesbian and gay officers in consultation with close colleagues, and often without the knowledge of their com-mittee chairs. In conjunction with their own personal/political agendas, officers considered what was achievable; the issue's importance or priority; its timing—whether it was likely to be blocked for electoral or public relations reasons; and the impact of financial constraints.

If the decision was made to go ahead, consultation would then take place with a range of other actors. Where staff-based equal opportunity or lesbian and gay working parties existed these would often provide an initial means of consulting with depart-mental officers. Emmy Doye describes the situation in Camden:

> There were monthly meetings of the lesbian and gay
> workers groups with LAGU [lesbian and gay unit].
> Extensive consultation would take place with them.
> They were also used as a forum where employees could
> make suggestions.[6]

Certain issues, principally personnel, required consultation with
local authority trade unions. The response of union representatives to lesbian and gay issues tended to vary between workplace
and between unions. While some unions proved innovative and
supportive, in other cases the hostility of union branches made
progress difficult. In Haringey, attempts to issue a questionnaire
to all staff, to elicit lesbian and gay employees' experiences, were
delayed by the personnel department and by key trade union
bodies. Well after the local radio station had announced the
survey's imminent arrival, Lesbian and Gay Sub-Committee meetings were taken up month after month with the latest 'union
concerns'—questionnaires could not be sent to employees' homes
because spouses would think they were gay; they could not be
handed out at work because this might lead to harassment and
ridicule. While many of the concerns were legitimate, the climate
of antagonism was frustrating for the lesbians and gay men
involved. Yet the actual degree of hostility from predominantly
blue-collar unions remained a moot point as did the extent to
which senior officers were manipulating the situation. As one
specialist lesbian officer remarked:

> I don't know whether it was the unions objecting as
> much as was represented by management. We didn't
> liaise directly with the unions. There was little direct
> contact. (F. Otitoju)

Where proposals concerned outreach, community development, or
funding of a particular group or project, early consultation with
activists might take place. Public meetings were also organised on
particular issues, such as education. Although attendance was
unpredictable, when successful, community meetings provided an
opportunity for specialist officers to test proposals and get a sense
of activists' concerns. According to Femi Otitoju, in Haringey:

> Co-optees were very involved in developing the unit's
> work plan... We had a lot of meetings to test the political

> *response because many lesbian and gay activists were*
> *active in the Labour Party and so would check things*
> *out at ward meetings. They would report back and that*
> *shaped what we put forward.*[7]

However, as Femi Otitoju states, the role played by community activists changed during the lifetime of Haringey's unit.

> *At the beginning they felt they owned the unit. But as*
> *we became more confident, more local authority*
> *officers, they felt less in control.*[8]

While some actors at the pre-committee stage acted in a principally consultative or supportive capacity, others worked to contain and control policies being developed. In Islington, where there were no lesbian and gay officers and agenda decisions were taken by councillors, monitoring took place through party political channels, with ultimate responsibility held by the leader. In Manchester and Nottingham equal opportunity units, almost all draft reports were seen in advance by the co-ordinator—a process that had the potential to be supportive or coercive depending on personal management styles and prevailing pressures.

In units without internal co-ordination or management, managerial decisions on whether to develop or halt work tended to be taken at a higher or, in the case of Camden, highest level. However, even in councils where specialist lesbian and gay officers were managed by co-ordinators, many leaderships had become so sensitised to the public relations implications that they demanded senior management monitor all lesbian and gay committee agendas. In Manchester, every report concerning lesbian and gay issues had to be submitted to the chief executive. In Nottingham, Betty Higgins, the council leader, took on this role, asking for copies of all reports prior to the dispatch of the Gay Men's Sub-Committee's agendas.[9]

In the case of council members involved with lesbian and gay work, participation took place at different points during the pre-committee stage. The complexity of the relationship between councillors and officers undermines any notion that councillors were passive bureaucratic pawns as well as the idea, already contested, that they were the principal policy makers. Generally, councillors' input occurred before final reports were drafted, since it was easier then to suggest certain items were inappropriate for committee or should be abandoned than to do so after a significant amount of discussion and writing had taken place. Although some of this contact was initiated by councillors, much of it also came from officers anxious not to develop initiatives which would not have member backing.

> Lesbian and gay issues were referred to the leadership and from there to the [Labour] group, if officers were concerned. (H. Joshua interview)

Yet, in a constantly changing political environment, not all problematic issues could be identified and resolved in advance. Often they were not picked up until the chair's meeting with officers just prior to committee. These meetings were used by chairs 'to weed out sensitive issues'.[10] 'The chair looked for pitfalls and political embarrassment.'[11] Decisions taken at these pre-meetings did not tend to result in reports being withdrawn, although this could happen. Rather, they were used to discuss the approach chair and officers would take in relation to specific items and to explore points that would be pertinent or useful to make at committee. Often this was as much about officers briefing the chair as about the chair controlling officer output.

In the case of committees chaired by co-optees as some lesbian and gay committees were, pre-committee meetings performed a different function since community representatives tended to be less concerned about avoiding political embarrassment for the council. Such chairs used pre-meetings to feed their own concerns or specific interests into the agenda-setting process. According to Paul Fairweather, Manchester gay men's officer, 'although they had an impact, it was not automatically their way.'[12] Despite the convention that committee chairs took the final decision on their agendas unless overridden by the leader, this was not the case for co-optee chairs who found it much harder to resist the advice or demands of senior management and councillors.

> The [co-optee] chairs were not very directive. Officers controlled the agenda. Chairs were told to change the agenda by officers and management. The chairs were weak and agreed. (P. Fairweather interview)

At this agenda setting stage, other officers too had an impact.

Delays or objections by the director of finance or legal services could mean a report would not be ready for committee. Even with the agenda complete, the committee secretariat could, and occasionally did, block reports at the last moment on grounds of procedural irregularity, confidentiality, or because the report was seen to be making unprofessional allegations concerning the practices of departments or senior officers.

Accommodation and Resistance

What then were the ideological implications of this process? This question needs to be addressed in two parts. First, how did specialist lesbian and gay officers respond? Second, what were the effects of interventions by other officers and members?

From the interviews carried out, it appears that lesbian and gay officers responded to the structures within which they worked in both a proactive and reactive manner. The former is explicitly described by Jane Skeates:

> It was schizophrenic because we were tailoring everything to meet members' ideas of what the 'problem' was....We rarely talked about choice...we rarely talked to heterosexual members about the benefits to them of freedom of choice around sexuality and freedom from sex-role stereotyping....We were really into statistics, that is, 10 per cent of the population are lesbian or gay. In reality we did not think the statistic was useful or relevant...but we used it to gain us allies and credibility....We fed it to them in the right way. I don't know otherwise how far we'd have got.[13]

Femi Otitoju from Haringey lesbian and gay unit makes a similar point:

> Many of the members were not very conversant with the issues so couldn't defend them from stroppy officers. Even those who were with us, were not very articulate in supporting the steps agreed, so we watered down reports before they got to members and put things in the simplest of terms.[14]

More progressive approaches to sexual politics were, therefore, consciously organised out at this stage by some specialist lesbian and gay officers in order to have the best possible chance of achieving limited goals. And yet notions of 'freedom of choice', without an analysis of heterosexuality and gender, remained rooted within liberal-pluralist discourse. Hence, *moderately* progressive ideologies discussed among lesbian and gay officers (that is those which in a limited manner made it through the first stage), were already by this second stage being organised out. This occurred not so much because of explicit structural constraints as the fact such ideologies were deemed to conflict with or threaten the attitudes of dominant municipal actors. According to a lesbian and gay officer in Ealing council, 'We chose languages and structures to ameliorate the fears of members.'

Conscious discursive manipulation to achieve desired results contrasted with the practices of other, less confident lesbian and gay officers, who, rather than exploiting ideologies that might win support, played down or dropped issues seen as contentious. Frequently, they involved children—the main focus of media outrage. For instance, in Lambeth council, matters blew up over the possibility of children's homes stocking lesbian and gay books. In Manchester, lesbian and gay work in social services was kept out of the limelight for similar reasons. The effect of abandoning or suspending such work was to minimise discourses which emphasised sexual choice, the notion of equally valid sexualities, and the sexual rights of young people.

The second mechanism of ideological organisation at the pre-committee stage was that of prolonged consultation. While it sometimes led to initiatives possessing a more open textured ideological form as draft proposals tried to encompass and respond to the many concerns raised, more often it weakened proposals. Sometimes ambiguous policies were agreed, thereby postponing the problem to the stage of implementation. Alternatively, when disagreements arose with the trade unions or senior management, it sometimes seemed easier to remove the offending sentence or draft recommendation than to spend vast amounts of time and energy winning agreement for it.

The third and most explicit way in which progressive ideologies were organised out emerged from the filtering of reports and the proscribing of particular initiatives. Proposals would become increasingly inconsequential as specific suggestions were deleted by senior officers and councillors, or simply watered down.

In London boroughs, this process was performed most power-fully through resource constraints—a means which protected senior actors from having to identify their own personal opposi-tion. Lesbian and gay officers either knew or would be told that there was no point including a certain set of recommendations in a report or developing a particular initiative because the funds simply were not available. For Camden lesbian and gay unit, commencing work in the midst of a major budget reduction process, this was a serious and constant problem. To focus on what was possible meant focusing on minor, incremental changes, since even work which did not directly involve resources required the input of a certain level of 'officer-hours'.

Electoral pressures performed a similar structuring role. After a while, lesbian and gay officers no longer needed to be told to cease work in the six months run up to a general or local election. The problems this caused were not only to any attempts to sustain major pieces of work. The clear embarrassment of politicians and management towards lesbian and gay policies revealed traces of an underlying conservatism—that really homosexuality wasn't quite nice, and helping hardly something to be proud of. Demoralising and, at times, humiliating for lesbian and gay municipal actors, this constantly recurring process produced a siege mentality, a sense of working within an atmosphere of shame that was hardly conducive to healthy policy development.

Yet, despite the ideological impact of resource constraints, electoral and management pressures, few lesbian and gay officers gave in without a struggle. Although the values and procedures of bureaucratic process tended to be absorbed so that major confront-ations were minimised, at the same time, as the accounts in Chapter 3 reveal, municipal lesbian and gay work involved ongoing and substantial intra-organisational conflict.

Specialist lesbian and gay officers unrelentingly resisted attempts by others to marginalise, water-down and trivialise their work. To varying degrees they succeeded, at least in the initial stages of policy formation. Femi Otitoju describes the situation in Haringey:

The leadership tried to have a containing role...but

> *because our politics were beyond a lot of them, they
> couldn't take us on effectively. One time Bernie Grant
> (the leader) demanded to see the unit in his office. We
> said we couldn't come because his office wasn't
> accessible. So he had to come down to the unit, onto our
> territory where there was eight of us and one of him.*[15]

The difficulty for lesbian and gay officers was in maintaining control over initiatives as they passed through the formal committee stage and then on to implementation. Nevertheless, at this earlier point in the process, Haringey proved one of the most successful units to resist management pressure, thanks to its size and collective structure.

> *As a unit we got on well, partly as a result of the
> pressure. We united around our stance over oppression.
> We were more radical and confrontational and learned
> a lot from each other....We acted more like the voluntary
> sector....There were some good things about being
> outsiders. It was easier to be critical....Because we were a
> collective, they couldn't single people out for heads to
> roll.* (S. Levy interview)

The ideological tensions that emanated from being a pressure group within a bureaucratic state apparatus were evident in the reports drafted by specialist lesbian and gay officers for committee. There, discrepancies existed between, on the one hand, the substantive nature of the proposals and, on the other, the EOPs discourses deployed. Pressures both explicit and implicit were placed on specialist officers to utilise the conceptual framework of equal opportunities. It gave their work legitimacy, made initiatives more easily understood, and facilitated acceptance by other officers and members. Operating within this discourse, reports emphasised the problems of institutional discrimination, prejudice, and community need.

While this was already a shift away from prior notions of equally valid sexualities, the actual recommendations proposed tended to be even more ideologically limited. Usually they involved one of three things: requests for future reports, consultation, and the establishment of working parties. According to Femi Otitoju, the ideological discrepancies within reports between

discourse and proposals reflected the divergence between address-
ing the causes of the oppression and simply trying to limit its
effects.

> The report addressed the infection, the recommendations
> just the symptoms. (F. Otitoju interview)

In addition, text and recommendations tended to address different
audiences. While the report mediated the conflicting concerns of
community and management, recommendations were targeted at
the officers responsible for implementation. However, this
bifurcation was rarely clear cut, creating a confusion of audiences
and purposes as I go on to discuss.

Power and Authority at Committee

Traditional organisational theory has tended to focus on committees as the main locus of decision-making; that is if ideologies
were organised anywhere this is where it would happen. By
examining the development of lesbian and gay initiatives I have
demonstrated the extent to which such an analysis oversimplifies
actual practice. By the time an initiative is placed on a committee
agenda and then discussed there, it has been filtered and reshaped
through a complex process of self-censorship, consultation and
monitoring.

Actors, Roles and Influence

Aside from officers, journalists and members of the general public,
co-optees and councillors comprised the main participants at
lesbian and gay committees, with community representatives
forming the largest contingent committed to the development of
lesbian and gay work.

The opportunity for community representatives to make their
views and opinions known occurred in a variety of different ways:
through informal meetings with officers and councillors outside of
committee; at pre-meetings, where officers and chair went
through the agenda to brief majority group members, to which co-

optees were sometimes invited; and at the committee itself, where they could (i) put items on the agenda in advance; (ii) raise matters under 'Any Other Business'; (iii) ask questions or comment on any of the reports discussed; and (iv) suggest, amend or oppose recommendations.

The reality of formal community participation was, however, very different from its ideal. Three problems (all interconnected) surfaced: lack of knowledge, lack of confidence and lack of power. Despite local authority attempts to involve community represen-tatives in the policy making process, few councils instituted the necessary changes to facilitate this properly taking place; nor did many councils give adequate consideration to the consequences or implications of community participation.

At the most basic level, co-optees complained that agenda papers and reports were rarely received more than 24 hours prior to a committee meeting making it impossible for them to be adequately read and discussed in advance. In conjunction with suddenly rearranged or cancelled meetings, this made proper accountability to the lesbian and gay community impossible. According to Emmy Doye, it was a matter of guesswork about what people thought.[16] Coming to meetings unprepared, without adequate information, further lowered co-optees' confidence. It also undermined their sense of legitimacy as community repre-sentatives since they could not speak meaningfully on their community's behalf.

A second factor contributing to co-optees' lack of knowledge and consequent lack of confidence was the paucity of training offered to them by the council. Induction sessions were sometimes organised, but these were rarely sufficient, and, particularly in the case of high co-optee turnover, seldom coincided with new committee membership. The content of training was also limited since it frequently neglected or played down the importance of *informal* municipal processes—vital to progressing controversial policies such as lesbian and gay initiatives. Further, aside from information on the decision-making process, few co-optees possessed sufficient understanding of the workings of different departments to be able to translate broad demands for lesbian and gay equality into concrete proposals. As Emmy Doye said, when interviewed, 'it was often hard to articulate issues'. According to a Manchester gay men's officer:

*Lesbian and gay co-optees didn't have a clue what to
ask for; they were so unaware of their own power and
of how far they could push things.* (interview)

Many community representatives found contributing to formal,
minuted discussions with councillors and senior officers present,
with much of the emphasis on highly procedural matters, an
intimidating and inaccessible process. In Lambeth, co-optees
complained about the jargon used.[17] Emmy Doye describes how
off-putting it was being a co-optee on Camden Women's Committee, meeting in the main committee room and having to speak
through microphones.[18]

Given this context, how much impact could community representatives have on the decisions made? Those I interviewed all
expressed doubts regarding their efficacy. David Dawson and
Emmy Doye describe how co-optees' views and suggestions might
be minuted, but were rarely acted upon if not backed by council
members. Despite their formal status, co-optees lacked the real
decision-making power of councillors. Their decisions could be
overridden, ignored (without too many formal or informal
repercussions), and put to the bottom of the pile. Harry Joshua
argues one problem was they lacked the lobbying power of other
groups.

*Lesbian and gay co-optees were relatively skilled at
local authority procedures. They were more middle-class
and educated [than other co-optees], but [other sub-
committees were] more effective, because the lesbian
and gay community had less political clout.*[19]

The second group of members on lesbian and gay committees—
councillors—encompassed a diverse range of opinions, ranging
from the hostile and ambivalent through to the supportive and
openly gay. 'Out' councillors often took the chair at committee,
sometimes facilitative, other times more directive, setting the
terms of the discussion, and fending off hostile comments. Other
sympathetic councillors might intervene with helpful procedural
comments (Haringey's Lesbian and Gay Sub-Committee, for
example, included the chairs of all major committees for this
purpose), or raise issues of particular personal importance, but
otherwise tended to remain silent. In some authorities, Labour

councillors played a less supportive role. In Nottingham, apart from openly gay councillor Richard McCance, Labour members often intervened, according to Jo Fraser, 'in a negative capacity of what was not possible'.[20]

In the case of opposition councillors, their position was ambivalent. On the one hand, most were totally opposed to the very notion of a lesbian and gay committee; on the other, as committee members, there was an implicit expectation they would make helpful suggestions. Moreover, the process of being on such a committee over a period of years seems to have had a socialising or co-opting effect. On Haringey Lesbian and Gay Sub-Committee, the Conservative member over a four-year period shifted from a position of derision and antagonism to one of cautious understanding.

While community representatives saw their accountability quite specifically to the lesbian and gay community or to a particular faction within it, councillors tended to be influenced by the views and demands of a wider, often conflicting constituency. Consequently, their decisions were affected by comments in the local media, pressure from hostile residents, and other adverse concerns. This influence did not usually lead to negative opinions being expressed at lesbian and gay committee meetings, but was a factor influencing suggestions for how work on particular issues should be progressed, and in decisions made away from the scrutiny or observance of lesbian and gay communities.

Political Lacunae and the Locating of Decisions

For lesbian and gay committees in Manchester, Nottingham and Southampton, a major restriction on autonomy was their reporting lines through an equal opportunities committee.

> The sub-committee was theoretically the decision-making body, but because it needed the authorization of the Equal Opportunities Committee it was not really. (J. Fraser interview)

A similar situation existed in Ealing where according to a lesbian and gay officer:

> Decisions made by the Gay and Lesbian Consultative

Forum if not to the liking of Policy and Resources
Committee could be easily overturned. (interview)

Aside from the sometimes uneasy relations between the 'sub' and
its parent committee, a more pressing issue was the avoidance of
lesbian and gay committees altogether. While proposals involving
substantial resources automatically went before committee, other
initiatives involved a cost-benefit analysis. For instance, would the
extra support and legitimacy gained from committee consideration
outweigh the drawback of public attention? In the case of controversial policies, committee backing and assumption of responsibility might be particularly important, but at the same time,
media interest would also be greater. In a lot of cases, the 'cost'
outweighed the committee benefit. Officers interviewed described
how many contentious initiatives were developed outside formal
committees, particularly in the run-up to an election. In Camden,
for instance, as a result of local media interest in the council's
heterosexism awareness training, a concerted effort was made to
keep it out of public forums.

The growing separation in some authorities between the content of lesbian and gay committee agendas and the work of
specialist officers had serious implications for community involvement in the decision-making process since representatives tended
to have less access and knowledge about work being developed
outside of committee. While avoidance was often to give
potentially controversial projects more chance of success, at the
same time it meant major initiatives received less visibility. One
effect of this was that if work was suspended before implementation (as was often the case), it would not even have the
reverberations from being raised and discussed at committee with
the subsequent publicity such an action would incur. A further
consequence was that it led to lesbian and gay committee agendas
being frequently filled with trivial items since the important issues
were kept away, and in some instances, as Richard McCance
describes in Chapter 3, it became difficult filling the agenda
altogether.

Finally, many decisions relating to lesbian and gay work were
decided in meetings of the majority group. Sometimes this was
prior to committee, but not always since committee decisions were
not regarded as final. Hence, if a conflict arose between the lesbian

and gay committee and the relevant departmental committee over an issue, the Labour group might make a determination. Such determinations tended to reject more radical approaches since the departmental committee chair, usually a more senior member than the chair of the lesbian and gay committee, would most often have majority support. As well, away from the pressures to demonstrate a pro-gay position, other factors frequently held more weight.

Texts, Implications, Audiences

The ideological impact of lesbian and gay committees manifested itself in two principal ways. First, their status as public forums enabled meanings to be conveyed directly to the general public. Although few people actually attended, discussions and decisions tended to be widely reported thanks to the presence of opposition councillors and the press. Although co-optees were often intimidated, and although their comments were usually dismissed or later overturned by other bodies, in terms of the impression given to people attending, their more radical statements were important; statements which could not with certainty be contained, or mobilised out in advance by senior management and the leadership. It was this public outlet in the midst of the policy-implementation process that many senior councillors and officers underestimated—to their cost. Their cynical belief that the implementation process would weed out troublesome initiatives and water down others neglected the impact committee discussion and decisions could have, just by being communicated to the wider community.

The second means of ideological communication was via implementation. The text of committee reports, recommendations and minutes passed on to those responsible for operationalising pieces of work incorporated a range of meanings, norms and values. While readings will differ according to a range of social and individual factors, analysing the texts gives us some indication of the ideological processes that took place.

Services such as housing, education and social services tended to draw heavily on weak liberal-pluralist arguments, legitimating their comments and proposals by reference to pre-existing council

EOPs. Although the language of reports was usually carefully worded to seem constructive or at least neutral, committee members and specialist officers perceived many reports to be (implicitly) negative and defensive. This defensiveness was characteristic of a civil-rights paradigm that granted lesbians and gay men rights on account of their human status, but refused to validate homosexual choices or desires. A report presented by the director of social services to Lambeth Working Party for Gay Men and Lesbians is a typical example.

> There is very little research available to answer even basic questions related to the ability of gay people to provide good parenting.[21]

Reports commonly claimed that lesbians and gays were treated the same as heterosexuals by the service, that there were no issues of lesbian or gay interest, or, alternatively, that the resources were just not available. In Lambeth, for instance, a report by the director of finance stated:

> The directorate...is keen to take positive action on the subject, but, as stated, little or no resources are available. If however resources were made available, the directorate would be more than delighted to play its part in improving the opportunities for lesbians and gay men.[22]

Although written reports and their recommendations were important in shaping the ideologies conveyed to implementation officers, in terms of the meanings conveyed to the general public, verbal comments were just as significant. The greater freedom for verbal contributions was utilised by specialist lesbian and gay officers to elaborate on points and to make arguments that could not for political or bureaucratic reasons be put into print. Specialist officers chose those verbal strategies which would be most effective given the particular committee's composition. Jane Skeates, in her interview, describes the use of 'sob stories' to convince heterosexual councillors.[23]

However, the ideological limitations on officers' contributions meant community representatives were sometimes used as their mouthpiece. In this way, co-optees might give voice to ideologies or proposals organised out, against lesbian and gay officers' wishes, at an earlier stage in the policy process. Femi Otitojudes-cribes how this happened in Haringey:

> People [co-optees] were primed and set up....We would
> know if an issue was going to be sticky and we'd go to
> the community who'd want it even stronger than in the
> report. We would say if you want it stronger, then say
> this or that at the committee....People lost their rag at
> committee. Things that could never be put in a report
> were said. If it had come straight from the unit we
> would have been reprimanded. Co-optee suggestions
> strengthened the recommendations. Nobody would say
> no and it would go through.[24]

In Haringey, co-optees' verbal contributions tended to be carefully planned in advance. Elsewhere this was not the case and even in Haringey, a few co-optees would make suggestions—sometimes provocatively—at variance with the officer-co-optee consensus.

A key form of verbal input was the addition of recommenda-tions to reports. This might seem a strange 'addition', since formally it was the job of the committee to make recom-mendations. However, reports were always written with recommendations included, and, in the main, these officer-chair 'suggestions' were accepted by the committee. When recom-mendations were added at lesbian and gay committees these tended to reinforce the already existing organisational bias of setting up working parties, increasing consultation, and referring the report to other committees. The ideological effect of such suggestions was ambivalent. Ostensibly, it gave an impression of municipal interest in, and commitment to, lesbian and gay 'equality'. However, for people more 'au fait' with local authority procedures, it demonstrated the lack of any substantive action to be taken. Lesbian and gay reports would be passed from committee to committee with little concrete progress. At the same time, this passage gave legitimacy to opponents' claims that lesbian and gay matters were dominating council business.

Conclusion

In Chapter 5, I continue this examination of the 'organising out' of more radical approaches by considering what happened during implementation—in other words, were policies further watered down? But first, let us briefly reflect on the analysis thus far. In general, my argument has been that as proposals became formalised and developed, with the exception of unpredictable committee moments, a liberal discourse of civil rights and minority status increasingly prevailed. As I have shown, this was not simply an effect of different actors with less radical politics becoming involved. The exertion of control and authority to constrain initiatives in part reflected senior actors sexual politics; inextricably caught up with this was the role played by financial, electoral and media considerations.

This chapter thus illustrates the limitations of relative autonomy as a conceptual framework of bounded freedom. There is no arena within which actors simply do as they please. All decisions, as well as interests, processes, values and demands, are affected by a range of considerations that congeal or condense in particular ways at any given moment. While actors can choose to ignore financial constraints or electoral unpopularity, such choices have implications, as I discuss in Chapter 9. Moreover, disregarding 'political realities' tends to be perceived as foolish, irrational and irresponsible, bringing with it its own political consequences.

In examining the interplay of organisational culture, structural factors and political interests, I have tried to demonstrate the relative ease with which they reproduce each other. This is a point poststructuralist theories of the state often neglect, focusing instead on the *difficulties* of reproduction, and the contested nature of the process. Yet, while it may be easier to reproduce status quo social relations and meanings than oppositional ones, the process of 'structuration' is not closed. As I discussed here and analyse in more depth in Chapter 6, absolute containment by local government bureaucracies of more radical approaches proved an impossible guarantee, and some policies managed to slip through. Even for the majority that did not, the task of maintaining control, in an area where reproducing the status quo involved sustaining normative heterosexual narratives at the unarticulated level, proved a fraught and stressful business for the authorities involved. One many were pleased to give up.

5

Implementation Failure, Appeasement and Prefigurative Practice

Within traditional political science, implementation has not been seen as a major problem. It was assumed that once a decision had been made, it would then be carried out as planned. More recently, such assumptions have been widely challenged. My research also reveals the highly contested nature of implementation; the post-committee stage of lesbian and gay work was as much a period of negotiation, lobbying and compromise as its earlier counterparts. Again, this is not unique to lesbian and gay policy development; few initiatives are operationalised exactly as decided by politicians on committees. This is not surprising, for in many ways it is these 'decision-making' committees which are anomalous. The power balance they represent—minimal officer influence, parity between committee members—is substantially different to the rest of the policy formation-implementation process. One might therefore anticipate that the format of policies developed for committee would undergo revision once the committee stage had been passed. Yet while this process is a 'normal' one, what lesbian and gay (and comparable strategic) work faced was not the resumption of a pre-committee paradigm but rather the imposition, post-committee, of a substantially different agenda: an agenda which aimed to minimise, ignore or discard lesbian and gay policy altogether.

In this chapter, I consider why such severe implementation problems arose, the strategies developed to overcome them, and the ideological implications both held. In particular, what was conveyed to different 'audiences' by the structuring of this crisis?

Yet the lack of implementation raises a further question: why bother offering to do anything in the first place? In exploring this issue, I examine the relationship between symbolism, ideology and material change.

A Crisis of Implementation

Autonomy, Hierarchy and Role

Implementing lesbian and gay initiatives took a number of forms. Sometimes the work was carried out by specialist lesbian and gay officers, who organised, for example, cultural events or staff training. Other times, implementation was the responsibility of particular departments, either alone or in conjunction with specialist officers.

In general, the involvement of specialist lesbian and gay officers in departmental implementation was very limited. Whilst the formal expectation was that specialist officers would liaise with departmental staff to ensure appropriate action was being taken on committee recommendations, this rarely occurred. In most local authorities, individual departments possessed considerable autonomy from the centre despite attempts in the 1970s and 1980s to improve corporate practice. Equal opportunity units found this departmental decentralisation of power a major obstacle in their attempts to monitor and influence changes to provision.

> People [in departments] go to their line manager and the decision [of the lesbian and gay committee] is sat on, particularly where no groundwork's been done. (J. Parker interview)

Departmental autonomy was not the only organisational obstacle. Even more significant, perhaps, was the hierarchical and role-dichotomised nature of public bureaucracies. This meant that those workers actually providing front-line services, *implementing* anti-discriminatory initiatives, were relatively uninvolved in their development. The traditional bureaucratic structure, whereby one set of officers 'formally' make policy and another carry it out, was left largely untransformed by the new urban left, the main initiators of municipal lesbian and gay work. Although lesbian and gay specialist officers attempted to work with front-line staff in developing initiatives, these ventures were too ad hoc and too unsupported to make much impact.

Leaving aside for the moment those initiatives which actually originated with 'street-level' staff (such as, social workers, librarians, teachers), divisions between policy-makers and implementing officers had a number of consequences for the execution of lesbian and gay work. First, front-line officers were often unaware of the details of policies they were expected to implement. In many instances, this bred a sense of hostility and resentment in workers who felt they lacked 'ownership' of policies identified with management. This frustration would have played out differently between workers used to high degrees of professional autonomy and those whose work was organisationally highly structured. However, both kinds of front-line staff resisted what they perceived as state *impositions*, in many cases irrespective of the content. Particularly in the case of some manual workers, their sense of 'us' and 'them' generated the negative equation of lesbian and gay initiatives with 'them'. This problem did not just affect lesbian and gay work. However, the newness of the policies, combined with their controversial nature, and the mixed messages received from middle management meant many front-line workers perceived them as an illegitimate interference.

Front-line opposition when it occurred proved a particular problem because of the nature of lesbian and gay work. Whilst some lesbian and gay initiatives were redistributive, for example, purchasing particular library books or obtaining funding for gay groups, the majority concerned 'protective-regulatory' strategies, that is, restructuring council work to reduce levels of discrimination and prejudice. In comparison to redistributive policies with clear resource implications, agreeing protective-regulatory policies such as EOPs, proved a relatively uncontentious process since not very much was committed by the mere process of committee approval except a nominal show of support. The real difficulty was in implementation. Attempts to tackle discrimination and prejudice in the provision of council services heavily depended on front-line officers *actually* not discriminating. Although authorities set up complaints procedures and in other ways tried to structure and contain officer discretion, it proved difficult to ensure that council officers abided by EOPs unless they were actually committed to doing so.

In cases where lesbian and gay officers were not in post, some councillors tried to intervene in the implementation process, pressurising front-line officers and middle management to ensure policies were put into effect. The results were rarely successful. Where councillors did get closely involved, this tended to reinforce council staff's perceptions that lesbian and gay policies lacked legitimacy, being the self-interested whim of one or two councillors. For not only were the policies themselves perceived negatively as too ideologically purposive, that is, *setting out* to change social meanings, but the very act of councillor intervention in the implementation process revealed their illegitimacy. If the policies had been proper, they would have been developed within the appropriate channels. The implications of such perceptions were serious. According to a former lesbian and gay officer at Ealing council:

> If officers think things are 'loony', they won't do anything.[1]

In discussing implementation problems it needs to be stressed that obstacles did not invariably come from front-line staff. In many cases, individual council employees—teachers, childcare staff, housing and social services workers—attempted to put into practice lesbian and gay anti-discriminatory policies. The difficulties they faced arose from the lack of support, advice, encouragement and, at times, even the dissuasion of colleagues and management within their departments. As a result, many front-line workers were put off, fearing the prospect of public complaints. If they put lesbian and gay policies into practice, would anyone back up their actions?

Overcoming Difficulties: Organisational Strategies

Frustrated by the lack of action, specialist officers made a number of attempts to overcome the implementation difficulties faced. Undoubtedly, their organisational location in the strategic 'centre' of the bureaucracy reinforced street-level staff's resentment— what did these people on big salaries know about the realities of rubbish collection, property maintenance or homelessness? Nevertheless, member, officer and committee structures were used in an attempt to expedite matters. At member level, one approach involved the chair of the lesbian and gay (or parent) committee taking up the matter with the chair of whichever service was causing problems. This strategy sometimes worked if the departmental chair was sympathetic and effective. Usually, however, they chose to endorse the decisions of their own departmental officers—mirroring the words of their director as to why work could not be carried out.

A second approach was for lesbian and gay specialist officers to request that their line manager resolve the problem with her or his equivalent within the relevant department. Where a good relationship existed between lesbian and gay officers and their manager, such as in Haringey, this was sometimes attempted. However, in authorities like Camden, the line manager was either too senior to be willing to intercede or, as in Nottingham and Manchester, too closely identified with lesbian and gay work to be effective.

A third strategy entailed using the formal decision-making forum.

> We used the committee to put pressure on departments because [lesbian and gay] officers had no status. (C. Root interview)

Lesbian and gay committees would request or even try to insist on implementation updates from departments. However, the production of reports was infrequent and tended to be preceded by a long time lag from the date of request. Robert Crossman states that his committee in Islington never received implementation reports. Consequently, he had no idea whether initiatives were implemented or not. On the whole, committee members did not force the issue. Two reasons for this stand out: first, many, particularly those who were less experienced, assumed implementation was taking place; second, questions of implementation appeared more frustrating and less interesting than going on to develop new work.

Using the authority of chair, line manager or committee to pressure a department into acting tended to be a last resort. The more frequently adopted procedure was to use informal networks, and to work in areas where influential and senior officers were more sympathetic. This, though, had its own problems. It meant work tended to be fragmented, developed in services where officers were interested, but not where they were hostile. As a result, some of the worst departments tended to be neglected. Informal networks also had their limitations.

> The coordinator said to use supportive workers in departments: but they don't have the power. (interview with Manchester gay men's officer)

Lesbian specialist officers found this particularly a problem. Lesbians tended to be at lower levels in departments than gay men and therefore were less able to advance initiatives. Moreover, Chris Root found that many closet lesbians avoided her in order that their own sexual orientation would not be called into question.[2]

Interpreting the Implementation Process

When interviewing, I asked people if the lesbian and gay initiatives implemented differed significantly from the decisions made at committee. What ideological change did policies and projects undergo between formal decision and implementation? The general response was that policies were not usually watered down, or changed. Rather, they were just not implemented, or, if implemented, put into effect in a highly ad hoc manner with little dissemination to the public or workforce as to what the policies meant or entailed.

In any implementation, new officers become involved, working with different 'policy frames', that is different interpretive frameworks through which they understand and conceptualise what the policy or project entails. The extent to which this differs from the initial 'policy frame' depends on the outlook of the implementers and the degree to which the original developers are involved.[3] Thus, in the case of lesbian and gay work, where specialist officers worked closely with those implementing initiatives, the interpretive shift was less than where departments passed on responsibility to implementing officers acting without the involvement of central units. Such an ideological shift was not automatically to the right, however. In some cases, implementation could potentially be more radical than earlier policy development if carried out by committed people away from the scrutiny and control of unsympathetic, anxious senior management.

However, in general, the lack of large-scale changes and the emphasis on individualistic implementation forced lesbian and gay work even further in the direction of marginal modifications. Senior management's refusal to *insist* on implementation meant the kinds of work that could take place tended to be small-scale projects that individual workers could implement with minimal (or no extra) resourcing. In cases where front-line workers acted on their own initiative, developments tended to be cautious and incremental. Within such an environment, it was also hard for policies to 'stick'.[4] Without adequate resourcing and monitoring, even policies that were implemented tended to fade quickly and disappear as soon as attention moved elsewhere.

These problems confirmed perceptions of lesbian and gay work as tangential and peripheral. Anti-discriminatory discourses, prevalent in the earlier stages of policy development, were barely apparent in what was conveyed to the public by the way initiatives were actually carried out. Rather, the ad hoc, individualised manner of implementation conveyed the impression that such initiatives were both ridiculous and unnecessary, lacking municipal legitimacy and support. Those officers who did attempt to put into practice policies in this area were frequently perceived as acting in a self-interested, unprofessional manner, giving disproportionate time and attention to an insignificant (and probably personal) minority interest.

This attitude was compounded by the measures adopted to overcome implementation obstacles. Taking matters to Labour group and senior management meetings or placing them on departmental committee agendas meant many council officers and committee members increasingly perceived lesbian and gay issues as inappropriate, diverting attention from 'real' and serious governmental affairs. In addition, the minor proposals or concerns, raised in these senior bodies because of resistance, contrasted unfavourably with the more substantial matters, for which these bodies tended to be used. This difference was exacerbated by the fact that lesbian and gay matters like other EOPs, because of their organisational location and political sensitivity, had relatively easier formal access to senior decision-making bodies than equivalent issues of service provision which also possessed a denser hierarchical structure.

Whilst anti-discriminatory measures for lesbians and gays generally failed to be operationalised in any meaningful way, targeted provision within lesbian and gay communities, for example, arts events and youth groups, was more successful. Yet the ideological impact of the latter was equally problematic. On the one hand, lesbians and gay men received benefits, in particular, a strengthening of community identity as a result of cultural initiatives. At the same time, specially targeted provision tended to reinforce the view amongst less sympathetic people that lesbians and gay men were hedonistic and privileged, receiving special treatment from local authorities at a time when other work was being cut.

Political Commitment and Symbolic Policies

Implementation of lesbian and gay work failed for many reasons. So far I have focused on bureaucratic factors, but equally as significant were the attitudes and behaviour of politicians. Throughout the 1980s Labour councillors were prepared to publicly articulate support for lesbian and gay equality. Most, however, were satisfied for the commitment to remain a purely formal one. For, questions of priority aside, Labour politicians were uneasy about the political implications of putting lesbian and gay equality into practice.

The desire to maintain political stability was a key consideration. Although the depth and extent of politicians' electoral anxiety varied between authorities, a correlation existed with the size of the Labour group's majority. Where it was greater, such as in Haringey, Manchester and Camden, the necessity of placating voters could be jettisoned in the short term. In Nottingham, on the other hand, where Labour nursed a one-seat majority, councillors remained perpetually conscious of the need to maintain sufficient support to stay in control and implement their priorities. Yet the

differing emphases on stability also highlighted ideological divisions. In Haringey, during the mid-1980s, the leadership was left
wing, with a commitment to change. Hence, they were willing, if
not entirely prepared, to take on the upheaval that might follow
any challenge to vested interests. The same was not true, however,
for more moderate leaderships, such as in Nottingham and, after
1986, in Islington (see Chapter 3).

Nevertheless, in the long term, no authority felt able to
operate effectively in a politically unstable situation. This point
has particularly important implications for initiatives whose
implementation would run over several years. For example, in
the case of Haringey's curricular proposals (see Chapter 6),
educational changes would not have come into force for three or
four years, but by that point not only could government legislation step in (if required), but Haringey council, under a more
moderate Labour leadership, was no longer prepared to withstand the opposition and destabilisation such an educational
strategy might provoke. Thus it seems that where policies were
likely to be controversial, implementation only transpired in
circumstances where it could occur quickly. Electoral and other
political reasons (for example, the desire to implement a range of
priorities) meant few councils were prepared to withstand long
periods of disruption. Even if leaderships were prepared to, their
party might not.

Symbolic Initiatives: A Challenge to the Policy/Implementation Dichotomy

Why, if many Labour councillors feared the implications of
implementing lesbian and gay policies, were they prepared to
offer statements of support? What did they think verbalised and
written declarations of commitment would, alone, achieve? These
questions shift the focus of this discussion. Instead of examining
the gap between policy and implementation, I ask: why promise
policies when there was no serious intention to deliver them?

This is a paradox witnessed in many areas of equal opportunity
work, in anti-sexist and anti-racist initiatives, as well as in
developing lesbian and gay equality work. Pfeffer argues, using
Edelman's work, that political language and symbolic outcomes are

deployed to placate sections of the community who are either unable to distinguish between 'reality' and 'symbols', or where 'symbolic' outcomes are what is desired (see Chapter 3).[5]

Barrett and Hill claim that development of symbolic policies is also facilitated by the division between policy makers and implementers.[6] Maintaining a distance from the implementation process makes it easier for councillors to offer token or symbolic gestures. They can make promises, heighten the sense of political dynamism,[7] whilst knowing and publicly asserting that, unfortunately, implementation is out of their control.

Yet why was there felt a need, by those politicians who remained ideologically unconvinced, to placate lesbian and gay communities? To consider this question we need to go back a decade. As I discussed in Chapter 2, Labour authorities' development of EOPs in the late 1970s and early 1980s, their critique of prejudice and discrimination, largely unwittingly laid the ground work for lesbian and gay policies. To have subsequently rejected or ignored this latter, emergent community, with its experiences of hardship and disadvantage, would have necessitated producing arguments that distinguished the needs of lesbians and gays from those of other 'minority' groupings. Within the new urban left's liberal-pluralist paradigms, this would have been difficult to achieve. Yet it was not just patronage and ideological coherence which led Labour councils to act; in addition, certain Labour-run districts began to consider it pragmatic and appropriate to respond to the growing political resources possessed by lesbians and gays. The alternative of dismissal might be risky, bringing with it the possible hazard of protest and opposition, as occurred in a number of authorities where council leaderships refused to include lesbians and gays in formal EOPs statements (see Chapters 2 and 3).

Yet, despite the fact lesbians and gays did not tend to mobilise against authorities that *formally* committed themselves to lesbian and gay policies, the extent to which activists or communities were 'satisfied' by political statements alone is uncertain. Whilst some may have taken statements as a promise of subsequent municipal developments, for others, acceptance was pragmatic, a belief that verbal offers were the most that could be expected at that given juncture. These responses assume a clear distinction between formal policy and concrete implementation. However, many lesbians and gays accepted formal commitments because they perceived such statements themselves as an important component of the change process.

In making this point, not only do we begin to problematise the distinctions between policy formation and implementation but also that between 'symbols' and 'reality'. The dissolving of such polarities was evident in lesbian and gay municipal work where the focus on bigotry and ignorance meant that the production of symbolic or specifically ideological texts were seen both as constitutive of 'reality' as well as helping to shape the process of social change. Yet how great was this impact? In Chapter 3 I briefly discussed the nature of symbolic policies: initiatives which attempt to achieve change by prefiguring desired norms and meanings. What symbolic policies ignore, however, intentionally or otherwise, is the need to work at other levels too if change is to be achieved. It was not enough, for example, to simply put 'lesbians' before 'gay men' in a committee title to achieve the social transformation—a challenging of sexism—that was being prefigured.

However, one might argue, it was largely because of this inadequacy that 'private' symbolic policies were permitted by senior management and councillors. (Public symbolism, such as the laying of pink wreaths on Remembrance Day, was more dangerous.) At the same time, even these gestures had a cost, as witnessed in the vigorous opposition generated by right-wing forces to purely formal lesbian and gay policies. For, despite the fact that change can rarely be achieved through symbols alone, at the same time, in the case of ideological policies, less disjuncture existed between verbal articulation and actual implementation. Hence, formal 'non-implementation' would not necessarily appease opposing forces. For example, a policy aimed at encouraging lesbians and gay men to adopt and foster cannot be separated from a strategy of rearticulating the parenting-sexuality nexus. Thus, the policy would, in part, be achieved by statements normalising non-heterosexual families and by meetings on the initiative's development within the lesbian and gay community.

However, though *communication* of council policies became part of the very process of implementation, the nature of such implementation was limited. Not only was this because implementation of most policies required more than their public announcement, but also because of the care councils took as to how and where they discussed or publicised initiatives. This was apparent in the limited arenas in which councillors and officers were prepared to talk about controversial policies, such as Haringey council's educational policy of 'positive images' (see Chapter 6). Although speeches were made in the council chamber and statements given to the press, little discussion took place outside of the traditional arenas of public debate, for example, amongst the intended beneficiaries of the policy: children in schools.[8] This problem of communication provides the central theme for the next two chapters which explore the struggles between the right, gays and the council to provide and convey the authoritative interpretation of the 'positive images' initiative.

6

With God's Help and Common Sense:

Policy-Making, Discursive Struggle and Homosexuality

> A little boy I know was going along the road with a dog one day; it was a boy dog. The boy dog met another boy dog and started doing what boy dogs don't generally do together. [gallery: whoops of laughter—you mean fuck?] Hang on. A mating ritual, yes. The little boy looked at the dog and said, 'I don't know why they're doing this, they're two boy dogs'. Two teenage girls standing alongside started to laugh and had a good laugh at this and said, 'the dogs must have gone to a Haringey school!'
>
> Cllr. Salim, Full Council meeting, 20 October 1986

It was a dark night with autumn already turning towards winter. A hundred yards from Haringey civic centre, I could already see the police cordons separating councillors from activists, and pedestrians from the gathering crowds. The meeting began outside, with activists several hundred strong. Councillors addressed the crowds, first from the town hall steps, then from a balcony overlooking the forecourt—the height of 'municipal royalty'? Finally, loudspeakers set up in the council chamber broadcast the formal meeting to those unable to get balcony seats. Yet this was no 'formal' meeting; a civic chamber converted into a site of urban struggle. Amid the speeches, heckles and laughter, eggs were hurled, a cushion flung, councillors expelled, and deputations censured. 'The national anthem has not been elected a member of this council', one Labour member quipped as the meeting drew to a close with 'Land of Hope and Glory' blaring from a Conservative councillor's tape recorder, the beat sustained by Tory councillors banging their tables with hastily removed shoes.

With over one thousand activists, politicians, council officers and journalists crowding in and around the civic centre chamber, this 'performance' of a full council meeting crystallised the tensions but also the theatricality of new urban left politics. This was an expressive politics of ideological assertion, a politics that rejected as trivial and uninteresting the 'bread and butter' issues of clean streets and repaired gutters. For a brief moment, Haringey was the epicentre of this revolutionary spirit, with lesbian and gay policies its chief mascot. But what had happened to get us to this place and how tendentious were its roots?

On 8 May 1986, Haringey borough elections returned a Labour leadership with an increased majority.[1] It was a victory that surprised many despite traditional Labour Party support in the borough. For in common with other authorities controlled by the new urban left, Labour in Haringey fought the elections on an unusually progressive manifesto prioritising the needs of oppressed and disadvantaged groups.

Haringey's commitment to challenging racism had become the focus of right-wing antagonism one year earlier. A Black leader who understood the tensions of an impoverished council estate, Broadwater Farm, and the racism that precipitated a small uprising proved too much for media, police and elite politicians alike. However, from April 1986 until the spring of 1988, Haringey came under attack for another of its political objectives: the implementation of equality for lesbians and gay men. One set of initiatives drew more attention than any other. This was Haringey's policy of 'positive images', which aimed to challenge the discrimination and inequality faced by lesbian and gay pupils and staff within the education system.

'With god's help and common sense' is an exploration of what happens when the internal mechanisms of ideological containment, as described in Chapter 4, break down. Broadly, my argument has been that most radicalism (or even progressivism) is contained, watered down or removed by state bureaucracies themselves. These processes, however, are not foolproof. In the context of lesbian and gay work, they were to different degrees abrogated, with Haringey's positive images policy providing perhaps the most extreme example.

What then followed? My argument is that *when* state contain-ment broke down, external forces intervened, deploying a range of power at their disposal. But such interventions, although they seemed from the outside pervasive, were in fact anomalous. In the main, central government and the right did not need to mobilise; the boundaries of municipal activism were policed with sufficient effectiveness from their interior. However, when they did organ-ise, a range of strategies were used. In the context of 'positive images', the right deployed textual strategies (written and oral) to reinterpret the policy, as well as other political techniques: administrative, juridical, populist. As Foucault argues in relation to torture, which functions both as violence and as signification, techniques and strategies often co-exist. Statutes, for instance, operate ideologically as texts as well as coercively through pro-hibiting, prescribing or facilitating behaviour.

This chapter also explores the concept of policy. By what means do we identify the parameters and substance of local government policies? To what extent are the meanings of policy fixed and unequivocal? Through exploring these questions, I wish to challenge the idea that a policy means what policy makers and implementers say it means. I also want to contest the notion that there are clearly defined policy makers and implementers. In this study of 'positive images' both categories were much more complex than the conventional policy-making view would suggest.

The Tale of 'Positive Images'

The 1986 Labour Party manifesto, which formed the basis of Haringey council's 'positive images' policy, only briefly referred to gays and education. However, it committed the council to support-ing the right of educational workers to be 'openly lesbian or gay at work'; supported students 'realising their own gayness', and aimed to 'begin the process of ensuring...lesbianism and gayness are treated positively in the curriculum'.[2]

On 2 June 1986, the manifesto was formally endorsed and adopted by the council at its annual meeting. Shortly afterwards, a letter was sent from the newly established lesbian and gay unit to all head teachers in the borough. It advised them of the policy and informed them of a 'fund for curriculum projects from nursery through to further education...specifically designed to be anti-racist, anti-sexist and to promote positive images of lesbians and gays, and of people with disabilities'.

The lesbian and gay unit's letter took Haringey council and the borough Labour Party by surprise. The council leadership and education service were furious that the unit had ignored the 'proper' procedures. They argued the policy should have been developed slowly and gradually with education taking the primary responsibility. That way, it was claimed, opposition would have been minimised. The unit, and lesbian and gay activists, disagreed. Had they not taken immediate action on the basis of manifesto commitments (subsequently council policy), nothing would have happened.

As a result of this letter, sent without consulting the education department, the storm over the council's lesbian and gay policies, brewing since the 1986 local election campaign, exploded. By the mid-summer of 1986, the Parents Rights Group (PRG) had formed with the ostensible purpose of opposing 'the council's policy to promote among children the belief that homosexuality is an acceptable alternative to heterosexuality'.[3] They and Tottenham Conservative Association spent the summer months distributing leaflets, petitions, and holding rallies against 'plans to introduce homosexual education'.[4] Meanwhile, questions were asked in the House of Lords,[5] and ministerial disquiet expressed by Secretary of State for Education, Kenneth Baker.

With the council angry and defensive at being caught on the 'hop', responsibility fell on community activists to take the initiative in opposing the right. In the late summer of 1986, Tottenham Communist Party called a meeting of sympathetic progressives 'to counter the Tottenham Tories on the Gay Classes issue'.[6] On 2 September 1986, Positive Images (PI), 'a community campaign for lesbian and gay rights in Haringey' was born.[7]

The autumn of 1986 saw a gradual escalation, as PI, Haringey Labour Party, the PRG, sections of the church, Tottenham Conservative Association and other groupings confronted each other over the proper response of an educational system to homosexuality. Within the coalition against a pro-gay policy, the church was a key participant. While some christian groupings, such as the Gay Christian Movement, were supportive of the policy, in the main the public response of Catholic, Anglican and Baptist spokespeople and particularly of fundamentalists was to back the stand taken by the PRG.[8] In the winter of 1986/7, opposition to the policy drew the support of the New Patriotic Movement, a far right religious group connected to the Unification church.[9] Yet it is important to make clear at this point that although the right dominated the membership and strategy of opponents, the policy was also opposed by non-aligned residents as well as by Labour Party supporters hostile to homosexuality. Martin Durham for instance, explores the tensions that arose within the PRG because some members were critical of the group's exploitation as a Conservative Party platform and puppet.[10]

In addition to these locally based groups, struggles over the validity and meaning of lesbian and gay rights in education took place in the media (see Chapter 7) and in national political forums. In these diverse locations, each side attempted to assert its definition and interpretation of 'positive images', as Haringey's educational policy on homosexuality quickly became known. At the same time, Haringey council, under pressure from all sides, hastened to set in motion development of its own corporate position. By the early spring of 1987, the education service, in conjunction with the lesbian and gay unit, had established a curriculum working party—promised the previous autumn—to develop 'guidelines for anti-heterosexist approaches in schools and colleges and to review and develop resource materials'.[11]

Nevertheless many supporters and advocates of 'positive images' considered the council's actions tardy. Some felt the council was simply shielding the unit's faux pas without any real commitment to developing policy. This perception was disputed by councillors and officers. However, the council's slow reaction did allow the right to gain the upper hand in setting the terms of the debate. Two events in particular illustrate this. One was the national outcry, in September 1986, over *Jenny lives with Eric and Martin*, a children's book about a young girl visiting her gay father and his lover, supposedly available to Haringey schoolchildren (see Chapter 7). The second was the hunger fast, in January 1987, of the Reverend Rushworth Smith, a local priest, who threatened to fast until death if the council did not retract its 'positive images' policy. Both events were extensively and sympathetically covered by the popular media, which, together with politicians and others, began to stimulate a moral panic that climaxed, according to Gyford et al. with the Conservative victory in the 1987 general elections.[12]

The right's use of 'positive images' to advance their electoral position can be seen by the following advertisement placed in several of the daily press. Incorporating a photograph of a leading PRG member, it contained the caption:

> 'My name is Betty Sheridan. I live in Haringey. I'm
> married with two children. And I'm scared. If you vote
> LABOUR they'll go on teaching my kids about GAYS &
> LESBIANS instead of giving them proper lessons.' Signed E.
> Sheridan

Yet despite the right's national victory in June 1987, at a local grass-roots level, PI and Haringey Black Action (a Black community group formed to challenge homophobia and racism) continued to proffer a challenge. On 2 March 1987 they organised a march through the streets of Haringey. Entitled 'Smash the backlash', it mobilised between 2,000 and 4,000 people in 'defending lesbian and gay rights'. The alliances formed around the march coalesced further in the winter and spring of 1987/8 in opposition to clause 28 of the Local Government Bill which proscribed the promotion of homosexuality by local authorities. Not only lesbians and gay men mobilised but others as well from artistic, political and legal communities.

Coterminous with the enactment of S.28, Local Government Act 1988, Haringey council published its report on 'positive images'. At over one hundred pages, *Mirrors round the walls* provided a thorough discussion on how educational provision could challenge heterosexism and provide a more adequate service for lesbian and gay students and staff. Although the report carefully located itself within the new statutory framework, its publication was too late for widespread implementation. The political, financial and legal climate of Haringey council had changed over the two years since 'positive images' was first mooted. As a result principally of central government (but also of Labour Party) policy, the council had neither the resources, political commitment, nor educational power to introduce such changes within its schools. Yet, despite this, the comprehensiveness of *Mirrors round the walls* ensured its demand by educationalists, local government officers and lesbian and gay activists both nationally and internationally.

Such then was the patterning of events surrounding 'positive images'. I now wish to consider how effective each side was and the means of power they deployed. I begin by discussing the portrayal of 'positive images' by Haringey council and the policy's supporters. Despite differences of interpretation within the council, and between sections of the council and organisations such as PI and HBA, the publicly pronounced, shared desire to see something positive happen created a working consensus around several broad themes.

'Positive Images' Discourse

Liberal-Pluralism and Multiculturalism

The council's liberal-pluralist approach to sexual politics, and to homosexuality in particular, strongly influenced its presentation of 'positive images'. Indeed, since the policy was never formally implemented, Haringey's public advocacy of a liberal sexual politics during the struggle was seen by some as the key contribution the municipal 'positive images' project made.

The council and its education service presented sexual orientation as an immutable, unlearned aspect of identity, and homosexuality as a quality possessed by a relatively stable proportion of the community:

> Many of the young people in our schools or colleges
> [estimates vary around 10 per cent] will be lesbian or
> gay.[13]

Since homosexuality constituted the reality of some people's lives, young people needed to be aware of this, both to understand their community's diversity and to function within it.

> We believe that everyone in the Education Service has a
> responsibility to the community which we serve to
> encourage social harmony and respect for...cultural
> differences.[14]

'Positive images' in this respect was a policy for *all* young people and educational workers. However, its primary focus was lesbians and gay men. The council and education service acknowledged the discrimination, prejudice and marginalisation homosexuals experienced. Perceiving such a situation as wrong, they wished to provide a remedy or at least ameliorate its worst aspects.

> ...the [Education] Service would wish to help deal with the problems which lesbians and gay men, their parents, their children and their friends face, arising from the way in which some people appear to deny their existence or exercise prejudice and discrimination against them.[15]

To Haringey council, homosexuality was, then, an issue of minority group need. Lesbians and gays were perceived as a section of the community whose 'problems' arose from their identity as 'other', inciting hatred and fear.

> Many groups within our Society are treated unfairly and put down because of who they are...Our attitudes can be shown in many small acts...added together they could make people feel unwanted and undervalued...Young people who are lesbian and gay need to build their own self-confidence...[many] still have to socialise away from the rest of society to support each other.[16]

Although terms such as 'heterosexism' were used (largely as a result of the work and politics of the lesbian and gay unit), emphasis was placed on challenging the repression of homosexual expression and identity, as well as heterosexuality's illusory claims to an *exclusive* truth. The connections between sexuality, gender and power, on the other hand, were largely ignored (see Chapter 10).

Haringey's ambivalent pluralism emerged out of an uneasy synthesis between the demands and politics of lesbian and gay communities and the liberalism of local government. As a result, PI and HBA, while publicly supporting 'positive images', also expressed unease that Haringey council lacked a real understanding and analysis of sexual politics. As a result, they argued, its position frequently dissolved into a sexual moralism. A Haringey councillor and member of PI put it this way:

Within PI there was a clear perspective on
liberation....Council policy was different...They supported
equal opportunities without any fundamental
understanding...that meant a liberal approach—not
wanting to be horrible, being nice to all people.

While the ideological framework of 'positive images' was fairly
apparent from the beginning, concrete details were slow to emerge
from the education service and were for the most part tentative.

There will naturally be a range of other related
development activities which will flow from the
committee's stated policy position....Members will wish
to consider the timing and scale of the financial
provision envisaged...(para 2.11)

All these are areas for detailed consideration, and for
the development of guidelines for schools and colleges
about education in personal relationships, curricula
content and support materials...(para 2.12 (b))[17]

Despite the frequent use of the term 'positive images' to represent
the policy as a whole, providing young people with role models
was only one part—indeed an underdeveloped part—of a wider
strategy. Other possibilities included:

staff in schools and colleges preventing name-
calling...supporting lesbian and gay staff who are open
about themselves...making sure all staff get to know
about this issue...in health and sex education...not
avoiding the mention of lesbians and gay men...making
students aware that lesbians and gay men have made
significant contributions...[18]

Yet even these were only 'possibilities'. This inability of Haringey
education service to come forward with an authoritative version of
what 'positive images' would mean, practically, in classrooms and
schools was a major strategic blunder, leaving the opposition free
to provide their own equally authoritative version.

Similarly problematic was the tone adopted by the education
service in discussing the policy and the progress it was making.
Particularly in its early stages (autumn 1986), the service was

determined to play down the policy. A letter from the chief education officer (CEO) to parents stated:

> There have been many newspaper and T.V. reports
> recently...some have gone so far as to suggest that the
> Council has asked schools to change their policy on sex
> education to include the 'teaching of homosexuality'. I
> would like to reassure you that these reports are not true...

Although this tone was largely a product of the letter's intended audience—parents—a similar manner is evident throughout most of the education service's literature on 'positive images' including committee reports targeted at councillors. In the 1987 leaflet, 'What every parent needs to know', delivered to all households in the borough, the format adopted was to answer hypothetical parental 'queries'. Yet to what extent did this reinforce notions that 'positive images' and homosexuality could be dangerous if incorrectly handled?

> Wouldn't this mean a lot of students will have 'gay ideas'
> put in their heads?...The newspapers said that four-year
> olds would be taught 'homosexual practices'. Is this true?[19]

Haringey education service, responding to concerns raised principally by the PRG about 'positive images', were anxious to assure parents nothing would happen without their involvement and that the policy's development would be slow. As the CEO stated in his letter to parents, '[a]ll this will take some time.' Thus, 'parental concerns', as pronounced by the PRG, that five-year-olds would receive homosexual lessons, were given some degree of legitimacy as being representative of the fears of parents as a whole. In this way, Haringey implicitly affirmed the right's assumption that parents were not only heterosexual but furthermore hostile to a 'positive images' policy. Moreover, by focusing on the policy's insignificance, the council was diverted from its primary textual objective: explaining how the policy's introduction was a response to the reality of lesbian and gay oppression.

The council's defensive posture contrasted with that of the community group, Positive Images (PI), who articulated an optimism about the policy. At Full Council on 20 October 1986, a PI spokesperson put it this way:

the council has four years to turn something, often just
a line in an equal opportunities policy into something
which through information and education becomes a
very positive thing which Haringey should be very
proud of and upfront about.

Promotion, Corruption and Liberal Education

In the discursive struggle over 'positive images', different sections
of the right—the Conservative Party, PRG and various christian
denominations—challenged the council and PI, contesting their
interpretation of the policy. The extent to which the right
intentionally and purposefully interpreted 'positive images'
against the grain of Haringey council texts is uncertain. On the
one hand, they undoubtedly 'distorted' the policy for political
reasons; on the other, ideological and religious factors also affected
the interpretations and explanations provided. It is important
also to remember that the right, like the left, was a hetero-
genous grouping, working with different ideologies, objectives and
perspectives.

The right based their reading of 'positive images' on a number
of texts, not all of which originated from Haringey council. The
council's vagueness, particularly early on, gave credibility to the
right's strategy of basing their interpretations on less guarded,
hence more explicit, secondary texts. These included comments by
other right-wing actors quoted in the press and the texts of PI. The
latter, the right claimed, reflected the true purpose of the policy,
despite the disclaimers of Haringey council and its education
service. A major discursive strategy of the right throughout the
mid-1980s was in finding the true—behind the scenes—leaders of
authorities like Haringey. According to a PRG member, speaking
in a deputation to Haringey council, 20 October 1986:

We have seen sneaking...moves by the council coupled
with frequent denials by council officials and employees
as to exactly what is going on. Not only are we concerned
about what the council states is going to take place, we
are even more concerned about what has remained unsaid.
I heard a member of PI on the local radio recently

*talking about mothers and fathers as unhelpful role
models. Unhelpful to whom? Unhelpful to the 90% of
children who will one day grow up to be parents
themselves, or unhelpful to the members of PI in their
present campaign?...*It is this underlying attitude of the
people who are to implement the policy.

Since the right argued Haringey council's own presentation of the
policy could not be believed, space was created for them to present
what 'positive images' really meant and was intended to achieve.
Two key strands were (i) promoting homosexuality by means of
'gay lessons', and (ii) social revolution (although this latter was
only explicitly identified by the far right).

From the first debate in the House of Lords when Lord Monson
asked whether HM Government approved of plans for 'compulsory lessons intended to promote "positive images" of
homosexuality',[20] through to the wording of S.28, the question of
promotion—could homosexuality be promoted?—remained
central. Interestingly, it was the right who took a social con-
structionist perspective on homosexuality, in contrast to the
essentialism and biological reductionism of Haringey council.
While the latter denied both the desirability and possibility of
promotion, the right argued that sexuality was fluid, influenced by
social relations, and that, therefore, it needed careful direction if
young people were to grow up heterosexual; a state of being,
which they argued was not only socially and morally desirable to
attain, but, paradoxically, natural and normal as well.

While neo-liberals focused on emphasising the absurdity and
ridiculousness of councils like Haringey, others took the argument
further. Baroness Strange, speaking in the House of Lords, claimed
that as a result of the policy, civilisation would be undermined,
families would disintegrate.[21] The Reverend Rushworth-Smith
and right-wing Haringey councillors argued this was just what
Haringey council desired. According to right-wing Conservative
councillor, Pat Salim:

*They are set to use our children, to politicise and corrupt
our children...all in the purpose of social revolution...*[22]

Thus, in contrast to Haringey council's attempt to understate the
policy, the far right's strategy entailed going to the other extreme—

linking the policy to objects of terror within dominant discourse. At Full Council on 20 October 1986, Conservative councillors equated 'positive images' with the violence and authoritarianism of both fascism and communism. The moderate leader of the Conservative group, less opposed to homosexuality than some in his party, focused on the issue of 'mind control'.

I can't help thinking there's an element of George Orwell's thought police...you may think in our way or not at all.

Yet the dominant discursive strategy of the right focused less on the nightmarish scenario of which 'positive images' was deemed part than on what would be taken away or lost as a result of the policy: parental rights, childhood innocence and the family unit.

Parental rights formed a major discursive element and functioned on several levels. First, that parents were not being properly consulted or involved—the policy was being implemented 'over their heads'. Haringey council's repeated reassurance that parents would participate fully remained marginalised by the right and media in their presentation of the issues. Second, 'positive images' was seen as undermining parental rights to decide what children should know about sex and homosexuality, how they should be told, and when they should be informed. Third, by encouraging or promoting homosexuality, 'positive images' subverted the very notion of 'parent'. This claim assumed (as did the others) that only heterosexuals could be and were parents.

The notion of the innocent child corrupted was a second key theme. Like that of parental rights, it provided a resonance for people fearful of familial disintegration, feeling powerless in the face of rapid social change. Within the right's discourse, the child symbolised ultimate helplessness. They, whom the policy would most affect, could do nothing to stop it. To achieve the greatest rhetorical impact, the right emphasised those aspects of the policy involving young children rather than teenagers. Repeatedly, the council confirmed that the policy was primarily for secondary school children, but the image of five-year-olds learning about gay sex was a more powerful and seductive vision.

The third concern—the family—linked the other two (parents and children) to wider macro-structures. As Baroness Strange made clear:

the whole of civilisation...and most religions, are based
on the foundation of the secure family unit consisting of
father, mother, child and of course grannies and
grandpas, uncles and aunties...[23]

This depiction of the family as the basic building block of a nation
was central to new right discourse which rejected the notion of
'society'. If the only units were family, church and nation, then
homosexuals and others, outside such units, were an aberration.
Indeed, as the wording of Local Government Act 1988, S.28 makes
clear, lesbian and gay family units can only exist as 'pretensions',
second-rate copies of the real thing.[24]

The right's contention that knowledge of homosexuality would
harm young people by leading to sexual experimentation was
rooted also in a particular understanding of the educational
process. Indeed, hostility to 'positive images' needs to be seen
within the context of ongoing attacks on progressive education.
The long history of opposition to 'new' educational methods
enabled the right credibly to present promoting homosexuality as
yet another example of misguided 'modern' teaching. At the same
time, their depiction of the policy's effects was rooted in traditional pedagogic assumptions that pupils uncritically accepted
everything they learned—empty receptacles to be filled up with
knowledge—thus new ideas such as homosexuality would confuse
and corrupt them.

The effectiveness of the right's portrayal in influencing public
beliefs is difficult to ascertain. What is apparent however is the
way the right were able to use *dominant* discursive themes,
exploiting Haringey council's lack of clarity. Thus, promoting
'positive images' became promoting homosexuality; opposing
heterosexism became opposing heterosexuality. Yet, despite such
advantages, the discourse of the policy's opponents also lacked
ideological and political autonomy. In public statements, almost all
of the right, excepting sections of the church and far right,
emphasised their *opposition* to discrimination against lesbians and
gay men. At Full Council on 20 October 1986 at which 'positive
images' was debated, the PRG representative began by stressing
the 'common ground' that existed.

We acknowledge gays and lesbians living in communities

> *are subject to prejudice. We are not inciting hatred*
> *against gays and lesbians. We don't object to the*
> *existence of this element of our society or their right to*
> *be regarded as people.*

Whatever their personal beliefs, the fact such a statement was deemed necessary for the right's public credibility demonstrates the dominance of a quasi-liberal sexual politics. Nevertheless, the hegemonic nature of such a politics was equivocal as the right's attacks on 'positive images' revealed.

Discursive Style and Techniques of Power

The right's desire both to eliminate and exploit 'positive images' relied not only on argument but, as well, on political style and the exercise of different techniques of power. Five stand out: (1) populist, (2) representative, (3) bureaucratic, (4) participative, and (5) elitist. Below, I outline how each operated, and consider their effectiveness in shaping the discourse, mood and political responses to 'positive images'.

Populist

While most sections of the right drew on popular sentiment, particularly around the family, children, education and sexuality, the main right-wing group to use a populist strategy was the Parents Rights Group. Exploiting their public persona as a group of predominantly working-class 'mothers', the PRG attempted to talk directly to, and on behalf of, 'ordinary, concerned parents' like themselves. Media access was exploited to draw people's attention to what was happening in Haringey, and to depict the PRG as championing parental rights through their vigorous and high profile opposition to 'positive images'. Perhaps the best example of their strategy was the panic they helped engineer over the availability of the book *Jenny lives with Eric and Martin* in local libraries (see Chapter 7). In this instance, the PRG gained media publicity with their claims of 'raiding' Haringey libraries to remove copies of the book which they would then subsequently burn on mass fires.

The populism of the PRG lay in the way they attempted to capture and then mould public feeling, drawing on people's fears. According to one member of the pro-lesbian and gay rights group, Positive Images, this was where the left fell down, unwilling or unable to 'manipulate' public sentiment in the same way.

> We were in a weak position because we were only able to
> use rational arguments. Most of the debate wasn't
> conducted very rationally at all. That was the strength of
> groups like the PRG, they could tap hidden fears...[25]

The PRG and their supporters not only made full use of a sensationalistic media to convey their stance, they also drew on demagogic traditions to capture and hold an audience. The speeches of Conservative councillor, Pat Salim, illustrate this. Her vitriolic attacks against Haringey council were constructed out of a seamless flow of images whose logical flaws were largely lost due to the speed, drama and intensity of her delivery. Unlike more middle-class Conservatives, Cllr. Salim spoke with a raw anger. Thus she appeared as one with the parents she claimed to represent against an authoritarian council.

Populist style and discourse had a significant impact on Haringey council. Exercising their weapon of electoral power, the PRG repeatedly referred to the number of Labour voters supporting their stand. While the Labour leadership and party dismissed such claims, they nevertheless felt sufficiently concerned, particularly with the 1987 general election approaching and Bernie Grant's Tottenham candidature, to dampen development of 'positive images' and to offer an appeasing consultation with parents.

Representative

In the 'positive images' struggle, representation was drawn on by MPs, councillors, and the fasting priest, the Reverend Rushworth-Smith. Yet, for each, the role meant something different. MPs predominantly saw themselves representing people confused by, and opposed to, the kinds of policies Haringey council was introducing.

> Mr Greenway [MP for Ealing]:....If one has a policy as
> Ealing Council has, of appointing teachers regardless of
> sexual orientation how can the House be surprised at the
> parents' fears that their children will be put in the hands
> of perverts, practising homosexuals who are interested in
> children....Of course they are frightened, concerned and
> feeling violent...[26]

Haringey Conservative councillors took a similar position, focusing on the policy's unpopularity and the undemocratic nature of its
implementation. A key target was the manifesto process. Tory
councillors threw doubt on 'positive images' political legitimacy by
arguing that, even if it was in the manifesto, few people had seen
the long document and even fewer had read it. Labour councillors
challenged Conservative insinuations. They argued the 1986 election manifesto had been well publicised and was the popular
mandate through which they represented the wishes of the
borough's electorate.

    In contrast to councillors and MPs, the Reverend Rushworth-
Smith, a local Baptist Minister, disclaimed democratic forms of
representation and presented himself as the spokesperson of God
and christian people. By proposing to fast to death in protest at
'positive images', Rushworth-Smith deployed traditional christian
imagery: a servant of God sacrificing himself for his 'flock'. Thus
while Labour and Conservative politicians fought over the
legitimacy of their mandates and their competing interpretations
of the electorate's wishes, Rushworth-Smith used his body to
speak the nature of his representation as sacrifice.

    Throughout the early part of 1987, the mass media covered
Rushworth-Smith's apocalyptic comments on the effects of 'positive images'. Yet the impact of his remarks was insignificant
compared to the visual impact of his presence—first with a
walking stick, then in a wheelchair covered by a blanket, too weak
to stand or walk, sipping hot water from a flask. For over a month,
Rushworth-Smith was ritually wheeled in to attend journalist-
filled council meetings, his deteriorating physical condition
symbolic of the harm and destruction 'positive images' was
wrecking around him. His sacrifice and altruism accentuated, by
contrast, Haringey council's aggressive, selfish policies.[27]

Bureaucratic

Bureaucratic discourse played an equivocal role in the struggle over 'positive images'. Whereas the bureaucratism of Haringey council reinforced the impression of 'positive images' as an autocratic imposition, that of the Department of Education and Science (DES) assisted their opposition by constructing a façade of professional neutrality.

On being informed by a Conservative councillor about Haringey council's new policy, the DES wrote a series of letters to Haringey's chief education officer (CEO).[28] Ostensibly requests for further information, the DES's letters acted as a reminder to the council of their limited discretion. Any belief that Haringey was free to pursue the policies of its choice was sadly misconceived. As an instrument of statute working within a legally circumscribed framework, its discretion was bounded and limited.

The discursive and practical impact of legal regulation was not the DES's only resource. Disciplinary power also operated through a detailed questioning of the authority on its intentions, practices and knowledge. The DES asked precise, formal, juridical questions, for instance:

> How [does] the Authority reconcile these policies and steps with...statutory powers and duties...in relation to the secular curriculum, under [sections of the Education Acts].

In this way the DES presented itself as rational, logical and positivist, accentuating by contrast the depiction of Haringey council as propagandising and biased. Such a textual effect in turn generated the question—could a council as irrational and misguided as Haringey adequately run a borough?—particularly since it appeared unable to provide adequate, confident answers to the detailed questions being asked.

Yet it was the DES and central government who were largely responsible for creating an environment in which ministerial questions could not be properly answered. For their legislative enactments created an educational regime inconsistent with the spirit of 'positive images'. This is apparent in the DES letter (29 January 1987; 4(c)):

> *let me have...an explanation of how the Authority*
> *reconciles these policies...with the statutory duties under*
> *S.46 of the 1986 Act...to secure that any sex education is*
> *given in such a manner as to encourage pupils to have*
> *due regard to moral considerations and the value of*
> *family life.*

As well, the DES's questions and comments boosted levels of anxiety in Haringey education service. As a result, rational policy models, targeted at eradicating prejudice and discrimination, were abandoned for incrementalist approaches which stressed the relevance and importance of the statutory framework to any developments that would take place.

Participative

Utilised by the three grass-roots organisations, the Parents Rights Group, Positive Images and Haringey Black Action, a participative strategy focused on mobilising local people around one or other discursive polarity in order for them to become active in the 'positive images' struggle. Involvement included drawing up and circulating petitions, letter writing, organising and attending public meetings, leafleting and lobbying, as well as participating on marches and demonstrations.

The impact of grass-roots activity on the abortive development of 'positive images' is uncertain. Haringey Labour councillors claim none of the groups made a direct impact on policy development within the education service, although PI and HBA were an important source of municipal support. PI members, on the other hand, argue that their presence and energy was *vital* to strengthening the backbone and commitment of Labour councillors, and to maintaining the policy's existence. In addition, as I have argued, despite the denials of Haringey council, the level of support generated by the PRG did affect municipal behaviour.

However, the principal impact of grass-roots activism was on the constantly changing equilibrium of micro-power relations within the locality. The appearance on Haringey streets of the PRG and Conservative Association, giving out leaflets, collecting signatures and holding rallies, granted the right a physical and ideological presence it had not previously possessed at that level. Such an adjustment of power precipitated claims by a number of lesbian and gay activists that they felt uneasy shopping and being visibly 'out' as gay on the streets. Left-wing parties running weekly street stalls also found themselves challenged on what they saw as their terrain, in a discursive battle they had not anticipated.

As a result, the 'Smash the Backlash' march, organised by HBA and PI to defend lesbian and gay rights in Haringey, represented an important contestation of the right's apparent grass-roots hegemony, and a symbolic reclamation of the streets. Subsequently, the activism against S.28 reinforced the left's local, urban, political presence.

Elitist

Compared to the right's more explicit populism, the elitism of senior Conservatives proved a marginal discursive practice in the struggle against 'positive images'. Nevertheless, in the speeches of peers, a paternalistic attitude towards parents, depicted as powerless victims, crept in. The Lords also ridiculed Haringey's policy from an aloofness and detachment that permitted them to see the absurd side. In so doing, the House, at times, trivialised the fears and concerns of those who perceived 'positive images' as a very real threat.

> Lord Beloff: My Lords, does my noble friend share my amazement that the Labour Party, which derives its inspiration from those two very active heterosexuals, Karl Marx and Friedrich Engels, now seems determined to confine its appeal to homosexuals?
> Baroness Hooper: My lords, I note my noble friend's remarks and would refer your Lordships to the date on the Order Paper (April 1st).[29]

The elitism shown by the House of Lords patronised both sides struggling over the policy, though their attention reinforced the notion that 'positive images' was a major issue of concern. Beyond that, the political authority of peers and central government ministers gave added credence to the discursive theme of family. Kenneth Baker, Secretary of State for Education, spoke against lesbian and gay educational initiatives, not from the standpoint of government minister, but from that of parent. Thus he raised the status of parenthood within the debate by demonstrating that even he, a government minister, felt his principal authority to speak came from his parental role. Bob Hall, leader of the Conservative group on Haringey council, did the same. In doing so, he even sought to question the legitimacy of those who were not parents speaking in the debate.

> I'm a parent of four children and I know what they're
> [parents] talking about. I rather doubt that Steve King
> knows what I'm talking about because he's not a
> parent....Is Davina Cooper a parent? Does she have
> children? (Full Council, 20 October 1986)

In this way, the voice of 'parent' was epistemologically privileged over and above other identifications.

To conclude, both sides of the struggle deployed different styles, strategies, and means of power to elevate the authority of their respective interpretations and agendas. While the council found itself deploying a bureaucratic style and means of power that alienated many, and that allowed the right to depict it as an authoritarian body imposing policies without any consideration of community feeling, opponents of 'positive images' utilised a wide range of strategies and approaches. Despite their frequently contradictory nature, such schemes enabled right-wing forces to engage the support or acquiescence of many different sections of the community. Indeed it is possible that their achievement was not so much to win adherents to their position as to attain the status of authoritative interpreters of what Haringey council was doing.

During the course of the debacle over 'positive images', I was rung up by a children's counselling phone-line to ask if it was true that *Jenny lives with Eric and Martin* would be delivered to every household in the borough. Aside from the implication that the book promoted child sexual abuse, I was amazed that anybody could think a London borough like Haringey had the resources (even if it had the political will, which it didn't) to buy and distribute approximately 80,000 copies of the book. The concept of the Town Hall waist-deep in such literature made me realise that, thanks to right-wing attacks, many people had no idea what to believe; their sense of judgement about what was plausible or likely had evaporated; thus they were suggestive to the most ludicrous and ridiculous possibilities. Even among people sympathetic to lesbian and gay equality, many, accepting that there must be some truth in what they heard, felt councils like Haringey were going too far.

Conclusion

In this chapter I have discussed the struggle over Haringey council's lesbian and gay educational policy 'positive images'. In the first part I explained how a letter sent by the lesbian and gay unit to local head teachers, by-passing the formal policy-making procedures of local government, also managed to by-pass the complex means of ideological containment described in Chapter 4.

My second objective in this chapter was to problematise the meaning of policy. Despite never being formally implemented as its initial designers intended, few would query 'positive images'' existence. But which of the many conflicting interpretations was 'positive images'? What did the policy *really* entail? Haringey council and supporters argued that the right were interpreting the policy incorrectly, distorting its true meaning. Yet this assumed first that the policy had a 'true' meaning, and secondly that such a meaning was determined by Haringey council. Below, I discuss this first assumption. But what grounds are there for the second?

Haringey's claims were based on its assumed status of initiator and developer of the policy. However, such a status can be undermined in several ways. First, it is doubtful whether Haringey can be treated as a single, coherent entity in this respect when interpretations and understandings of 'positive images' differed widely between sections of the council involved: lesbian and gay unit, education department, council leadership, press office. Second, gaps and uncertainty regarding aspects of the policy existed among municipal actors; thus, what was presented to the public lacked both closure and completeness. Third, Haringey's development and eventual abandonment of 'positive images' was largely the result of external pressure. Not only did the right shape Haringey's development of the policy, but they provided as well its dominant interpretation. Indeed, it is likely many of

Haringey council's own staff learned more about the policy from opponents' comments broadcast on television and in the press than from council reports and policy statements.

Since 'positive images' cannot easily be said to 'belong' to the council, an alternative perspective would be to argue that there were many different 'positive images' policies possessed by the right, the council and by groups such as PI and HBA. One might argue that each group tried to implement its 'policy' and that the right was most successful, since its 'positive images' policy not only aided the re-election of a Conservative government, but also facilitated the emergence of a new right-wing moralism and the subsequent disbandment of Haringey council's own initiative. Yet does this kind of analysis confuse policy with strategy? Moreover, is it useful or meaningful to talk about several separate policies?

In the case of a policy which worked principally as a political metaphor it seems unhelpful to talk of distinct policies or to focus on which was the *correct* reading or interpretation. More important, perhaps, are the ways in which interpretations varied and the effect such diverse 'readings' had.

Using 'positive images' as a case study, I have tried to demonstrate how the meaning and content of such policies are neither fixed nor determined by the designations of their initiators or 'owners'; rather, they are the result of an ongoing process of negotiation and conflict. Thus the meaning ascribed varies according to the time and place at which the policy is 'pinned down' to provide 'answers',[30] reflecting the balance of power between forces at that particular juncture. For example, the constitution of meaning in a *Sun* editorial will be vastly different from that of a lobby organised by the 'policy's' supporters. Yet, in the case of 'positive images', the balance of forces was rarely equal. Why were opponents generally more successful in shaping and interpreting the policy?

'Positive images', despite its origins in a left-wing Labour council, existed within a broader political, social and economic framework unsympathetic to its progress. It was a policy beyond the council's power to control, for it could determine neither its development nor the (pressure) groups given access to the decision-making process. The weakness of 'gatekeepers' in this context contrasts, interestingly, with the experience of progressive organisations kept from participating within Conservative councils' policy-making partly as a result of those restricting access.

In part, opponents' success was due to better strategy and tactics. However, I would argue, their ideological congruence with the status quo whose discourses they were able to deploy, and their physical composition as a constellation of powerful individuals and groupings was more significant. They used against Haringey's lesbian and gay educational policy ministerial directives, legislative enactments, financial restrictions and the outrage of media and establishment.

Yet such dominance in the struggle was never complete. Not only were the right obliged to articulate elements of a liberal sexual politics in order to retain credibility, but their very attack on 'positive images' increased the visibility given to homosexuality. Although lesbians and gay men were forced on the defensive, heterosexuality to a lesser extent was as well, both by the policy of 'positive images' and the struggles that surrounded it. Although neither this struggle nor that around S.28 involved the deconstruction of heterosexuality nor disidentification with it, the lesbian and gay counter-discourses articulated provided a first step. Heterosexuality's exclusive claims to the 'truth' could no longer be taken for granted.

7

Mad Bouncer Killed My Baby:

Queer Coverage and Political-Media Activism

If you teach four year olds about sex, it's a good read. Sex is a good story. Gay sex is a better story.

B. Harris interview

Homosexuality and the Production of News

In recent decades, the British mass media has responded to homosexuality with a fascination, both tempered by coyness and accentuated by horror. The contradictory message that homosexuality both is, and is not, a suitable subject for the delicate eyes and ears of the British, heterosexual public pervades the issues that receive coverage. In the press, stories or items have tended to centre around the following: the homosexual practices or identity of public figures; intra-gay violence; 'sordid' sexual activities; 'bizarre' practices such as self-insemination; and, since the turn of the 1980s, AIDS. Within accounts, certain images prevail: seduction, particularly inter-generational; sexual permissiveness; degradation; secrecy; and cross-gender identification.[1]

The media's treatment of homosexuality has been the subject of extensive criticism from within the lesbian and gay community. One useful British publication is *Out of the Gutter* by Gary Armitage et al., published by the Campaign for Press and Broadcasting Freedom. Much lesbian and gay disapproval has focused on the tabloid press. Yet how much better are broadcasting and the broadsheet press? Despite broadcasting's obligations to achieve a 'proper balance' under the Broadcasting Act 1981, and its reputation for being the mass medium which provides the most accurate, detailed information, diverse perspectives on homosexuality do not receive equal treatment. The Glasgow University Media Group has provided detailed critiques of television bias.[2] Yet identifying bias depends on an acknowledgement that *valid* differences of opinion exist. What does this mean in the context of homosexuality where general public opinion considers lesbian and gay sexuality a less legitimate option, and where heterosexuality remains unproblematised? Is television biased for not deconstructing heterosexuality? What does neutrality or equal treatment practically entail? This is an important issue. Perceptions of broadcasting as ideologically impartial facilitate its ability effectively to convey particular interpretations and perspectives, as I discuss below.

Since the late 1980s, broadcasting has begun to widen its current affairs coverage of homosexuality. Channel 4, established in part to cater for unmet tastes,[3] has been the most pioneering in this regard. Their series 'Out', introduced in the late 1980s, depicted a different paradigm of homosexuality, one more in line with the liberal-pluralism discussed elsewhere in this book.

A change of tone and content has also appeared more recently in the coverage of lesbian and gay issues by the broadsheet press. The disdainful, patronising distance of the 1970s and early 1980s has been replaced with more sympathetic, interested coverage. Ironically, the Local Government Act 1988, S.28 provided a turning point for the broadsheet press by placing lesbian and gay issues firmly on the national political agenda. Coverage was no longer of marginal and salubrious concern but part of the mainstream. The late 1980s and early 1990s witnessed press reporting of new lesbian and gay organisations deploying creative forms of political action, a gay 'wed-in', a 'kiss-in', leafleting of schools; television stars and other influential figures began to speak on behalf of lesbians and gays—in other words, on their *own* community's behalf.

Yet, despite growing broadsheet press interest in lesbian and gay struggles for legal equality, discussion of heterosexism and homophobia has remained minimal. Moreover, during the decade of municipal sexual politics, papers such as the *Guardian, Inde-*

pendent and *Observer* were largely silent. Haringey's policy of 'positive images', for example, was treated—when not ignored— as a misguided effort, a red herring that was enabling the right to detract attention from more important issues.

The silence of the broadsheet press contrasted with the extensive coverage given to lesbian and gay municipal policies throughout the 1980s by the tabloids. Homosexual initiatives were deployed, through a process of 'escalating signification',[4] as a way of attacking progressive local government in general. Thus policies such as 'positive images' became a metaphor for the new urban left project. Moreover, despite opposing party political affiliations, the *Daily Mail*, *Evening Standard* and *Mirror* were all clear in their opposition to policies which treated homosexuality as an acceptable sexual and social lifestyle. George Gale, writing for the *Daily Mirror*, 9 July 1986, described Haringey's policy as

> lessons that threaten life. The left-wing conspiracy to brainwash children into the subversive belief that homosexuality is just as good, natural and desirable as heterosexual activity continues.

Media Tales of 'Positive Images'

Between May 1986 and the spring of 1988, Haringey council's lesbian and gay educational policy, 'positive images', rarely left the news. During this period well over 100 items appeared in the press and more than 20 television and radio programmes were devoted to the issue.

Although coverage all concerned the same policy development, the stories themselves tended not to focus on 'positive images' directly. Instead, they clustered around particular incidents or episodes connected to the policy struggle. The first major story to break, in the early autumn of 1986, concerned the children's book *Jenny lives with Eric and Martin.*[5] Apparently, Kenneth Baker, Secretary of State for Education, suddenly became aware of the book's existence within the ILEA's school library service and demanded its removal. At approximately the same time, the Parents Rights Group (PRG) discovered the book in Haringey libraries (see Chapter 6).

As interest in the book died down through the late autumn and winter of 1986, a second story hit the media in early January 1987. This concerned the Reverend Rushworth-Smith's proposed fast until death unless Haringey council withdrew its policy.[6] Finally, in the spring of 1987, after Rushworth-Smith had ceased his fast, a third story emerged concerning a day's event for young lesbians and gay men organised by Haringey lesbian and gay unit in conjunction with the authority's youth service.[7] According to media reports, a woman arriving to witness the event was assaulted by a council officer; the police were called and subsequently, as a result of the attack, the woman miscarried. A private prosecution then commenced, at which the plaintiff, Parents Rights Group (PRG) member Rosemary Johnson, was represented by the Reverend Rushworth-Smith. However, when the defendant (a lesbian and gay officer) entered the court, Johnson declared the council had provided her with the wrong man's name.

In this chapter I examine the media's portrayal of 'positive images' and the struggles that surrounded it in order to explore more general issues about the media's role in political conflicts. The nexus of sexuality and state provides a prism for close examination of media activism. In the first part of this chapter I consider the techniques adopted by the mass media to maintain and convey a discursive authority to different audiences. Subsequently, I go on to consider the relationship between the mass media and the parties involved in the struggle. Did a special relationship between the media and right exist? What was the effect of this on the mobilisation of forces, and on the development of 'positive images'? And to what extent was such a relationship the result of political and ideological congruity or the product of other factors, that is, the political environment and the requirements of newsworthiness? Finally, I return to the issue of communicating sexual politics, and ask whether local government would have been more successful if it had found alternative strategies that did not involve competing and negotiating with dominant media discourses.

Textual Strategies

Mediating Between Radio Interviewees

As interest in Haringey council's lesbian and gay educational policy began to heighten in the early summer and autumn of 1986, several radio programmes chose to deal with the issue. Such shows were intended to present a balanced set of opinions, by including for example, a Labour councillor as well as a member of an opposed pressure group in discussions. Nevertheless, the ideological steer was visible from the start because of the very nature of the problematic. This was not the construction of sexuality, nor even how schools should deal with questions of sexual orientation, but the much more limited issue of 'should homosexuality be taught in schools'. Below I consider two examples of radio interviews about 'positive images'.

In the first, 'The Way It Is',[8] the guests were Martin Mallen, Conservative opposition leader from Ealing council, Michael Duffy, incoming president of the Secondary Head Teacher's Association, and Diana Minns, Labour member of Haringey council, and the only panellist publicly to support 'positive images'. The presenter commenced the short programme by introducing the 'deep concern' of Conservative councillors, MPs and 'worried parents' and asked Councillor Minns how it was possible to present homosexuality in a more positive light *without encouraging it*'. After she had briefly replied, the presenter then asked Councillor Mallen to state his objections, which the presenter emphasised by reiterating the fact that the policy applied to 'quite young children'.

In contrast to the interrogative stance adopted with Councillor Minns, the presenter went on to clarify the opposition's position by confirming that they were not hysterical; that is, that their fears were reasonably held and they were not reacting inappropriately. The programme concluded with another short statement by Councillor Minns, preceded by the presenter's comment, 'such negative attitudes about the council's approach don't move Haringey Councillor Minns and she's got this message for the critics'.

Thus, in this four-and-a-half minute radio item, although opposing views were given approximately equal airtime and Councillor Minns was given the final word, the depiction of the issue by the interviewer was clearly more favourable to opponents of 'positive images'. Their arguments were presented as those of 'parents genuinely worried', while the Haringey representative was constructed as rigid and 'ideological'.

In a longer, twenty-seven minute item on the Gloria Hunniford Programme,[9] a similar ideological steerage was apparent in an exchange of views between a representative of the PRG and one from the Gay Christian Movement. In part, this was again the result of the interview structure, the advocate of 'positive images' being placed on the defensive while the opponent was assisted in presenting his point of view. Hunniford's comments, questions and the issues she emphasised affirmed a dominant sexual politics: that the policy affected parents; that the primary issue was the age of the children concerned—young children would become sexually confused; that it put pressure on teachers at a time of cutbacks; that they were being *forced* to teach pro-gay material; and that children emerged exclusively out of heterosexual unions. Attempts by the Gay Christian Movement representative to challenge the assumptions implicit in Hunniford's representation of the issues were undermined through interruptions by Hunniford and the other interviewee, her sudden topic changes, the use of callers to shift attention and to back up Hunniford's point of view, and her reiterated insistence that certain issues were *crucial*.

Plots and Sub-Plots: Press Coverage

Textual strategies within the press's portrayal of 'positive images' had similar effects. Here I focus on the media coverage of the *Jenny lives with Eric and Martin* episode, one of the most extensively reported lesbian and gay stories of the period prior to S.28. While newspapers covering the item were less concerned to present a balance of views than were broadcasting programmes, the need for coverage to appear credible was equally strong. For this reason the vast majority of the items took the form of news stories rather than editorials, since the latter function more explicitly as interpretive directives, that is the paper's opinion on an issue. Moreover, the narrative or story format facilitated the use of elaboration, making the tale more interesting and memorable. This enhanced rather than detracted from its ability to shape and confirm public attitudes.

During the period 16 to 22 September 1986, over 24 items on *Jenny lives with Eric and Martin* appeared in the nation's press. The main plot concerned the apparent widespread availability of the book and, by implication, its curricular use in London schools. Since the book was seen as symptomatic of general changes wrought by left-wing local authorities, a sub-plot became the simultaneous *removal* of other books from schools and libraries, such as Biggles and Enid Blyton novels, on the grounds of racism and sexism. The key theme was the danger of revolutionary transformation, the forced eradication of traditional forms of pleasure enjoyed by generations and their substitution by joyless propaganda.

In response to these charges, local authorities stressed the highly limited availability of *Jenny lives with Eric and Martin*. Nevertheless, the media's use of carefully woven textual strategies enabled the views of local authorities to be marginalised, and their story maintained credibility.

Headlines and Text
Studies have shown that people reading newspapers absorb headlines and opening sentences to a much greater extent than comments at the end of a story or press item.[10] Local knowledge of this kind influences journalists' and editors' choice of layout and was widely utilised in the tabloid press's coverage of *Jenny lives with Eric and Martin*. To begin with, nearly all items opened with a statement of opponents' fears; only towards the end of articles, if at all, was the position of the local authorities revealed. Second, sensationalistic headlines were used even where these were contradicted or at least modified by the story below. Such headlines during this period included: '"Don't ban Biggles", Minister tells Public Library';[11] 'Hit Squad of Parents to Burn Gay Schoolbook';[12] 'Parents Say "Withdraw that Book"';[13] 'Gay Book is on Loan to Children';[14] and 'Baker acts over Gay Schoolbook'.[15]

These headlines reveal several textual strategies. First, word association: *Jenny lives with Eric and Martin* was never conceived of as a school book. Although written for young people, it was not intended as part of a structured curriculum and indeed sympathetic educationalists have rejected it for use on that basis. Nevertheless, in both headlines and the items that followed, the book was consistently referred to in this way. Why? One possible explanation is that for the majority of people reading the story who had never come into contact with the book itself, the notion of 'schoolbook' conjured up images of instruction and mass readership by young people. According to the *Daily Telegraph*, 17 September 1986, almost 3,000 copies had been sold. Thus the implication was of books being widely purchased for school use. (The reality was that the book had fairly low sales until the right's publicisation put it out of print.) This raised a further question: what was the curricular framework that precipitated the need for such a book? The answer: promoting homosexuality.

The use of curt, abrupt headlines also created a sense of urgency. The need for immediate action was accentuated by the active subjects within the headline syntax—predominantly parents and ministers—followed by transitive verbs. Normally quiet, highly respected figures had been so angered by the book's availability that they were taking unprecedented action.

Other devices emphasised the extent of parental anger at the amount of money spent on lesbian and gay initiatives when insufficient funds were available for other projects. The *Haringey Advertiser*, 17 July 1986, quoted 'mothers' as 'furious that a reported £250,000 is being made available to schools to implement the equal opportunities policies'. This excerpt demonstrates several journalistic mechanisms. First, the generic term 'mothers' does not specify which are angry or how many. Instead it suggests that all mothers are or would be angry since the policy is by implication a direct attack on their parental role. Second, the information, while clear in its thrust that considerable sums were being spent on lesbian and gay educational policies, is actually very vague. Where does the figure come from? Who told the parents? Did the journalist suggest the amount to the women in order to get a reaction? If the figure came from the women, this enables the journalist and newspaper to convey it as factual information without taking responsibility for its accuracy.

As well as conveying anger, press stories and headings also stressed the degree of power possessed by the book's opponents. This was a double-edged tactic. On the one hand, the press presented the local authorities in question as authoritarian, bent on indoctrinating their borough's youths. At the same time, it was important to portray opponents as able to resist; otherwise, people reading the articles might sink into apathy—opposed to a policy they could do nothing about. Indeed, I would argue, one of the implicit objectives of many of the articles was to incite opposition to municipal gay initiatives and to left-wing councils in general.[16] In one *Daily Mail* article, 17 September 1986, Pat Headd from the PRG actually states that the reason her organisation mobilised locally in Haringey against *Jenny lives with Eric and Martin* was because of the press's coverage of Baker's angry comments:

> The Minister's message in your own paper was a sign
> for us to act...and use our own initiative.

Photographs

Alongside or just underneath the headings of many of the stories were photographs. Most depicted Kenneth Baker, the story's central figure, looking alternately angry, upset or masterful. Others reproduced the photographs from *Jenny lives with Eric and Martin*.

One photograph in particular stands out. Although only a few of the papers chose actually to print it, nearly every article alluded to it. The *Haringey Advertiser* even went so far as to reduce the entire text of the book to this one visual image which 'shows two gay men naked in bed together',[17] and sitting between them, the five-year-old daughter of one of them. This picture became central to the debate over *Jenny lives with Eric and Martin*, symbolising as it did opponents' fears. The photographic image equated homosexuals with sex; that was the implication drawn from two men lying (semi-)naked in bed. Furthermore, it showed a child in close proximity to such sexuality; 'youthful innocence' juxtaposed with corruption. The book was therefore all the more dangerous because it depicted the experience as innocent fun. The child would develop a tolerance or even worse a liking for deviant sexual activity. The image also resonated with connotations of sexual abuse, connotations sufficiently powerful to outweigh the contradictory message constituted by gay male adults and a female child.

A similar set of associations are manifested in the illustrations accompanying an article on 'positive images' by Paul Johnson of the *Daily Telegraph*.[18] The piece focuses on what is described as: 'an "official" sex industry...at work in the classroom...poisoning the minds of children'. On the article's first page, an illustration of the cover of *Jenny lives with Eric and Martin* is placed adjacent to one of two men with National Union of Teachers (NUT) placards supporting 'Haringey's "positive images" policy for homosexuals'. The proximity of these two images suggests that Jenny, laughing, innocent, young and blonde is in danger, despite (and because of) her obliviousness to the threat posed by these grim-looking, dark-haired union men. (The racism in the imagery is not terribly subtle.)

The connotations here are not only of child abuse and homo-sexual proselytism but also of children being used as instruments in a militant cause. The two men carrying placards with political slogans are teachers. They are the 'enemy within', able actually to implement 'positive images' in the classroom. Unlike other texts which have distanced education workers from the policies of authorities such as Haringey and ILEA, this image links teachers and authority together.

On the following page of Johnson's article, the juxtaposed photograph and drawing continue the theme of the previous page. The illustration is of the book cover, *The Playbook for Kids about Sex*. Adjacent is a photograph of people struggling outside Haringey's civic centre. The caption accompanying the two images reads, 'last week's confrontation between North London parents and activists favouring the new sex education orthodoxy. Right: textbook for beginners'.

Despite the ironic tone of the comment, the suggestion, once again, is that what might seem initially innocent, a book with funny pictures of parts of the body, leads people on to less harmless behaviour. According to Jill Knight MP, *The Playbook for Kids about Sex* uses pictures that appeal to a child.[19] Thus it is the most frightening piece of propaganda. Moreover, if the book is being promoted by 'violent' radicals—Socialist Workers Party (SWP) placards are just visible in the photograph—then it must be even more politically charged than it might otherwise appear.

References to the SWP's supposed involvement in defending 'positive images' were included in several papers. For example, the *Herald*, 9 October 1986, refers to: '200 supporters of council policy including local gay and lesbian groups and the SWP' and the London *Evening Standard*, 1 October 1986, states 'parents were met by an equal number of gay and lesbian and SWP activists'. A similar point is made by Baroness Cox, undoubtedly influenced or informed by the national and possibly local press.[20]

> [I]t is necessary to understand that there is a political dimension which we cannot ignore and that is the involvement of the hard line far left in local government and also in local politicised branches of the National Union of Teachers.

> At the council meetings where there has been such violence, there is a forest of banners including those of the revolutionary [sic] Communist Party, the Socialist Workers Party and in Haringey the Haringey Branch of the National Union of Teachers.

Who's Using Who? The Contested Terrain of Media Access

For different participants in the struggle, expectations and perceptions of the mass media varied. For the council, press and broadcasting were something of a Trojan horse, untrustworthy, but impossible to ignore. Few council spokespeople thought their comments would be sympathetically received and fairly reproduced outside the small progressive press. But the fear was not only of distortion. Haringey council leadership and senior officers lacked confidence in how the policies, even if 'accurately' conveyed, would be received by the general public. They also feared how such information might be used by the right. As a result, their response tended to be defensive; emphasis was placed on protecting the council from attack rather than on effectively conveying the reasons why a policy such as 'positive images' was necessary (see Chapter 6).

Anxiety about the media percolated through the different council levels. The message I received in my early days as a councillor was: be on guard, give little away, and choose words as carefully as possible to evade misleading editing. While these strategies may have formally 'protected' the council, I doubt they conveyed a good impression to audiences who tend to prefer open and engaging personalities to stiff, uncommunicative spokespeople

My first television experience as a councillor involved being cornered by the presenter Kilroy Silk who wanted to know— indeed badgered to know—if Haringey was prepared to break the law in the implementation of lesbian and gay work.

It was situations like this—the leader's anxiety at what might be said by inexperienced and 'foolhardy' members—that triggered an instruction that Haringey councillors were not to issue press releases independently of the council leadership. Instead, all press contact was to be through the official press office and members' comments via the deputy leader.

Nevertheless, despite misgivings, few requests by the mass media for information and interviewees were actually turned down (with the exception of the Murdoch press which the council was boycotting at the time). To reject requests out of hand, it was felt, would give a completely free hand to opponents' interpretations of the policy. Furthermore, despite councillors' reservations, the mass media was seen as the only way of reaching a wide public.

But what about the council's own texts? Attitudes towards these varied. For some councillors, officers, and community activists they were essential as a means of 'putting the record straight', maintaining editorial control and as a discursive weapon within the political struggle. For others, their limited availability beyond Haringey meant they were peripheral to the national arenas within which conflict was taking place. In addition, council literature was less influential than mass media texts. In part, this was because of the council's position as a partisan player within the struggle but also because of the language and discourse it deployed. The council could not compete for effectivity with the media's expressive language, and aural and visual imagery.

Haringey's defensive strategy contrasted with the right's pro-active, assertive use of the media. The PRG, for instance, structured their campaign with a view to what would attract the greatest media interest: burning copies of *Jenny lives with Eric and Martin*; the vicar's timely supposed fast to death; the claimed assault on a pregnant member of the PRG attending a lesbian and gay youth day; 'parents' picketing outside school gates to persuade other parents to keep their children at home in protest. Dramatic, entertaining, ludicrous, each of these events became, as I have said, the focus for a batch of media stories.

The right also had the advantage of key public figures. Church

leaders, government ministers, conservative academics such as
Roger Scruton, all added their names to protests against the
policy.[21] The ability to deploy well-known and influential actors
gave the right a number of advantages. As Young discusses, the
social, economic and political connections between elite figures
and controllers of the media assisted the former in obtaining
access to the media, in particular to the press, as did shared goals
and perspectives.[22]

However, media bias cannot be entirely explained by the
political complexion of the newspapers and mass media in
question. It also emerged as a result of the congruence that existed
between the right's strategy and media interest. Unlike the left,
who focused on policy goals and objectives, the right emphasised
the characters in their narrative—the fasting priest, angry minister and assaulted pregnant woman—whose actions took place
against a backdrop of worried 'mothers' and 'parents'. This is not
to say that the right did not also talk about issues. As I discussed in
Chapter 6, they certainly did. However, such issues were always
articulated by well-defined characters; and it was the characters
rather than the issues that were placed under the spotlight. Media
researchers have suggested this kind of strategy is more compatible with the requirements of newsworthiness as currently understood by the mass media which perceives people as more
newsworthy than both underlying forms of discrimination and the
mechanisms adopted to tackle them.

Thus the right's success in shaping media coverage was partly
the result of its own strategising, but also, to a large degree, the
consequence of media values and 'bandwagon' interest which led
journalists to *choose* to focus on the right's point of view. The
extent of the skewing of access in the press coverage of *Jenny lives
with Eric and Martin* can be illustrated by the *Daily Mail*. In their
four items on the topic,[23] quotations were only included from
Kenneth Baker and the PRG. This trend was replicated throughout the tabloids, the local papers,[24] and the right-wing press
generally.

Yet the issue of media access does not simply relate to the
proportion of coverage allotted to supporters or opponents of
'positive images'. It also encompasses the question of *who* was
allowed to represent either side. In the case of opponents of the
policy, access to the media tended to be available to a wide variety

of spokespeople, including politicians, clerics, pressure groups and 'parents'. However, this was not the case for supporters of the policy.

Pressure groups on the left were rarely given the opportunity to present their views. Instead, spokespeople for Haringey's educational policy tended to be councillors or officers. In a survey of about two-thirds of the press-cuttings on 'positive images' from the summer of 1986 until the end of 1987, unidentified council spokespersons were most frequently referred to as the source of information or quotations,[25] senior councillors were quoted a handful of times, Positive Images (PI) once and Haringey Black Action (HBA) once.

One explanation for such limited exposure was journalists' decisions not to interview left-wing, grass-roots activists. This may have been for a number of reasons. First, the policy was seen as *belonging* to Haringey council—an important discursive element in the right's attack. Second, PI and HBA were seen as constituted around their support for an unpopular, potentially dangerous cause. Third, their very identity as gay, Black and radical was perceived by the media as affording them no legitimacy or credibility as spokespeople.

An alternative explanation for the omission is that although interviews took place journalists or editors chose not to use them because grass-roots groups refused to say what the press wanted to hear. PI and HBA included a number of experienced activists well used to dealing with the media. Thus it is likely that journalists did not get statements from them that would have assisted the mobilisation of people against the policy. Also, one might conjecture, the media feared that reporting PI and HBA's comments could win people over to the policy. For it is quite likely that the groups' spokespeople were more able to convey effectively the purpose and objectives of the 'positive images' policy than apprehensive politicians were capable of doing.

However, PI and HBA's exclusion was not solely the result of media selectivity. When journalists and broadcasting researchers wanted an interviewee they tended to approach the council, usually the press office, for possible names. While the local Conservative Association, when approached, would suggest that journalists contact the PRG, the council tended to be more reluctant in referring journalists and researchers to PI and HBA.

This might have been because they feared what such groups might say and wished to maintain greater control over statements to the media. Equally important, however, was the tenuous nature of the links between most officers and members, and HBA and PI. Moreover, whereas the Conservative Party recognised the importance of the PRGs maintaining a high profile, the council saw supportive pressure groups as having at best an ancillary function, since council members believed they themselves had sufficient legitimacy to promote their policies effectively.

This was the paradox councillors and officers worked within. On the one hand, they believed their policies would not be adequately conveyed by the mass media; on the other, they did not consider other progressive actors to have any greater chance of success. While it is extremely unlikely PI or HBA would have received a better reception from much of the press and broadcasting stations, at the same time, assisting progressive community groups to have greater media exposure would have helped the council address part of its communication problem. But this the council failed to recognise, for it ignored the ways in which its own role as spokesperson played into the criticisms of the policy as authoritarian and unrepresentative of the community's wishes.

Constructing a Common Currency: The Deployment of Media Texts

I have discussed above how the mass media was used by right-wing participants in the struggle over 'positive images' to publicise particular 'facts' and opinions and the differential access granted by the press and broadcasting to particular actors and perspectives. I now want to consider the use made of already produced media texts by participants in the struggle.

Since most media texts were hostile to 'positive images', the use supporters of the policy could make of them was clearly limited. Perhaps their principal value for the left was in demonstrating the degree of hostility that existed, to keep supporters abreast of their opponents' plans, and to rally people around the threat posed by the right. Their focus on the frightful misdeeds happening in Haringey in some ways strengthened people's resolve more than the stock council denials, and more than left-wing actors' own perceptions of the watered-down reality of the situation.

Some stories and media items were also sufficiently open-textured to be read as parody and found humorous.[26] Despite the levels of hostility and resentment such texts represented, they did provide a source of shared amusement for supporters of the policy at what was perceived as the excesses and distortions to which the mass media would go. Moreover, the explicit lack of neutrality or balance within the tabloid press was also, on some level, politically comforting. Articles in the *Daily Mail* and *Daily Express* made clear that a conflict existed, that a struggle was taking place between opposing values and lifestyles. In a sense, this was more satisfying to left-wing actors than the stony-faced silence of the broadsheet press who treated the issue as insignificant, rejected any notion of essential contestability, and affirmed council claims that very little was actually taking place.

Beyond this, media attention had a negative effect on proponents of 'positive images' since it pressurised Haringey council to contain policy development and implementation in order to avoid adverse coverage. A leading Haringey councillor argues that up until the 1987 general election, the council was always on the defensive as a result of media interest. Consequently, what emerged was a contradictory situation. On the one hand, council spokespeople repeatedly informed the press that no withdrawal was taking place from manifesto commitments; at the same time, immense public and media pressures meant little developmental work on 'positive images' could be carried out.

For opponents of 'positive images', news stories played a vital part in popularising and giving credibility to their position. First, they provided a constant reiteration of conservative sexual politics. Second, they generated stories that could be used with authority despite the fact that many came from right-wing sources in the first place. As a result of a general acceptance of the media's primary, fact-finding role, press stories were deemed to possess a truth-value unmatched by the more explicitly partisan constructions of right-wing groups. A story was more credible if its source was a newspaper, particularly one of the quality press, than if it came directly from Conservative central office.

Mass media narratives also made available a common currency from which opposition to 'positive images' could be constructed.

First, because as stories they were memorable. The announcement of Jill Knight MP, for example, that Haringey lesbian and gay unit had made a video on how to be a lesbian in 35 minutes, shown to 'mentally handicapped girls' was a powerful rhetorical gesture that extrapolated aspects of the event in order to turn it into something unintended by the council bureaucracy.[27] Second, such stories, by being nationally known, provided shared points of reference. Even Labour MPs appeared to accept uncritically the reality of 'loony' left-wing councils as propounded by the nation's press.[28] Labour peer, Lord Graham, stated in the House of Lords,

> I don't deny what the booklets pleaded in aid in debate
> are said to contain and I abhor it as well as anyone else.[29]

The significant level of media coverage also assisted the right by exaggerating the degree of support they possessed. According to Lord Halsbury:

> ...there is overwhelming support from all over the
> country and a very good press.[30]

So much attention by the media, so many quotations from outraged parents and others must mean considerable and widespread opposition. Just as the media used the comments of right-wing politicians to legitimise otherwise dubious statements of intention and fact, and to avoid their own responsibility for such statements,[31] so politicians used the media for similar purposes. For instance, Lady Saltoun of Abernethy commented in the House of Lords:

> ...did the noble Baroness see the report in The Times of
> 17th March about the pregnant woman who went to a
> meeting of gays and lesbians in Haringey and was sworn
> at, punched in the stomach and thrown to the ground?[32]

In this way a self-affirming cycle of information and opinion was constituted, beneficial to the right and the media alike.

Yet, in this cycle of knowledge gathering, little information about lesbian and gay educational policies was conveyed outside of the series of isolated incidents which tended to possess only a tangential connection to the central issue. As an article in the *Guardian* stated,[33] right-wing politicians such as Jill Knight evaded demands for 'hard' evidence that homosexuality and homosexual literature were being 'pushed' in schools. This was not surprising since, as the local authorities in question constantly reiterated, widespread implementation of lesbian and gay educational initiatives did not exist. What was surprising, however, was the right's ability to engineer a moral panic on the basis of a few isolated incidents, such as, for instance, the girl described by Sally Oppenheim, MP, who supposedly had a nervous breakdown after being given Kate Millett's *Sexual Politics* to read.[34]

To do this, the right relied on the metaphorical value of the stories it told. News items on gay books, the assault on a PRG member, and the bonfire to burn *Jenny lives with Eric and Martin*, all stood for something else, larger and more coherent than these fragmented events. By adopting this strategy, the right was able to focus attention on the underlying problem such incidents revealed and thus argue the need for widespread regulation. Lady Saltoun of Abernethy stated in the House of Lords,

> as a mother and grandmother I am appalled by 'The
> Playbook for Kids about Sex'. Corrupting children is one
> of the worst crimes anyone can commit....This is a David
> of a Bill to kill a Goliath of an evil.[35]

The adoption of this approach by the right forced the Labour Party into a corner, arguing over the details—how accessible was *Jenny lives with Eric and Martin* to children?[36] Was Ms Rosemary Johnson really assaulted?—rather than the wider issues. In this way, they reinforced the right's argument that such policies were widespread, although the particular details concerning certain resources or events may remain contested or in doubt.

Conclusion

These last two chapters have explored the struggle over the communication of a lesbian and gay sexual politics, and in particular the battle to provide and be constituted as the authoritative interpreter of 'positive images'. Within the context of this struggle, the mass media played a role that would surprise few. Yet herein lies the problem. Not only lesbian and gay work, but a range of progressive policies, depended on the mass media for their communication. But how could councils rely on a mass media that they knew full well would be unsympathetic? Why was not more time and resources put into developing alternative forms of communication, especially for initiatives which both aimed to achieve, and required for success, changing social attitudes?

Probably the most successful authority to communicate its politics was the GLC. In its campaign against its own abolition it used billboards and public advertising with great effectiveness. In fact it was so successful that the government subsequently outlawed 'political' municipal advertising. However, some messages are more suitable for billboards than others. A 'say no' campaign is probably more appropriate than one attempting to develop a multicultural sexual politics. Councils did try other approaches, printing their own magazines and newspapers. However, as I have described, the ban on political publicity combined with what one might call civic journalism tended to render them less than exciting and convincing.

At stake for local authorities in their struggle to communicate innovative policies was the perceived need to win consent and support prior to implementation. This is a contentious point. Many observers of the new urban left have argued that the problem was the converse—moving too quickly without winning the necessary backing, underestimating the importance of taking 'ordinary' people along. However, this suggests that backing and consent can be obtained in advance. For councils faced with a hostile and antagonistic press creating hegemony in advance proved extremely difficult. Moreover, aside from difficult questions about democracy where policies precede majority consent, the strategic privileging of consent also implies that values and beliefs only change through explicit ideological struggle, that is, one has to win the war of words in order to pre-empt the war of action. Yet one does not have to prioritise the material aspects of practices to argue that ideology is not autonomous, but rather shaped by changing social relations and processes.

If we start from this premise, it is possible that if councils such as Haringey had gone ahead and implemented a multicultural sexual politics, they might have found this a more effective way, not only of contesting conservative interpretations of events by providing examples of 'real' practice, but also of changing social meanings away from homosexuality's negative articulation. Local councils, I would suggest, made the mistake of entering the mass media's terrain of communication and abandoning their own. But the state cannot compete with the press—broadsheet or tabloid—in the dissemination of information and norms. What they can do, however, is something the mass media could not: that is, adapt and transform the running of public, local services and provision.

This was urban government's strength in the 1980s, its advantage, but one it failed thoroughly to use. Cultural initiatives, such as anti-racist festivals, were a start in conveying alternative meanings through social practices; but, as I discussed in Chapter 5, their seemingly 'luxurious' nature meant they often backfired. The focus needed to be on the 'bread and butter' issues of education, housing, social welfare, rearticulating practices to an oppositional equality politics. Councils held back, scared to go ahead.

Yet the potential and capacity to re-form services was one of which the right was only too aware. It answered by diminishing local government powers. As I discuss in Chapter 9, responsibilities moved, some to the centre, others to newly established bodies. Within this changing environment, what opportunities remained for municipal radicalism? Could local councils still be used to convey an oppositional sexual politics? I return to these issues in Chapter 10.

8

Pushing Us Off the Pavement:

Ideological Challenges to State Boundaries

So far, this book has explored the emergence, development and opposition faced by lesbian and gay state policies. I began by recounting how and why lesbian and gay issues surfaced on the local government agenda in the early 1980s, and then went on, in Chapter 3, to examine the rise and fall of institutionalised sexual politics in four British authorities. Chapters 4 and 5 continued this analysis by exploring the ideological steer that took place during the policy-implementation process, the 'organising out' of more progressive proposals, and the crisis of implementation. But, as I discussed, this process of containment was not foolproof. In Chapters 6 and 7, I explored what happened when it broke down in the emergence and subsequent struggle over Haringey council's educational policy, 'positive images'.

While my focus has been on the specific nature of lesbian and gay municipal projects, the analysis of *Sexing the City* has wider implications. Similar experiences have been recorded in other areas of progressive local government practice, in particular around race and gender policies. Moreover, in Australia, Canada and the USA in particular, where comparable initiatives have been attempted, the processes of containment and watering down, combined with external pressures, have similarly limited the extent to which social progress can be achieved by activists working within state structures.

Pre-emptive Mobilisation of Bias

Yet this 'mobilisation of bias'—a term developed by Schattschneider to describe the process whereby some issues are 'organised' into politics and others organised out[1]—does not just happen after proposals have been made and work begun. It also happens at a previous point to render certain ideas unspoken or even unthought. This is the issue I wish to explore in this chapter. How does power work to silence particular possibilities? My focus here is ideology both as a form of power and as a political strategy—a double take.[2] My argument is that the ways in which local government is generally understood and discursively constructed places limitations on state strategies, especially those concerned with changing social meanings and norms.

Taking local government as a body with these limitations, we can, perhaps, better understand the horror when local authorities appear to transgress their role and boundaries. But the intense opposition lesbian and gay work provoked was not due simply to local government breaching the ideological prohibitions placed upon it; also at stake was the nature of these particular breaches: intruding into the private realm, and conveying progressive attitudes towards homosexuality. Having set out the theoretical framework for the rest of this book, I return to questions about the public/private divide and homophobia.

The Ideological Terrain of Local Government

Arguing that certain political perspectives remained unthought as a result of the workings of a particular form of power is a tricky issue. While we can as a matter of fact identify ideologies that seemed to be absent from municipal sexual politics, for example, revolutionary feminism, lipstick lesbianism, gender bending or gay liberation politics, why this was so is a harder question. A liberal response might be to explore the personal politics of the actors involved and conclude that since they did not advocate these particular perspectives it is not surprising nor very meaningful that they were absent. However, this raises a question about why municipal actors personally advocated some politics rather than others—was this to do with dominant lesbian and gay sexual ideologies or because other activists were stopped/discouraged from getting involved in municipal politics? Perhaps local government is organised in ways that make it appear irrelevant or unhelpful to certain communities. Thus, even if there was no disjunction between the personal politics of the lesbian and gay actors involved and the ideologies they articulated within the state arena, one might still identify local government's closure against particular ideological perspectives.

But it would also be wrong to say no disjunction existed. From the research carried out and the many comments of interviewees in Chapters 3 to 5, it is clear that certain approaches to sexuality were deemed inappropriate for local government. On some occasions this was a conscious process, whereby activists, councillors and officers chose not to articulate a politics that they purposefully advocated in a non-state setting, such as, within a community organisation. At other times, ideas seemed so outrageous to a municipal politics that they were not even thought within *that* context.

How can we understand this process of ideological closure? On what basis were certain perspectives or approaches defined as beyond the municipal bounds? Was it simply a matter of degree—the more radical, the less acceptable, or something else? And why were legitimate community ideologies deemed illegitimate when proposed by local government? None of these questions can be answered in any trans-historical manner. The proscriptions on local government are constituted within a particular juncture and need to be read as such. However, it seems apparent from other people working in similar fields that the prohibitions operating in British municipal politics over the past decade were also present elsewhere.

A Conceptual Framework of Ideology

In exploring these issues, I want to make use of four concepts. They are 'dominant ideology', 'oppositional ideology', 'structural ideology' and 'instrumental ideology'. While these have tended to emerge within fairly rigid paradigms, such as Marxist notions of false consciousness, none is used here as a fixed, quantifiable category. Rather, they are relative concepts, locations on a continuum of meaning. Let me set out what I mean by each of these terms.

By 'dominant ideology' I refer to those networks of meaning which are both generally accepted and which *appear* to legitimise and perpetuate existing relations of power.[3] Thus, I exclude meanings which might justify the status quo but do not command widespread support.

Throughout this book, I have stressed that my analysis of ideology proceeds from a comprehension of power as multiple, and of oppression as diverse, involving relations of race, economic class, gender, disability and residency amongst others. From this perspective—a kind of working relationship between neo-Marxism, feminism and poststructuralism—there is no *one* dominant set of meanings issuing from one dominant relation of power. Meanings are instead contradictory and inconsistent. For example, the tension between capitalist and patriarchal norms has been expressed in the question: is women's 'place' the home or the workplace? However, to treat capitalism and patriarchy as separate systems ignores the ways in which ideology and social practice *condense* different relations of power. Thus, although there are contradictions and inconsistencies within dominant ideology, the articulation of different power relations tends to produce 'coherent' dominant images, the excess removed beyond the onlookers' line of vision, for example, the butch, white, upper-class lesbian, or the masculine, working-class, gay man.

The second term 'oppositional ideology' refers to frameworks of meaning which challenge, negate or undermine the maintenance of current unequal social relations. They may function (counter) hegemonically, that is, have gained broad consent, but are more likely, by their very nature as oppositional to the status quo, to lack general acceptability.

The third, 'structural ideology', comes out of a neo-Marxist, structuralist trajectory which depicts ideology as a system or level that impacts *upon* people. Althusser and others, who have worked within this framework, refer to the process of subjects being 'hailed' or 'interpellated'.[4] By this they mean that a reified (or deified) ideology calls to people, who, in recognising themselves as being 'hailed'—such as a woman who responds (positively or negatively) to a wolf-whistle or who, working as a prostitute, approaches a slow-moving car—become both subjects of, and subjected to, the meanings ideology constructs.

Loosely based on this approach, I use the term 'structural ideology' to refer to those meanings generally perceived as non-ideological or non-political; that is, those meanings taken as commonsense, that refer to 'the way things are'. While structural ideology *encompasses* dominant ideological meanings, it is also broader. This is a crucial point. Structural ideology includes as well generally accepted, that is, naturalised, oppositional meanings, such as, in our society, norms of formal equality. Yet despite this inclusion, because of the hegemonic nature of power relations, most common-sense meanings affirm or justify the status quo.

The normalised or natural status that dominant relations and values thus achieve is crucial to their perpetuation; but how does it arise? One important method is through their communication and affirmation by authoritative institutions: the education system, legal system, the mass media and so on. Linked to this is their pervasiveness. Seeming to be everywhere, conveyed by a number of institutions and through a multitude of social relations, their 'self-evident' nature is strengthened.

The concept 'structural ideology' is helpful in drawing attention to the common-sensical, uncontested nature of certain meanings, and to the role institutions such as local government and the education service can play. However, at the same time, it is important to stress that structural ideology, as I have defined it, is also fluid and contradictory—even more so than dominant ideology since it encompasses some oppositional meanings as well. Second, that what is perceived as common sense will vary according to time and place; and third, that people do not simply accept the interpretations conveyed to them, but rather synthesise meanings within their own conceptual and normative frameworks.

The final concept that requires explanation is 'instrumental ideology'. Of all the terms discussed here, instrumental ideology is probably closest to the meaning of ideology within liberal political discourse. In contrast to neo-Marxism, liberal theory treats ideology as functioning within a 'market-place' of meanings. People, it is suggested, freely choose the ideas and interpretations that appeal to them most. By focusing on conscious ideological choices, liberal political discourse tends to ignore the ideological nature of meanings which are not contested or consciously articulated, that is, it ignores structural ideology. I use instrumental ideology to refer to those ideologies or meanings considered not as common-sense but rather as explicitly political. Generally held *consciously*, they are usually advocated as part of a process of purposive social change. Instrumental ideology thus includes programmes for material transformation as well as ideological change. In this chapter, however, I am concerned with the explicit promulgation of new ideas, norms, truths and values rather than with ideologies which advocate, for instance, the reallocation of resources. While the former may and probably would lead to the latter, it is the up-front attempt to change how people understand the world—conveyed through material practices as well as through more obvious 'texts'—that precipitated the controversy discussed in this work.

Purposive Ideologies Beyond the Realm of Common Sense

Having set out at some length the key concepts for the rest of this book, I can now return to my original question: why were certain more progressive approaches to homosexuality organised out of the policy-making process of local government before even being raised? In part this question has been addressed through my discussion of structural ideology. Those ideologies which operated *exclusively* as normal or natural could not have been contested since at that point in time no oppositional interpretation existed. However, of more concern here are those radical meanings or approaches advocated outside of local government but suppressed or *unthought* within it. For instance, lesbianism as a strategic challenge to male power; policies based on a polymorphous approach to sexuality; critiques of Eurocentric social structures such as the nuclear family, current social mores and so on.

My argument is that the reason such meanings or approaches were either not thought, or else not articulated, concerns local government's inability, legitimately, either to articulate oppositio-nal ideologies beyond the realms of common sense (structural ideology) or else to deploy ideology in a purposive (instrumental) manner. Let me take each of these points in turn, beginning with the second.

The *conscious* communication of progressive ideas was a major aspect of new urban left politics which aimed to use the local state to create a counter-hegemony around alternative values and norms. Within this context, lesbian and gay initiatives had an explicit ideological role: to alter people's attitudes around homosexuality in order to eradicate discrimination and prejudice. Yet attempts to deploy ideologies instrumentally, as I have discussed in this book, did not go unchallenged.

Opposition concerned not only lesbian and gay policies; nuclear free zones, anti-apartheid initiatives, anti-racist and anti-sexist strategies all came under attack.[5] However, what became increasingly evident was that the attack was not principally directed at the *substance* or content of the policies—a content firmly rooted within (equivocally) oppositional, structural ideologies such as equal opportunities and liberal-pluralism. Rather, the opposition was directed at the *purposive* character of the initiatives: their conscious attempt to use local government in an ideological way. Why?

To address this question we need to consider the discursive construction of local government—the meanings generated as to its role and purpose. Within the wider polity, according to Leach, local government's role was deemed one of provider and promoter of public services.[6] Other roles included representing local residents, responding to their needs, and helping to maintain or regenerate the local economy. Within any of these projects, conflict was deemed inevitable and even acceptable,[7] providing it was kept within certain bounds. Even the Widdicombe Committee on local government considered it appropriate for councils to have a political function with regard to conflicting perceptions as to how and which public services should be provided.[8] *Explicit* attempts to achieve ideological restructuring were, however, another matter. Mather describes how 'The Thatcher government [was] vigilant to police the borders of what it [saw] as acceptable local policy innovation'.[9] And the Thatcher government was not alone. Not only the right but others also perceived the role of local government as something less than an agent of ideological change.

In identifying the reason for this prohibition, some neo-Marxists and socialist feminists have pointed to the relationship between local government and political power. At this historical juncture, it is argued, one of local government's tasks is to mystify and depoliticise social relations in order to hide both the constellation of power that exists and the way it is facilitated and reproduced by state machinery. It is therefore crucial that local government is perceived beyond the realms of ideological machinations, a basically a-political, non-partisan apparatus. This assists the local state and, thus, the state itself to maintain legitimacy and operate with greater hegemony.

While this argument may accurately point to some of the *effects* of state practice, to see mystification and depoliticisation as the state's *role* seems unduly functionalist. It also suggests a state that is coherent, unitary and trans-historical unless the source of its 'function', for example, the 'ruling class' or the mode of production, changes. This book challenges the notion of a unitary, coherent state by demonstrating the tensions and contradictions between different state bodies, and more particularly within local authorities themselves. At the same time, I argue, certain trends and 'logics' seem apparent—in this case, the mobilisation of bias within and against local councils that appeared ideologically purposive.

But why were local councils differentiated from the legitimate, ideologically purposive political parties that ran them? One source of possible answers is in the operation of liberal discourse. Within its frameworks, local government is there to mediate conflict, to treat us equally as citizens, not to advocate explicitly a particular version of the 'good life'. Conveying instrumental ideologies, as urban left authorities attempted to do, breached all three discursive tasks; it entailed the 'creation' of conflict, a re-settlement of the balance of power, and the promotion of particular lifestyles. While, one might argue, reproducing status quo social relations and norms also privileges certain choices and social forces, the naturalised nature of these relations and norms renders them less explicit and less political.

The generation of public anxiety about ideologically purposive state practice was also linked to concerns about state power. Despite the critique of centralised authority by foucauldians, for most people the state appears extremely forceful and dominating. Thus, within liberal discourse, boundaries are placed on the exercise of its power. In the case of local government, these limits highlight areas of life that the state should stay well clear of, and rules of government it should not transgress. The discursive dominance of liberal frameworks meant that councils who developed lesbian and gay work could be construed as Stalinist, megalomaniac, and even fascist. As Conservative councillor Pat Salim put it at a Haringey Full Council meeting:

> If these people are in power in the land as a
> government, believe me, you in the gallery [general
> public] will be the first to be kicked into line. You won't
> be allowed to behave by them as you are behaving
> now...I repeat, I thought the 1930s were behind us, but I
> see we have a good fascist mind in the people
> opposite....(20 October 1986)

Yet liberal frameworks, while dominant, were not totalising. Left-wing municipal activists identified local government as a legitimate site for the communication of new ideologies, and, to an extent, the right did as well. These challenges to dominant discourse are important in reminding us that although hegemonic notions such as local government impartiality may be an important factor in shaping (responses to) municipal practice, both are open to change.

The second, and even more powerful, prohibition on local government's ideological role concerned the actual *substance* or content of the meanings conveyed. The strength of this interdiction can be seen in the fact that although the new urban left attempted to deploy local authorities in a purposive or instrumental ideological manner, almost no examples exist, that I know of, where councils conveyed oppositional, counter-intuitive meanings. This is perhaps a surprising point. Lesbian and gay policies, in particular, were lambasted by the mass media and opponents for proposing 'loony' nonsense. Yet, I would argue, the policies and initiatives referred to in this way, such as gay men's swimming sessions or anti-heterosexism training, while possibly unusual, were located within broadly liberal paradigms; thus, they did not constitute oppositional meanings beyond the realms of commonsense.

But perhaps this is putting the point too strongly. Such policies did entail the articulation of homosexuality with liberal precepts, a conjunction which may have given previously mainstream notions a radical tint. Indeed, defining the point at which social meanings go beyond the confines of structural ideology is awkward since the concept, as I have said, is more a matter of degree than operating within hard and fast boundaries. Why, then, was it that although some councils deployed ideology instrumentally, they generally refrained from articulating non-consensual, oppositional ideologies, in particular those that explicitly challenged or deconstructed conventional meanings?

One response is that counter-intuitive meanings and even more such norms seemed inappropriate, that is, they did not appear suitable, even to many radical municipal actors, as a basis for local goverment work. Few lesbian and gay municipal actors could seriously envisage, for example, a sex education teacher detailing homosexuality as the most 'normal' kind of sexual practice, despite the fact that the opposite was a routine occurrence. However, as well as feelings of inappropriateness, equally powerful was the perception of *latent* opposition. While the opposition that mobilised against purposive ideologies, such as lesbian and gay equality of opportunity, was significant, many municipal actors feared that such opposition would intensify considerably if more radical discourses were articulated. At least in the case of the former, municipal actors could point to the *common-sense*, reasonable nature of the ideas being conveyed; but if radical, counter-intuitive ideologies were communicated, both prohibitions would have been breached, since such a public project would only function instrumentally.

In this section I have developed a way of understanding why certain approaches to lesbian and gay sexual politics were unthought, or, if thought, were not articulated publicly by municipal lesbian and gay actors within the state arena. My analysis is based on two injunctions within dominant discourse. First, it was deemed inappropriate for local government to conduct itself as a political actor advocating a prescriptive social vision (instrumental ideology). Second, councils were not to convey ideologies which challenged or went outside of existing notions of commonsense (structural ideology).

My argument is that left-wing actors either believed in these injunctions (consciously or otherwise), or alternatively, knew that transgression would precipitate explicit conflict and the mobilisation of opposition against them. However, as this book illustrates, these injunctions were violated, albeit to a limited degree. In the chapter that follows, I return to this issue of transgression, and use the analysis developed above as a way of explaining what happened.

Understanding Intensity of Prohibitions and Opposition

So far, I have developed my argument at a level that would be equally true for radical economic initiatives as for sexuality policies. Was there anything special about sexuality, particularly lesbian and gay sexuality, that intensified the two ideological prohibitions discussed above, and that caused—when they 'appeared' breached—the desperate responses shown. And I mean desperate. As a local resident at a Haringey education meeting said to me, 'I've never cared about anything so much.'

In this section, I wish to explore two possible characteristics that lesbian and gay equality work possessed. The first—penetrating the private—contributed to the perception that purposive ideological initiatives were 'exploiting' local government power, using it inappropriately beyond the boundaries of the public realm. The second concerned the homosexual content of the strategy in a context where homophobia proved a key element in the construction of a sexual common sense.

Homophobia has been identified by many as the root cause of opposition to lesbian and gay work. I am not sure that alone, it was quite that powerful; as I have argued here, other factors were also at work. Nevertheless, it was clearly a central reason for the tightness of the ideological boundaries, and a primary motivation for the communities who mobilised to police local government's slackening borders.

Local Government and the Private Domain

The meanings attributed to the private sphere have varied politically and historically. Here, my concern is with the private sphere in two senses: (i) the domestic realm and (ii) as encompassing, if not synonymous with, sexuality and personal beliefs.

The domestic realm is an area of life in which the state's role has traditionally been an ambivalent one—a combination of absence and presence. In the context of local government, both direct penetration as well as structuring by omission are evident.

Through policies and services relating to council housing, education, social services and planning, local government has both
assumed particular family structures and through its provision and
ideology helped to create or maintain them. At the same time,
despite municipal interventions into the family and home, particularly of Black and working-class households, council practices
reproduce meanings that entrench the ideology of domestic
privacy.

The power and pervasiveness of privacy as an ideology assisted
in structuring the limits of local government activism. For those
developing lesbian and gay policies, it provided a set of boundaries,
issues that were 'off limits'—for example, sexual practices, erotica,
discrimination and bigotry beyond the public realm. Yet the
ambiguous nature of the pubic/private divide, particularly in the
context of sexuality, made operating within state borders difficult.
Thus councils developing work in this area were repeatedly
perceived as going beyond their legitimate political remit.

The right argued that lesbian and gay policies infringed people's personal belief systems by forcing them to accept certain
attitudes or behave in particular ways. Oft-cited examples
included council employees being sacked for refusing to follow
the new credo, or parents losing the right to decide when and
how their children learn about sex education and procreation. At
a more general level, the new policies made possible a discourse
of state penetration, bullying and interference by which the right
could mobilise others.

Local authority claims that their policies were unconcerned with
people's private practices and dealt only with public relations were
further challenged by opponents' arguments that homosexuality
was an inappropriate matter for public society. Despite the
emphasis placed on the private within dominant discourse, a
certain credibility and status has also tended to be accorded to
issues and practices that enter the public—an arena within which
weighty matters are dealt with and acceptable behaviour practised.
Equality for homosexuals was considered neither. While liberal
discourse was shifting from the 'private harm' foundations of
Wolfenden to an emphasis on lesbians' and gays' right not to have
an 'irrelevant' consideration counted against them, conservative
discourse maintained that, at best, homosexuality should remain a
private sin.

Thus, the right mobilised to keep the public sphere out of the private and the private sphere out of the public, to maintain a divide that the welfare state had increasingly come to challenge. Lesbian and gay policies operated at the interface of the 'divide'. Not only did they concern the relationship between sexual/ domestic practices and social identity, but the initiatives developed aimed to challenge private inequality—child rearing, housing, information, leisure access—through public policies.

Opposition to state intervention, however, did not just come from the right. Progressive forces also expressed mistrust of policies which seemed to entail an activist state going beyond the boundaries of previous municipal governance. At the heart of this animosity lay a distrust of state practice, a belief that the state was ruled by social forces or agendas antithetical to progressive demands. People pointed to state treatment of Black and working-class communities and questioned the notion that the state could be an ally. Lesbian and gay municipal actors were naive to think the state could represent their interests, and wrong to disregard the implications of giving the state greater legitimacy and permission to enter community's lives.

An illustration of this naivety was the suggestion, made in several authorities, that the council monitor employees' sexual orientation to ensure discrimination was not occurring, a proposal that ignored the dangers of the state acquiring such information. There was also a real contradiction for gay men, in particular, who, on the one hand, were being asked to trust municipal goodwill, and who, on the other, faced state arrest and prosecution for breach of discriminatory public order legislation, some of which emanated from local authority bye-laws.

As well as fearing municipal interventions into the private, some lesbian and gay radicals also questioned the benefit of state legitimisation. What processes would homosexuality have to undergo to prove its credibility—would people, for instance, have to 'confess' or 'prove' their sexuality to win positive treatment? How transgressive could it be, if lesbian and gay orientations became state policy developed by committees and paid government bureaucrats? And would all lesbian and gay identities receive validation or only those whose lifestyle fitted in with municipal norms and values?

The project to make homosexuality safe—'we are just like

you'—did not unleash on local government an equivalent radical constellation of forces to those mobilised by the threat of municipal socialism. What it did do, however, was limit the degree of support council initiatives received as many sexual activists maintained a sceptical or simply impassive distance. In addition, as the 1990s rolled on and council policies failed to provide the 'goods', a modest community backlash took place emphasising danger, desire and the radicalism of queerness over public conformity.

The second issue I wish to raise here is less concerned with pushing forward the boundaries of the state (instrumental ideology) than with the nature of the meanings conveyed (structural ideology). Despite deploying liberal equality discourse, lesbian and gay policies remained at the borders of common-sense meaning. What was it about homosexuality that rendered its articulation with rights and citizenship so counter-intuitive? Why was it seen as fit only for the private realm of self-harm and sin? Does homophobia provide us with any purchase on the hostility and hatred homosexuality engendered?

Fear, Mistrust and Hatred: Homophobia

> It is part of the softening up propaganda that lesbians and gays are nearly always referred to in that order. The relatively harmless lesbian leads on to the vicious gay...but...the loony left is hardening up the lesbian camp and...they are becoming increasingly aggressive. (Lord Halsbury)[10]

The concept of homophobia, as a way of understanding and identifying anti-gay feeling, has gained considerable influence over the past two decades. However, more recently, it has been criticised by a number of writers and activists who argue that it individualises and pathologises the problem. Instead, many have preferred heterosexism since it focuses on the institutional privileging of a particular sexual orientation, that is, heterosexuality. However, while institutional processes are central, it is still important to understand the intense hostility and fear homosexuality generates in people, whether as individuals or collectivities. While we may be able to explain the mobilisation of bias and opposition to lesbian and gay policies in a range of different ways, to ignore anti-gay feeling would indeed be to miss what is perhaps the most obvious motivation for what happened.

But what is homophobia? How do we understand these intensely hostile feelings? Social psychology, feminism, lesbian and gay studies have produced a range of possible responses, many of an instrumental or functional nature, for instance, 'queer-baiting...serves to keep all men in line',[11] or anti-lesbianism maintains women's servicing of patriarchy. The difficulty with these explanations is that they rely on an overarching set of interests—patriarchy, capitalism—which strategically deploy sexuality. While patriarchy undoubtedly benefits from the hegemony female heterosexuality achieves, male hatred of gay men is more complicated; as Frye claims, in a 'male supremacist culture' not to love men is the worst possible sin.[12] Similarly, while it is arguable that capitalism requires the control of sexuality and exploits the production of a sexual surplus, this might not have to take a heterosexual form.

Thus it seems problematic to explain homophobia as the direct effect of a particular set of interests or social structuring. A more complex analysis might relate it to the condensation of a range of power relations: race, gender, class, religion at a given juncture. But perhaps this too presumes too high a degree of determinacy. Sexual feelings, beliefs and attitudes develop as a result of many different factors mediated through a person's own experiential trajectory. While dominant beliefs undoubtedly exist, rather than searching for their origins in particular interests or structural requirements, one might ask: by what means are they reproduced and affirmed and how powerful are the social forces that aim to transform them?

Anti-gay feeling is clearly reproduced by media, religious bodies, local communities and by the state not only at the level of explicit, derogatory practice but also by rendering homosexuality marginal and invisible; and through the privileging of heterosexuality. Lesbian and gay initiatives witnessed the largely unsuccessful attempt (particularly in the short term) to contest such attitudes. As I discussed in Chapter 6, one reason given for this was the inability of municipal actors to fully understand what people's fears entailed. It is within this context that homophobia as a description of community reaction reveals its inadequacies. There was fear, but there were also other elements not reducible to fear—dislike, antagonism, ridicule, trivialisation, political differences, interest conflict. Can one say that underlying these responses was a common emotion? Is it helpful to posit an authentic truth lying beneath the responses people gave?

Anti-gay feeling operated at different levels of consciousness and expression. One cannot assume that the arguments actually made by opponents reflected their greatest concerns since strategic requirements were also a consideration. For instance, the right's emphasis on parental consultation and its insistence that it was not anti-gay was partly a tactical decision not to appear homophobic. At the same time, how do we ascertain and identify feelings that remain unexpressed, particularly when traces cannot be found in the statements made? And are such feelings, if and when 'uncovered', any more valid than the more conscious, explicit discursive meanings and norms that are publicly circulated?

These questions concern not only authenticity but also coherence. There is a danger in using the charge homophobia as a way of suggesting that certain feelings, albeit irrational and incoherent, were nevertheless totalising. Within the struggles over lesbian and gay policies, many opponents expressed and seemed to experience a range of *conflicting* emotions. Progressive activists tended to scoff at opponents who talked about gay friends in the same breath that they opposed lesbian and gay policies. It was assumed that even if such friendships existed (and this was often doubted), the anti-gay attitudes described were the more authentic emotion and the friendship built on pretence. But if we treat the range of responses as equally 'real', condensed in different ways at different moments, that is, different when socialising with gay friends than when speaking at a council meeting, then acknowledging their variation and fluctuation might be useful in developing a strategic response. For example, it might be more productive to work *with* the positive emotions shown than to respond purely to the negative ones on the assumption that they are overriding and, at a deeper level, totalising.

It is also important to acknowledge and explore the *range* of hostile emotions and attitudes displayed. In the anger and fear shown to lesbian and gay work, a key theme was that of uncontrollable sexuality. In Camden, local women opposed the establishment of a lesbian centre on the grounds that the proposed venue was near a girls' school. Women claimed that, as mothers, they feared for their daughters' safety finding themselves at the mercy of passing lesbians' uncontrollable lust. Emotions were so intense that at council consultation meetings, women articulated fears of predatory lesbians putting their hands down young girls' knickers. Although these manifestations of emotion were perhaps more expressive than some others, these women were not alone in their fears and stereotypes. MPs and Peers formulated arguments based on similar images. According to Mr Greenway, MP:

> If one has a policy, as Ealing council has, of appointing teachers regardless of sexual orientation how can the House be surprised at the parents' fears that their children will be put into the hands of perverts, practicing homosexuals who are interested in children, lesbians and so on. (House of Commons, col. 1091, 21 October 1986).

Linked to the threat of an uncontrollable sexuality was a further fear: if people transgressed sexual conventions—the most rigid of norms—they might well breach others as well. Thus lesbians and gays, according to Lord Halsbury, were closely linked with other radical social forces and with interests that conflicted with those of the status quo.

> They will push us off the pavement if we give them a chance. I am, in their jargon, a homophone [sic] a heterosexist exploitationist. (Earl of Halsbury, Lords, col. 310, 18 December 1986)

As Didi Herman (1994) has cogently written about in the context of the new christian right in Canada, what many conservatives felt they faced was a war of values, a war they were determined to win. To describe such feelings as homophobia ignores the self-interested aspect of the struggle. Conservatives may fear homosexuality but much of that fear is based on a 'rational' dislike of values they see lesbians and gay men as representing: choice, self-determinacy, progress, change, secularity and lack of discipline. One might argue that this is a distorted description—that lesbians and gays need not be articulated with progressive norms—however, given that the right perceived this to be the case, its response is not surprising.

This kind of reaction can be contrasted with a series of articulations that appear more overtly phobic. Rather than focusing on the political conventions lesbians and gay men might breach, opponents saw in their amorality a sensory transgression, one grounded in dirt, disease, odour and contagion. Although barely expressed in the public arena in relation to homosexuality, these condensed images became crystallised in public discourse on AIDS. Made to stand for savage sexuality and death, it became a focus for much of the opposition towards lesbian and gay municipal work. In the mid 1980s at least, comments could be made about AIDS which would have been deemed unacceptable if explicitly directed at homosexuals.

Fear of the animosity that would greet lesbian and gay work shaped and contained policy development. However, the measures taken by urban authorities proved insufficient. Opponents coalesced in their antagonism towards 'loony' homosexual knowledge and norms despite the variance between them. In treating these forces as one, the urban left made a tactical error. Not all the opposition could be described as homophobic, and as a blanket term it provided little insight into the different feelings opposing communities expressed. A better strategy might have been to attempt to fragment opponents, and to work with those whose opposition seemed the most incoherent and contradictory.

To an extent this approach was adopted in work with council employees. Here, lesbian and gay municipal officers treated the problem as ignorance and engaged in what one worker described as a 'mega-myth busting exercise'. The success many officers found adopting this approach may have also been achieved working with local residents who opposed lesbian and gay equality initiatives. However, local people tended to be pushed into the welcoming arms of right-wing forces. In the final chapter, I pick up this issue of strategy in engaging with opponents. Before doing so, let me briefly discuss some of the changes that took place in lesbian and gay work in the late 1980s and early 1990s, locating these changes within the shifting political climate.

9

Towards a New Equilibrium:
The Changing Nature of Equal Opportunity Work

Between 1987 and 1993, local government in Britain underwent a remodelling so that, by 1993, lesbian and gay municipal structures, along with the separate frameworks established for race, gender and disability work, had largely disappeared. How did this happen? In this short chapter, I wish to discuss four sets of factors: central government intervention, financial and legislative changes, the altered discourse of councillors and officers, and community disillusionment. I end with a brief survey of the changing nature of equality work.

State Intervention and a Crisis of Legitimacy

Lesbian and gay policies developed, in the 1980s, by councils such as Manchester, Ealing and Camden epitomised for central government what was wrong with local government more generally. Within this context of Conservative disapproval and dissatisfaction, the Widdicombe Inquiry was established in 1985, and subsequently legislation introduced, to deal with the 'cancer', the 'new corruption' that had penetrated the local state.[1] As Tory minister Ridley stated in *The Local Right* (1988),[2] 'where local responsibility breaks down there is inevitably stronger pressure for central intervention'.

According to Gyford et al., central government's sudden concern with local authorities owed much to the threat, or at least to the obstruction they posed to the government's dominant strategy for

securing economic and social welfare. However, in their discussion, Gyford et al. are scathing about the threat posed by 'sub-
revolutionary rhetoric', which they claim 'no serious observer
could have imagined...[would] have...possessed the resources
necessary to overthrow an elected government'.[3]

Undoubtedly this is true. However, what they ignore is the
substantive *ideological* challenge posed by authorities who
articulated oppositional meanings. Combined with a strategy of
explicitly seeking ideological change—of testing the boundaries of
state activity—left-wing councils faced the wrath of local Tories,
the mass media and central government. As a result, authorities'
legitimacy as state bodies became contested.

This became evident in a number of ways. First, outside forces
such as Haringey's Parents Rights Group, in intervening against
lesbian and gay policies, treated councils as if they were some 'off
the wall' community group rather than a public institution. This is
an important point. Because authorities (or sectors within
them)—by purposively seeking ideological change—behaved
more like grass-roots pressure groups, they were treated as such.
Thus the extra legitimacy and authority local councils had
possessed as governmental bodies, which assisted in the communication of dominant meanings, began to evaporate as they stopped
conveying such meanings. Accused by opponents of lies, diver-
sions, and misrepresentations (see Chapter 6), councils like Haringey, lost status as an 'authoritative constructor of social reality'.[4]

In Haringey, opponents of 'positive images' threatened publicly
to burn local authority books and to keep children out of schools
without any of the censure that usually followed such activities.
Instead, the council was censured for lawlessness and violence (see
Chapters 6 and 7). In the House of Commons, MPs described
opponents' feelings of violence as perfectly legitimate and understandable in the situation.

Second, the process of local delegitimisation was exacerbated by
central government intervention which pushed councils towards
crisis and then, by reasserting dominant relations of power within
the state, back towards 'normalcy'. The first stage was achieved by
heightening the discursive struggle already taking place, and by
lending support to opponents of policies such as 'positive images'.
The second entailed legislation, ministerial regulation and
derision.

This last technique of ridicule, deployed throughout the government's opposition to 'positive images', was an important factor in forcing Labour authorities to take their own action to contain and undermine lesbian and gay initiatives. Leaderships acted, motivated by a determination to regain legitimacy as a credible state body. While the central government introduced the Local Government Act 1988, S.28, demonstrating the political consequences of 'stepping out of line', it was left to political forces within the Labour Party and local government to do the rest. How intentional or conscious any of this process was is hard to say. However, the continuing assault on councils by the centre, combined with the Labour Party's desperate drive to regain political credibility, caused authorities to eschew policies that would escalate their delegitimisation to constituents and establishment alike. They were propelled to emphasise those aspects of their work which depicted their authorities as efficient and well-managed, providing the services required within the legislative framework operating.

Financial Crisis, Privatisation and Public Markets

In addition to central government's direct intervention in relation to particular policies such as 'positive images', its political agenda more generally impacted upon lesbian and gay municipal initiatives. Between 1987 and 1993, local government underwent a number of changes as the Thatcherite agenda of individualism, familial morality and private market mechanisms gained ground. The introduction of new housing policy, compulsory competitive tendering and educational reform, all had implications for the development of equal opportunity policies. However, I would argue that the major challenge to lesbian and gay initiatives, and to EOPs more generally, was the financial crisis that faced many authorities following the 1987 general election.

Banking on a national Labour victory, many new urban left councils had spent the preceding years using financial creative accounting techniques to expand their work in line with policy commitments or at least to maintain a steady level of service provision in the face of repeated central government attempts to reduce local authority spending. The 1987 Conservative victory, however, forced many local Labour parties to reconsider their financial position, both in the short-term and long-term (see Chapter 3). In some authorities, left-wing council leaderships refused to make cuts, arguing for a strategy of defiance and non-compliance; the aftermath of the general elections saw them replaced by leaderships from the centre. Elsewhere, left-wing leaders either stood down or, if they remained, were prepared to implement a new political and financial agenda.

Lesbian and gay initiatives suffered heavily in the budgetary reductions of 1987/8. Their perceived unpopularity meant they were offered up as savings in several authorities despite the limited financial difference this would make. The new political leaderships of the late 1980s, more closely aligned with the national Labour Party, tended also to be less sympathetic to lesbian and gay policy, prioritising instead political and electoral stability. Thus, aside from the financial cutbacks faced directly by lesbian and gay, and equal opportunity units, attempts to get other services to develop and implement lesbian and gay initiatives became increasingly difficult as officers sensed the issue's political deprioritisation.

Faced with growing workloads, shrinking budgets and reduced staffing levels from voluntary and compulsory redundancy programmes and the freezing of posts, management felt able legitimately to refuse or, alternatively, to stall on implementing new urban left agendas. Lesbian and gay work's lack of any statutory basis (apart from the discriminatory bases of Local Government Act 1988, S.28 and Education Act 1986) affected its position throughout the periods of budgetary reductions. As councils became financially leaner, the choice of what to cut grew increasingly harder as statutory provision had to be protected. It was also relatively more difficult to reduce or withdraw apparently popular services such as libraries, swimming pools and advice centres.

Ongoing financial crises did not hit all authorities equally. In Inner London, money remained the dominant issue right through the early 1990s; elsewhere resources were slightly easier. However, other financial modifications also affected lesbian and gay work. One key change was the financial reorganisation that followed the introduction of compulsory competitive tendering (CCT). In many authorities, recharging systems were introduced so that central services' costs would be paid out of departmental rather than centrally held budgets. In part this was required by government legislation so council bids for municipal tenders would not have a competitive advantage through having part of their running costs subsidised. However, being compelled to introduce recharging for tendered services, many local councils introduced internal markets throughout their authority.

It is too early to identify the full effects of internal markets on lesbian and gay work. However, from the start, new accounting techniques increased pressure on local authorities to keep their central costs, including those of equal opportunity units, as low as possible. In some authorities, equal opportunity officers within tendering services were made redundant and equal opportunities training for employees in those services deleted. Yet the impact of internal markets for municipal lesbian and gay work has not been in all cases entirely negative. The Service Level Agreements (SLAs) through which equal opportunity units negotiated work with departments raised the profile of work being carried out. In most cases, departments were not given a choice about whether part of their budget would go to pay for centrally organised equality work. However, their growing awareness that scarce resources were being 'siphoned off' in this way led many departments to demand greater control and direction over equalities work that they were now paying for directly. As a result, equalities units targeted their work more closely to the needs of services who, feeling in greater command, showed greater openness to implementing policies agreed.

> SLAs meant more scrutiny, having to prove ourselves. We tried to concentrate on practical things where we could make a difference and be seen to have achieved something concrete. Because the departments were paying, they wanted to direct more. Instead of focusing on, for example, developing policies from the centre, we send officers out into the services, so they see us. And we work with them so that they learn from us and we learn much more about the practical implementation of policies in different areas of the council's activities. Together, with a

department, we agree on the agenda, agree priorities and
objectives—it's like a contract. Some of the suggestions
are ours and come from the community and the equalities
committees, and some are theirs. (interview with
L. Alderson)

The introduction of internal markets was part of a broad shift in
the ethos of local authorities during the late 1980s and early 1990s
as notions of equality gave way to those of quality and efficiency.
Central government discourse began to be taken on by council
officers and councillors. Local government's role was changing.
CCT and other legislation meant that its primary function was
shifting from provider of services, to co-ordinating their provision
by other bodies—private and voluntary.[5] Thus, as well as the direct
impact of changes on lesbian and gay units, the newly emerging
role of local government further reduced units' remit. As more
services and provision were taken on by other bodies in the
voluntary and private sector, lesbian and gay officers and
councillors found it increasingly difficult to ensure EOPs were
applied. While, in theory, councils as purchasers of services and
provision should have been able to insist on EOPs, in practice this
was extremely difficult since council officers were unable easily to
monitor or co-ordinate work with external bodies.[6]

Reconstructing Equality Work

Attitudes to EOPs work among councillors and officers were also
changing, particularly in authorities seen as having led the way.
Gurbux Singh, chief executive of Haringey council, opening a
conference on 'Equalities' organised by the Local Government
Information Unit, argued that equal opportunity units were no
longer appropriate, that what was needed was 'mainstreaming',
getting the departments to take responsibility for equalities work.[7]
I do not intend here to go into criticisms of this approach, except
to suggest that one reason units were set up was because services
were deemed insufficiently sensitive or committed to EOPs.
Whether this has changed enough for units now to be redundant,
and whether the structures exist to ensure equal opportunity work
would not be marginalised in departments, seems unlikely.

  In conjunction with these changes, many authorities faced the increasing disillusionment of lesbian and gay communities (see Chapter 3). As several activists stated in interviews, lesbian and gay municipal policies happened because gays and lesbians, whether as officers, Labour Party members, community activists or councillors, demanded and fought for them. However, the realisation of how slow and difficult change was to achieve, the ineffectiveness of lesbian and gay committees, and the lack of implementation despite paper promises, led many lesbian and gay activists to lose faith in the possibilities local government offered (see Chapter 3).

Grass-roots dissatisfaction became exacerbated by lesbian and gay officers and councillors' inability to fulfil the demands placed upon them. To many on the outside they seemed increasingly complacent and co-opted, 'luxuriating' in high status and large salaries that distanced them from community concerns. While this characterisation would be unfair to most lesbian and gay equality workers, there was a sense in which they had become 'professional dykes and faggots', employed on relatively good salaries for their skills and knowledge of community issues. As a result, in some authorities the working links between officers, councillors and a committed, wider, gay community began to dissolve.

But these were not the only reasons. The late 1980s and early 1990s witnessed, in many areas, a mushrooming of the lesbian and gay commercial scene. New pubs and clubs diverted attention from the political arena. Combined with a changing cultural, sexual politics concerned with desire and danger rather than housing and social services, many lesbians and gays simply lost interest. During the height of municipal 'radicalism', local government became a fashionable and trendy cause, the town hall a 'cool' place to be on a mid-week night. But, as one officer described, equality work, once established, became suddenly less exciting—no longer a trans-gressive, controversial demand.

The effects of these financial, legal, political and cultural changes were evident in the general decline of lesbian and gay equality work, particularly in London. By 1992, all lesbian and gay committees, with the exception of Islington's had been abolished or downgraded, while units were dissolved or else merged into single equal opportunities units. One London lesbian and gay officer in a London authority, interviewed in 1992, felt that the change from separate to integrated equalities units might be an improvement, and lead to greater effectiveness and co-ordination. She argued that equalities work made more sense when one could link together different issues of discrimination.

> It's easier to get lesbian and gay issues on the agenda
> with an integrated approach, working with other
> officers, drawing parallels, and being consistent about
> all kinds of discrimination.

This approach was one that several lesbian and gay equality teams had already taken, refusing for political reasons to prioritise particular forms of oppression or to assume all lesbians and gays were white and ablebodied. Yet, for 'integration' to work successfully, other equalities officers had to 'take on' lesbian and gay issues, but in the main, for a range of reasons, this did not occur.

Other interviewees also stressed the need for equalities work to change. They argued that in many cases it had lost direction, was too focused on internal council affairs, and generally failed to produce change. However, speaking to people a year later, few felt happy about the reforms introduced. One officer argued that lesbian and gay work, and equalities issues more generally, had suffered constant demotion. In Camden, by 1993, for example, only a skeletal structure remained, demoralised and disempowered, but one authorities were wary of eliminating altogether for fear of political repercussions.

The passive disintegration of equalities initiatives was also evident in a number of authorities outside of the capital. Slowly, councils let the organisational frameworks ebb away, not replacing workers who resigned, demoting committees first to sub-committees and then to working parties, and leaving the work without resourcing. This gradual disbandment of work in the late 1980s and early 1990s mirrored, in reverse, the process of emergence a decade earlier.

Yet decline was not apparent everywhere. In Leeds, equal opportunity work seemed to be growing. In Manchester, despite plans for restructuring, lesbian and gay officers continued to develop innovative initiatives, particularly around staff training. In authorities as diverse as Newham, Brighton, and Rochdale lesbian and gay equality strategies were making headway. Elsewhere, lesbian and gay union and Labour Party members struggled to put sexuality on local political agendas. Activists in these authorities had watched and learned from mistakes made else-where, yet still many of the same demands were apparent, such as for lesbian and gay centres, specialist officers and committees. Nevertheless, despite the continuing emphasis on bureaucratic structures, the political climate had changed. Initiatives springing up in the early 1990s seemed less aspirational and more cautious, grounded in entrenching and normalising the contested achieve-ments of the previous decade.

10

Decentring the Local State:
Alternative Social Change Strategies

> *Money is still flowing out of Haringey coffers in small grants to voluntary groups. But the distribution of the 'handouts' is unfair, claims Cllr. Terry Pope, Conservative member....*
>
> *Cllr. Pope said: 'A little old lady was asked by Labour chairman [sic] Davina Cooper how many of her group were gay, lesbian or Black.*
>
> *'The poor old lady said "I don't know—they are just elderly people."'*
>
> Hornsey Journal, 7 December 1989

While the meeting described above did not quite happen in the way portrayed by Terry Pope, his depiction nevertheless captures, albeit crudely, some of the contradictions of state engineered social equality. In this final chapter, I want to explore this issue: the paradox of a hierarchy 'imposing' equality, and then go on to consider an alternative form of community engagement with the local state. In particular, I wish to examine the prospects of a decentred approach to municipal sexual politics.

An Agenda for Change

Impacting upon Social Meanings

In this book I have focused on ideology rather than collective provision and services since it was at the level of ideology that lesbian and gay council initiatives posed the greatest challenge to the status quo (see Chapter 8). Nevertheless, it is important not to neglect local government's key role in the area of providing public services. Linda Bellos, former leader of Lambeth council, when interviewed, criticised council politicians who concentrated on using local government as a campaigning tool rather than on improving services. She argued that few councils were able to do both jobs adequately and that since local government was neither well placed nor appropriate as an ideologue its primary objective should be to provide the best possible services for the *entire* community.

Yet service provision and ideological change are not mutually exclusive strategies. The nature of the relationship between them is crucial in rethinking local government's ability to convey a progressive sexual politics. To begin with, we need to question the extent to which collective provision of services can be seen as non-ideological. Enabling lesbians and gays to adopt and foster, for example, challenges traditional sexual meanings. As I discussed earlier, ideology is not autonomous. It is as much affected by changes elsewhere as by 'direct attack'. Thus, if the economic, social and cultural position of lesbians, gays and heterosexuals changes, through transforming local government's provision of services, this will impact upon sex/gender meanings.

Therefore, in considering the ideological potential of local authorities, we need to consider a wide range of municipal practices, not just those that ostensibly seem to be about conveying oppositional meanings. Yet whether the focus is on ideology specifically or council services more generally, local state attempts to transform social meanings create problems. In Chapter 4, I discussed the mobilisation of bias against more progressive policy proposals, and in Chapter 8, I explored the boundaries that stopped some ideas from even being raised. Both sets of limits arose out of the specific discursive construction of local government during the 1980s and early 1990s. Here, I want briefly to examine two further restrictions—less concerned with the substantive nature of local government organisation and practice than with its hierarchical form. These two restrictions are discursive closure, and the 'externalisation' of subjugated voices. In discussing these limitations, I lay the groundwork for exploring other possible strategies.

Discursive Closure

Let me begin with the problem of closure. In Chapter 6, I argued that municipal texts on lesbian and gay policies *lacked* closure, that is, they were too vague and tentative about what policies would actually entail, and, as a result, open to opposing interpretations. At the same time, however, at the level of discourse, certain positions, perspectives and analyses became (temporarily) frozen as authoritative. In part this emerged from the detailed mobilisation of bias described. However, at a more general level, the very nature of organisational inequality and hierarchy made the discussion and debate necessary for a plurality of discourses to proliferate bare impossible.

Senior managers rarely gave serious attention to manual staff's ideas and views. Councillors, as Terry Pope's account was intended to demonstrate, did not in the main share a 'dialogue of equals' with local constituents. Particularly when organisations were requesting money or other assistance, honest communication became tenuous at best. It would have taken a very 'brave', foolhardy group to challenge the questions asked of them, and when groups, on other occasions, expressed their views, municipal attentiveness depended on a range of other considerations— financial, electoral, political and ideological.

Discursive closure within urban left authorities was particularly apparent in the dominance of equal opportunities, under whose conceptual umbrella lesbian and gay politics had little choice but to be located. As I argued in Chapter 2, lesbian and gay policies became possible because a tenable paradigm for their development—equal opportunities—already existed. Yet, as several interviewees suggested, it proved a particularly inappropriate framework within which to develop an oppositional, municipal sexual politics. For against whose standards were lesbians and gay men to be compared? What kind of good life was to be on offer? Would equality only be gained where a heterosexual equivalent already existed? Municipal activists thus spoke the language of 'equal opps', while demanding something more. As a result, there was a gap—a disjuncture—between the rationalisations and justifications offered and the politics—radical pluralism, lesbian feminism—being sought.

The State and the Subjugated Voice

Linked to this ossification of particular discursive frameworks was the difficulty, within a hierarchical framework, of generating 'subjugated knowledge'—that is, oppositional knowledge from the perspective of subordinated communities.[1] Lesbian and gay policies, like other equal opportunity initiatives, were unusual in that they were ostensibly constructed from the perspective of the oppressed or disadvantaged subject. Thus their production was grounded in the agency of lesbian and gay municipal actors rather than of heterosexuals speaking on their behalf. Yet, at the same time, actual knowledge was 'produced' by municipal bureaucrats working through local state structures that located the speaking lesbian/gay subject as the minority Other.

For the discursive framework of lesbian and gay work to have been different, lesbian and gay community activists needed a stronger role, *independent* of municipal structures. That way, it might have been possible to develop initiatives ideologically removed from dominant municipal paradigms. This did not happen. Despite the co-optee structure, public meetings, community consultation and so on, too much control was preserved by the local council. It could not produce subjugated knowledge; at the same time, its hierarchical arrangements of power meant little space was provided for such knowledge to be effectively developed and communicated from any place else.

The Limits of a Liberal Sexual Politics

The impossibility of subjugated knowledge combined with the exclusive discursivity of formal equality generated a further limitation: local government's emphasis on sexual *identity* rather than sexual *politics*. As I have shown, councils attempted to construct, at most, a multi-cultural environment of lifestyles (see Chapters 3 to 6). Lesbians and gays were a constituency, with needs, demands, and experiences of discrimination which undermined status quo discourses of *prevailing* formal equality.

In trying to tackle the difficulties lesbians and gay men experienced, local councils were both unwilling and unprepared to ground their approach in an explicit discourse of sexual politics. While a liberal sexual politics based on rights, freedom and equality underlay council lesbian and gay initiatives, at the same time there was an inability to locate lesbian and gay policies, that is, both homosexuality and local government practices, in an explicit, wider analysis of power, heterosexuality and gender.

Lesbian and gay initiatives, in the main, not only ignored relations between heterosexuality and gender; they also ignored the political issues surfacing within lesbian and gay communities. Questions of butch and femme, cross-dressing, sado-masochism, for instance—all dimensions of internal gay and lesbian struggle— were neglected by municipal policies which aimed to treat all homosexual relations equally.

But should such issues have been ignored? How could local government have addressed them? These questions reveal the limitations of local government's policy choices. As a bureaucratic structure producing directives, regulations and initiatives, it could mandate, proscribe and facilitate. But, as I suggested above, it could not easily engage in an open, equal process of social change with its local communities. This is not to deny the discursive forums generated by municipal lesbian and gay policies—the discussions at committee, in the press, and in various local authority workplaces. However, not only were these discussions ideologically and politically constrained, but the generally narrow, bureaucratic conception of policy-making utilised within urban state politics marginalised their ability to impact upon social processes and relations.

What I am arguing for, therefore, is a shift of focus: a radical move away from identifying 'policy' as something generated by councillors and officers within formal organisational processes and from classifying lesbian and gay urban politics as an issue of minority group disadvantage and sexual identity. Homosexuality cannot be dealt with in isolation from a broader sex/gender politics and this cannot fully take place within traditional bureaucratic forms. What we therefore need to explore are ways in which local government *can* engage with how sexual politics is lived, organised and structured.

Strategy for Changing Times

Municipal politics in the 1990s is not the same as its predecessor a decade ago. People are less optimistic, have lower expectations, and, indeed, they are right to feel this way. As I discussed in Chapter 9, the role of local government is in transition. Legislative and political changes make it unlikely, for the foreseeable future, that activists will be able effectively to use local government as a base for ideological campaigning. In addition, the task of providing services is becoming less central to local councils' work as they become re-created as co-ordinator and contractor—facilitating the provision of private firms and the voluntary sector. Thus, both routes posed by Bellos, the one she propounds as well as the one rejected, seem to be becoming increasingly redundant.

A Decentred Strategy

Within this changing framework, the need exists for a 'decentred' strategic approach towards local government. So far this book has focused on the centre, the formal policy-making apparatus, in the main, because that was the strategy and approach adopted by lesbian and gay municipal activists. Yet, as I have stated, it was an approach with limitations: limitations, I would argue, which could not be overcome simply by means of better council reports or improved scrutinising of front-line workers. While both may have been of some benefit, also required—within a framework which focused on sexual politics rather than sexual identity—was an approach that located change at the municipal interface, in the multifarious interactions of people and resources.

In part, this is a pragmatic argument. Research carried out within the field of sociology of law as well as in the work of academics such as Lipsky on 'street-level' bureaucrats shows that policies (and laws) are not generally effective in changing people's behaviour and even less their attitudes.[2] In Chapter 5, I discussed the opposition to lesbian and gay initiatives from within the council organisation. This being the case, how was even the most minimal of changes to be achieved? How much coercion would be required? Who would do the penalising, the monitoring, and would this even work? To what extent can you *force* people to treat others equally? Rational choice theory might suggest that if the costs are sufficiently high, people will stop discriminating. However, effectively raising the 'costs' of unequal treatment is a difficult process, and, as this research has suggested, for many, the formal costs of discriminating proved a scarcely relevant consideration. While none of this is to suggest that anti-discrimination policies and laws are not symbolically valuable and a useful resource, by themselves they achieve little.

In addition to pragmatic arguments, there are also theoretical and political ones. I have already set out some reasons why a hierarchical, bureaucratic approach to sexual politics proved inappropriate: the oxymoron of the state speaking in a subjugated voice. Beyond that, there are also real problems in the notion of 'implementing ideology'. Progressive ideologies cannot simply be *implemented* like any other policy, nor are they best communicated through leaflets, reports and media interviews. Rather, they are affirmed and validated through experiences and practices—the interaction of people with each other, with institutions, and with resources.

A Differentiated Strategy for Street-level Interactions

If, instead of privileging council bureaucrats as agents of change, the focus shifted to encompass teachers, volunteers, childcare workers, housing office staff, cleaners and librarians; that is, to interactions within schools, community projects, parent-toddler groups, housing offices and libraries, we might have a more realistic and useful perspective on where progressive developments within the local polity can arise. Lipsky argues that it is *these* 'street-level' interactions which are crucial, because they are often one to one, based on flexible interventions and the exercise of discretion, and because it is within these relationships that people change.[3]

A strategy that focused on the specificity of different kinds of interactions, such as between a repairs service and tenants or social workers and children, would also require the contribution or role of management to vary, shifting away from broad guidelines, intended to be as applicable in the housing office as in the community centre or swimming pool, to a service or 'interface'-centred approach. In general, lesbian and gay municipal policies tried to adopt this more flexible approach—responding to the specific demands of particular situations. As one lesbian officer, for example, explained,

> We organised practical-based awareness training rooted in particular workplace needs. Training people working with lesbian families, for instance, around donor insemination.

However, the 1980s witnessed too much reliance by lesbian and gay municipal actors on traditional, policy-oriented strategies that emphasised impersonal interaction, rules, regulations, and the dispersal or shifting of conflict.

The limitations of this latter approach can be seen in the following illustration. A parent-toddler group, in which women members discussed their dissatisfaction with their partners' contribution to child care, might be deemed to breach its authority's lesbian and gay policy if certain monitoring requirements were not fulfilled or certain books not purchased. While these council requirements may be entirely valid, such policies would be problematic if they ignored the kinds of changes *actually* taking place, as well as underestimating the need to start with the sexual politics of the participants involved—a sexual politics that is as much about gender, race and class as it is about homosexuality.

> Sexism is central to homophobia. Working with day nurseries, it's clear how anti-gay and lesbian discrimination starts. Mothers who won't let boys wear face paints and dress up. Parents bring their daughters and say they can't play football, or send them in inappropriate clothes and say they want them to stay like that all day....When

*they bring their children, some parents say they don't
want their child turned into a 'queer'.* (Lesbian officer
interviewed)

A decentred childcare strategy, on the other hand, might be
initiated by community activists, parents, staff or, possibly, lesbian
and gay specialist officers. Proposals for developing a progressive
sexual politics could include training (as occurred in the above
example), inviting someone to facilitate a discussion with parents,
extending the range of non-gendered toys and books, altering the
composition of families using the provision and so on. Whatever
the requests and recommendations, these could then be channelled
through different decision-making systems depending on what
was appropriate. Thus they might get taken up by sympathetic
councillors on committees, lesbian and gay officers working in
units, departmental staff, trade unions or appropriate grass-roots
organisations.

But what if such requests did not receive council management
support? Or what if the childcare project was uninterested or even
hostile to the idea of developing a progressive sexual politics? Let
me take the second question first. If blanket opposition existed,
then no change in the short term would be likely to occur
whichever strategy was adopted. However, if there were a few,
lone, voices—staff or parents, perhaps—a strategy which
emphasised grass-roots activity might offer more hope than an
approach which posited local government as the repository of all
policy development. Yet I am not suggesting here that the role of
municipal support and policies is redundant—not by any means.
For in such situations, the existence of council policies *would* be
useful, a resource that advocates of a more progressive approach,
such as front-line staff, could draw upon to gain legitimacy and
municipal assistance.

Responding to Opposition

Let me now return to the first question: the problem of opposition
from within the bureaucracy. A decentred approach might make it
easier to challenge opposition from the council leadership or from
senior officers since any proposal which reached them would
already have the backing of people at a number of different points

and locations. It might also be a more effective strategy in dealing with resistance from front-line workers. By transferring ownership and control of initiatives away from senior management, front-line workers would perhaps be more *willing* to develop initiatives and more prepared to respond to criticisms.

I said above that a hierarchical, policy-oriented approach deflects and diffuses conflict since nobody takes responsibility, except possibly those too inaccessible to most complainants. Yet diffusion of conflict does not mean it disappears. Rather, it allows a build-up of tension and resentment which can then be exploited by right-wing actors as happened in Haringey. Moreover, if the objective is to change attitudes, perspectives and institutional practices, it is important that conflict is not suppressed, but rather *constructively* engaged in so that change and progress are possible.

In saying this I am suggesting that many of the people who opposed lesbian and gay policies may have been less antagonistic had they been involved and *understood* what was implicated. At the same time, it is important not to overestimate the power and impact of knowledge. Many on the right knew all the arguments put forward by advocates of lesbian and gay equality, yet still remained hostile. Thus, equally important in enabling conflict to lead to productive change is the fact that a decentred strategy shifts the balance of power away from elite actors. In this way, lesbians and gays, as well as progressive groups generally, might be more able to *assert* and *enforce* their demands against right-wing actors.

But could a decentred strategy be achieved *prior* to a shift in the political balance of power? Why would councils *agree* to such a project if it were ultimately disempowering for them? These questions raise the issue of who is being addressed in this discussion. It is important to emphasise that in a sense I am not here 'speaking' to local authorities but rather to progressive actors working in this area. Thus, in contrast to arguing for political, managerial or service-based decentralisation which *depends* on local government establishing appropriate structures, this exploration is about political strategy to achieve specific objectives: strategy which lesbian and gay actors can *choose* to adopt.

The approach I am proposing is not perfect. It is also not particularly novel. Activists have advocated it for decades. Indeed, many of the community-based municipal developments of the 1970s were a response to similar perceptions of the local state's limitations. In the 1980s too, many lesbians and gay men tried and to varying degrees succeeded in operationalising a less hierarchical politics. However, lesbian and gay municipal politics in the 1980s became too caught up with bureaucratic structures and processes. Perhaps though, this was inevitable. Throughout my research, I have indicated the structural constraints on progressive initiatives, and the power and impact of state processes and culture. The extent, therefore, to which municipal actors could have 'chosen' to construct an alternative approach is uncertain. For aside from obvious constraints, the more subtle considerations of socialisation, political judgement and personal interest problematise the very notion of choice.

The desire for policy, committees, reports and officers is also understandable in a structure which accords status to those particular things. Yet while these goals may have provided a modicum of legitimacy for lesbians and gay men, this book has suggested that such strength was almost entirely symbolic. Few changes occurred within the provision and structuring of local government services as a result of lesbian and gay policies. While changes in attitudes and perspectives, I would argue, did take place, these changes were principally among those actors directly involved in the political struggle rather than within the broader constituencies of the local polity.

As the 1990s continue to witness the diminution of local government's role of provider, as relations between local authorities and their communities become ever more complex, progressive attempts to direct change through *centralised* directives will become increasingly unsuccessful. The need to locate a progressive sexual politics first and foremost in the *multiple* relationships people have with council structures and practices will become ever more imperative.

The State-community Interface: A Blurred Realm

In this conclusion, I have questioned not only the top-down, but also the centre-periphery model of local government. Yet how far should such a contestation be taken? One could go further and deny not only the unequal distribution of power within and between local government and its environment, but also that any separation exists at all between local government and its community. Unfortunately, there is not the space to address this first issue. I do, however, wish to make a few brief points about the second as this is particularly pertinent to the theoretical perspective I am adopting.

To begin with, how do we know where local government 'ends' and the community 'starts'? One approach might be to consider whether there are any criteria which distinguish local authorities from the communities of which they are part. State pay-roll, for example, is not a distinguishing feature of the former, nor are legal constraints. Both apply to bodies and actors traditionally separated from local government. It would seem therefore that the municipal-community interface is not a clear cut boundary but blurred. Where, for example, would one locate voluntary workers in a council-funded and -run community centre, private companies with tenders to provide public services, or childcare workers on a council register? Indeed, it is this lack of clarity and complexity that makes decentred strategy crucial. At the same time, there are dangers with a thoroughly poststructuralist account which denies any distinction at all.

For, if we are all part of local government or the local state, do such terms then convey any useful meaning? My argument, in Chapter 8, that local government can legitimately neither deploy ideology instrumentally nor convey non-structural meanings, is grounded in an analysis which distinguishes local government from community activism since I suggest that neither prohibition applies to organisations within civil society. We might therefore try re-working Gramsci's useful, although somewhat confusing, approach which treats civil society as both part of the state, while, simultaneously, separate from it.[4] At the same time, I would suggest, there is a third area—a grey space, a realm of fluidity— which is both state and non-state. This paradox of the state reflects different levels of reality. It reflects the fact that what we observe when examining the local state depends on *why* we are examining it. At the same time it assists in developing a strategy.

If progressive, municipal initiatives can be developed within the grey area—at the interface of state and community—then it is possible that the problems identified in this book, those of bureaucratic containment and status quo opposition, may be reduced or even thwarted. In the case of lesbian and gay policy development, both kinds of difficulty occurred because initiatives entailed the *specific* utilisation of local state processes. Thus initiatives developed within the bureaucratic policy-implementation process experienced the consequences of a mobilisation of bias. Those that managed to escape, flying out through chinks in the processes' walls, precipitated and encountered tremendous levels of opposition.

Yet, if one develops municipal strategies outside such bureaucratic policy-making processes, containment is less possible. Instead of policies developed for future consumption, where an ostensible separation occurs between means and ends, the two become fused. In this way, there are fewer deep grooved channels through which initiatives flow, through which they can be controlled, contained, watered down and watered out, fewer points at which different permissions are requested and can be refused. Rather, the process of dialogue and interaction is the change.

In addition, since the *formal* policy-implementation structures of local government are not ostensibly reaching beyond their ideological boundaries, articulating non-structural meanings, and using ideology in an instrumental way, right-wing mobilisation becomes much harder. First, conservative forces cannot point to local government's illegitimate behaviour since the sexual politics is taking place outside formal, political arenas. Secondly, as I have said, it is less likely that there will be a reservoir of dissatisfaction all focused on the same target, for resentment would be lessened and the targets too dispersed.

Poststructuralists might argue that there is nothing to suggest that the problems experienced in developing lesbian and gay policies in the 1980s and early 1990s would be repeated in subsequent attempts. Formally, I would agree this is true. However, the limitations on local state activism happened because of *reasons*, and there is little to suggest that these reasons have substantially vanished or become transformed.

Shifting initiative to the 'peripheries' would also enable more lesbian, gay, and other progressive actors actively to participate, rather than depending on a minority or professionalised elite. Thus it might also reduce the likelihood that those involved would be socialised into bureaucratic ways of working, thereby lessening the co-optive tendencies of the local state. It is much easier to co-opt—socially, ideologically and politically—a few community activists sitting on a council committee than a large number of people, with varying degrees of involvement and sympathy, working to change a variety of state practices. For these reasons, as well as the greater political heterogeneity that would undoubtedly result from the participation of more people who were not council employees, actors would be less likely to perceive themselves as ideologically constrained by the narrow arena of acceptable municipal practice.

Yet none of this is to say strategies would necessarily be radical. Activists come in a range of persuasions and this would clearly influence the nature of political struggle and demands. However, if radical approaches were articulated, they would stand a higher chance of survival, free from the manacles of 'state activism'. Moreover, working beyond state boundaries would give activists greater political freedom and thus encourage the involvement of those put off or alienated by state participation.

This does not deny the need for action at a distance from the state (narrowly defined). Many writers and activists have addressed the importance of independent community organising and grass-roots provision as well as the process of politicising the home, workplace and a myriad of other arenas. Similarly, I do not wish to marginalise the importance of bureaucratic change and development. In this book, I have explored the symbolic and practical importance of municipal initiatives in improving conditions for lesbians and gay men. I have also examined the impact of such policies at a national level in precipitating a discursive struggle around issues of sexual politics.

As I stated in the introduction, it is important not to under-estimate what was achieved, including the gains that were once present but which failed to survive. From my own experience as both a participant and commentator, the attempt to enact a radical aspiration proved immensely worthwhile for the possibilities it revealed, as well as for the skills and lessons it granted. With the decline of urban EOPs in the early 1990s, lesbian and gay participants fanned outwards in a range of directions, many returning to the voluntary sector from which they had come a decade earlier. They—we—took with us a knowledge, but more importantly a sense of empowerment, that state activism, however contested and difficult, had provided.

Notes

The detailed source material on which this book is based can be
found in 'Sexing the City: Lesbian and Gay Municipal Politics,
1979–87', PhD: Warwick University

1 Sexual Politics and the Activist State

1. See Appendix A.
2. Davina Cooper, 'An engaged state: sexuality, governance and the potential for
   change', *Journal of Law and Society*, 20, 3, 1993.
3. See Sophie Watson (ed.), *Playing the State: Australian feminist interventions*,
   London, 1990.
4. See for example, Gerry Stoker, 'Creating a local government for a post-Fordist
   society: The Thatcher project?', in G. Stoker and S. Leach (eds), *The Future of
   Local Government*, Basingstoke, 1989.
5. See Peter Saunders, *Social Theory and the Urban Question*, London, 1981, and
   'Rethinking Local Politics' in Martin Boddy and Colin Fudge (eds), *Local
   Socialism?*, London, 1984.
6. See Patrick Dunleavy, 'The limits to local government', in *Local Socialism?*; W.
   Magnusson, 'Urban politics and the local state', *Studies in Political Economy*, 19,
   1985.
7. Andrew Cox et al., *Power in Capitalist Society*, Brighton, 1985, pp.204–6.
8. W. Magnusson, 'Urban politics and the local state', op.cit., p.117.
9. Ralph Miliband, *Capitalist Democracy in Britain*, Oxford, 1984.
10. See for example, Annette Kuhn and Ann-Marie Wolpe (eds), *Feminism and
    Materialism*, London, 1978; Anne Showstack Sassoon (ed.), *Women and the
    State*, London, 1987; Suzanne Franzway et al., *Staking a Claim: Feminism,
    Bureaucracy and the State*, Cambridge, 1989.
11. David Morley, 'Changing paradigms in audience studies', in E. Seiter et al. (eds),
    Remote Control, London, 1989.

12. By 'material' I mean those physical changes which interact with ideology to produce meaning.
13. See Lillian Faderman, *Surpassing the Love of Men*, New York, 1981; Adrienne Rich, *Compulsory Heterosexuality and Lesbian Existence*, London, 1981.
14. See for example, 'Forum: The feminist sexuality debates', *Signs*, 10, 1, 1984.

2 Agenda Politics

An earlier version of this chapter, entitled, 'Off the Banner and onto the agenda: The emergence of a new municipal lesbian and gay politics, 1979–86' has appeared in *Critical Social Policy* 36, 1982/3.

1. Lynne Segal, *Is the Future Female?*, London, 1987, p.224.
2. Martin Boddy and Colin Fudge (eds), *Local Socialism?* London, 1984.
3. John Gyford, *The Politics of Local Socialism*, London, 1985.
4. Stewart Lansley et al., *Councils in Conflict: The Rise and Fall of the Municipal Left*, Basingstoke, 1989.
5. John Gyford, *The Politics of Local Socialism*, op.cit., ch.2.
6. Organised by the GLC, Autumn 1985.
7. Funded by Edinburgh City Council, 1987.
8. Funded and partly organised by Camden, Hackney, Haringey and Islington councils, 1987 to 1990.
9. Derek Cohen and Richard Dyer, 'The politics of gay culture', in Gay Left Collective (ed.), *Homosexuality: Power and Politics*, London, 1980.
10. Interview with Linda Bellos.
11. Ibid.
12. Interview with Peter Tatchell, gay activist and Labour Parliamentary candidate for Bermondsey, 1982.
13. Lynne Harne, 'From 1971: Reinventing the wheel', in Amanda Sebestyen (ed.), *'68, '78, '88: From Women's Liberation to Feminism*, Bridport, 1988.
14. See A. Durrell of CHE (*City Limits*, 19 January 1985), quoted by Stephen Jeffery-Poulter, *Peers, Queers and Commons*, London, 1991, p.203.
15. Interview with Peter Tatchell.
16. See Philip Jones, *London Labour Briefing*, July 1981; Ann Tobin, 'Lesbianism in the Labour Party: the GLC experience', *Feminist Review*, 34, 1990, p.58.
17. Stephen Jeffery-Poulter, *Peers, Queers and Commons*, op. cit., p.165.
18. Stewart Lansley et al., *Councils in Conflict*, op.cit., p.162.
19. Peter Tatchell, *The Battle for Bermondsey*, London, 1983.
20. Interview with Peter Tatchell.
21. Jan Parker, 'No Going Back', in Bob Cant and Susan Hemmings (eds), *Radical Records*, London, 1988, p.261.
22. John Shiers, *Lesbian and Gay Socialist*, Spring 1985.
23. Lynne Harne, 'From 1971: Reinventing the Wheel', op.cit., pp.68–9.
24. Femi Otitoju, 'The Should We, Shouldn't We? Debate', in Bob Cant and Susan Hemmings, *Radical Records*, op.cit., pp.224–5.
25. Dennis Altman, 'AIDS and the reconceptualisation of homosexuality', in Dennis Altman et al. (eds), *Which Homosexuality?* London, 1989, p.35.
26. In the early 1990s the age of consent has returned as a priority.
27. London Strategic Policy Unit, *Lesbian and Gay Issues, Policy Development and Legislation, 1967–87* (1988).
28. Interview with Linda Bellos.

29. Interview with Ken Livingstone, former leader of the GLC.
30. Interview with Anne Matthews.
31. Jane Dixon et al., 'North London Young Lesbian Group: Specialist work within the Youth Service', in Carol Jones and Pat Mahony (eds), *Learning Our Lines: Sexuality and social control in education*, London, 1989, pp.233–4, 239.
32. Interview with Linda Bellos.
33. A. Armitage, *Gay Times* (November 1984, no.75:18–19).
34. *Gay Times* (December 1984, no.76:10–11). See also S. Jeffery-Poulter, *Peers, Queers and Commons*, op. cit., p.174.
35. *Gay Times* (October 1985, no.86:8, Dec/Jan 1985/6 no.88:9).
36. Ibid. (April 1986, no.91:9).
37. Ibid. (August 1986, no.95:6).
38. Interview with Jane Skeates.
39. Ann Tobin, 'Lesbianism and the Labour Party: The GLC Experience', op.cit., p.58.
40. Interview with Ken Livingstone.
41. Ibid.
42. K. Livingstone interviewed by K. Kirk (*Gay Times*, April 1986, no.91:50–2).
43. Femi Otitoju, 'The should we, shouldn't we? debate', op.cit., p.288.
44. Interview with Jan Parker.
45. Interview with Linda Bellos.
46. Ibid.
47. Femi Otitoju, 'The should we, shouldn't we? debate', op.cit., p.288.
48. Ann Tobin, 'Lesbianism and the Labour Party: The GLC experience', op.cit., p.57.
49. Ann Tobin, 'Lesbianism and the Labour Party: The GLC experience', op.cit., p.64.
50. Stephen Jeffery-Poulter, *Peers, Queers and Commons*, op.cit., p.204.

3 (Dis)trust, Hope and (Dis)illusionment

1. Association of London Authorities (ALA), *Local Government Directory*, 1988.
2. Ibid.
3. This changed with the abolition of the Inner London Education Authority (ILEA) in 1988.
4. Gay and Lesbian Sub-Committee, *Minutes*, item 6, 17 September 1984; item 6, 10 July 1985.
5. Interview with Robert Crossman.
6. Interview with David Dawson.
7. Interview with Robert Crossman.
8. This figure is based on the 1981 census. See *OPCS County Monitor*, publication of the Government Statistical Service, 26 January 1982.
9. Ibid.
10. Interview with Richard McCance.
11. Interview with Jo Fraser.
12. Gay and Lesbian Sub-Committee, *Minutes*, item 96, 6 February 1986.
13. Ibid., item 112, 6 March 1986.
14. Lesbian Sub-Committee, *Minutes*, item 33, 6 November 1986.
15. Gay Men's Sub-Committee, *Minutes*, item 84, 11 December 1986.
16. Interview with Richard McCance.
17. *Saturday Evening Post*, 14 March 1987.

18. Gay and Lesbian Sub-Committee, *Minutes*, item 70, 5 December 1985.
19. Ibid., item 135, 6 March 1986. See also Gay Men's Sub-Committee, *Minutes*, item 54, 9 October 1986.
20. Gay and Lesbian Sub-Committee, *Minutes*, item 45, 7 November 1985; ibid., *Minutes*, item 61, 5 December 1985. See also Gay and Lesbian Sub-Committee, *Minutes*, item 36, report of the chief executive on opportunities for lesbians and gay men through IAP, 8 October 1985.
21. Gay Men's Sub-Committee, *Minutes*, item 82, 11 December 1986. See also Lesbian Sub-Committee, *Minutes*, item 22, the response to Lesbian Line, 4 September 1986.
22. Interview with Harry Joshua.
23. Gay and Lesbian Sub-Committee, *Minutes*, item 16, 4 July 1985.
24. Interview with Richard McCance.
25. Gay Men's Sub-Committee, *Minutes*, 8 October 1984.
26. Report from Black Lesbian and Gay Group at second public meeting, 28 January 1985; Gay Men's Sub-Committee 2 February 1987, 6 July 1987; Lesbian Sub-Committee Work Review, August 1987.
27. Lesbian Open Working Party, 10 February 1985.
28. Gay Men's Sub-Committee, 16 September 1985.
29. ALA, *London Government Directory*, 1988.
30. Ibid.
31. Interview with Sandra Plummer.

4 Something Nice for the Poor People

1. Stewart Lansley et al., *Councils in Conflict: The Rise and Fall of the Municipal Left*, Basingstoke, 1989.
2. Report of the director of administrative and legal services, Lambeth Working Party on Gay Men and Lesbians, *Minutes*, item 6, 21 May 1984.
3. *Councils in Conflict*, op.cit.
4. Haringey Labour Party, *Manifesto*, section 5, 1986. Emphasis added.
5. Interview with Sandra Plummer.
6. Interview with Emmy Doye.
7. Interview with Femi Otitoju.
8. Ibid.
9. See letter from city secretary to committee secretary of the Gay Men's Sub-Committee, 25 July 1986.
10. Interview with Jo Fraser.
11. Ibid.
12. Interview with Paul Fairweather.
13. Interview with Jane Skeates.
14. Interview with Femi Otitoju.
15. Ibid.
16. Interview with Emmy Doye.
17. Lambeth Working Party for Gay Men and Lesbians, *Agenda*, item 14, 7 January 1987.
18. Interview with Emmy Doye.
19. Interview with Harry Joshua.
20. Interview with Jo Fraser.
21. Lambeth Working Party for Gay Men and Lesbians, *Agenda*, item 7(b), 21 May 1984.

22. Ibid, *Agenda*, item 7(i), 21 May 1984.
23. Interview with Jane Skeates
24. Interview with Femi Otitoju.

5 Implementation Failure, Appeasement and Prefigurative Practice

1. Interview with Ealing lesbian and gay officer.
2. Interview with Chris Root.
3. B. Hogwood and L. Gunn, *Policy Analysis for the Real World*, Oxford, 1984, p.119.
4. Ibid.
5. J. Pfeffer, *Power in Organisations*, London, 1981, ch.6.
6. S. Barrett and M. Hill, 'Policy Bargaining and Structure in Implementation Theory', in M. Goldsmith (ed.), *New Research in Central-Local Relations*, Aldershot, 1986, p.38.
7. Murray Edelman, *Constructing the Political Spectacle*, Chicago, 1988, ch.2.
8. Davina Cooper, 'Positive Images in Haringey: A Struggle for Identity', in Carol Jones and Pat Mahony, *Learning our Lines: Sexuality and Social Control in Education*, London, 1989, p.72.

6 With God's Help and Common Sense

1. The London borough of Haringey is situated in a high density residential area, approximately ten miles north of London's West End. It is a single tier authority and as an Outer London borough has been historically responsible for providing its own education provision. It has a population of approximately 200,000, almost half of whom are from minority ethnic communities (calculated by Association of London Authorities from 1981 census data).
2. Haringey Labour Party, *Manifesto*, 1986.
3. PRG leaflet.
4. Tottenham Conservative Association leaflet, part of campaign for 'normal family life' (undated).
5. See 'Haringey Council: School Lessons', House of Lords, col. 552–554, 28 July 1986.
6. Minutes of Positive Images, 2 September 1986. Tottenham is the eastern constituency within Haringey.
7. Ibid.
8. Bob Cant, 'The Limits of Tolerance', in Tara Kaufmann and Paul Lincoln (eds), *High Risk Lives: Lesbian and Gay Politics After the Clause*, Bridport, 1991, p.168.
9. Ibid.
10. Martin Durham, *Sex and Politics*, Basingstoke, 1991, p.113.
11. Education Committee, *Minutes*, item A162, 30 September 1986.
12. John Gyford et al., *The Changing Politics of Local Government*, London, 1989, p.312.
13. See Haringey education service leaflet, entitled, 'What every parent needs to know about lesbian and gay issues' (undated).

14. Ibid.
15. Education Committee, *Report*, 'Equal opportunities—lesbians and gay men', 30 September 1986.
16. 'What every parent needs to know', op.cit.
17. See Education Committee, *Report*, 'Equal opportunities—lesbians and gay men', 30 September 1986.
18. 'What every parent needs to know', op.cit.
19. Ibid.
20. House of Lords, col. 552, 28 July 1986.
21. Ibid., col. 572, 1 April 1987.
22. Full Council, 20 October 1986.
23. House of Lords, col. 572, 1 April 1987.
24. David T. Evans, 'Section 28: Law, Myth and Paradox', *Critical Social Policy*, 27, 1989/90, p. 83.
25. Interview with PI member, in Davina Cooper, 'Positive Images in Haringey: A Struggle for Identity', in Carol Jones and Pat Mahony (eds), *Learning Our Lines*, London, 1989.
26. House of Commons, col. 1090–1, 21 October 1986.
27. In the spring of 1987, Rushworth-Smith ceased his fast, see Davina Cooper, 'Positive Images in Haringey: A Struggle for Identity', op.cit., pp.58–9.
28. DES to Haringey's CEO, 25 July 1986, 29th January 1987, 31 July 1987.
29. House of Lords, col. 572, April 1 1986.
30. See Diane Macdonell, *Theories of Discourse*, Oxford, 1986, for comparable discussion in relation to discourse.

7 Mad Bouncer Killed My Baby

1. James Baaden, 'Sells Papers, Ruins Lives: Homophobia in the Media', in Tara Kaufmann and Paul Lincoln (eds), *High Risk Lives: Lesbian and Gay Politics after the Clause*, Bridport, 1991.
2. Glasgow University Media Group, *Bad News*, London, 1976; *More Bad News*, London, 1980; *Really Bad News*, London, 1982.
3. Caroline Spry, 'Out of the Box', in *High Risk Lives*, op.cit., p.131.
4. Alison Young, *Femininity in Dissent*, London, 1990, pp.52–3.
5. For instance, the *Daily Mail*, 16 September 1986; the London *Evening Standard*, 16 September 1986; *Today*, 21 September 1986.
6. See the London *Evening Standard*, 10 December 1986; the *Hampstead and Highgate Express*, 23 January 1987; the *Weekly Herald*, 22 January 1987.
7. See *The Times*, 17 March 1987; the *Daily Mail*, 3 April 1987; the *Hornsey Journal*, 3 April 1987; the *Sun*, 22 April 1987.
8. Capital Radio, 21 August 1986.
9. BBC Radio 2, 12 February 1987.
10. Alison Young, *Femininity in Dissent*, op. cit., p.121.
11. The *Daily Telegraph*, 19 September, 1986.
12. The *Daily Mail*, 17 September, 1986.
13. The *Haringey Independent*, 18 September, 1986.
14. The *Evening Standard*, 16 September, 1986.
15. The *Daily Mail*, 16 September 1986.
16. For example, George Gale, the *Daily Mirror*, 9 July 1986.
17. The *Haringey Advertiser*, 25 September 1986.
18. The *Daily Telegraph*, 6 October 1986.

19. House of Commons, col.999, 8 May 1987.
20. House of Lords, col.322, 18 December 1986.
21. Roger Scruton, *The Times*, 11 November 1986; see also Auberon Waugh, the *Spectator*, 10 May 1986.
22. Alison Young, *Femininity in Dissent*, op.cit., ch.6.
23. See the *Daily Mail*, 16, 17, 18 and 22 September 1986.
24. Access to the local press was an important factor since many of the national papers picked up local stories, often repeating them without any of their own investigation.
25. Usually the press office.
26. John Fiske, 'Moments of Television: Neither the Text nor the Audience' in E. Seiter et al. (eds), *Remote Control*, London, 1989, p.70.
27. House of Commons, col.999, 8 May 1987.
28. See the *Guardian*, 15 March 1988. The political centre accepted without question Conservative claims that homosexuality was being promoted by Labour councils. Until a change of heart on the Labour front bench, with the advent of S.28, few mainstream politicians were prepared to argue that presenting positive images in schools was promoting 'tolerance' not homosexuality.
29. House of Lords, col.327, 18 December 1986.
30. Ibid., col.311, 18 December 1986.
31. Graham Murdock, 'Political Deviance: The Press Presentation of a Militant Mass Demonstration', in Stanley Cohen and Jock Young (eds), *The Manufacture of News: Deviance, Social Problems and the Mass Media*, London, 1973, p.168.
32. House of Lords, col.572, 1 April 1987.
33. The *Guardian*, 15 March 1988.
34. House of Commons, col.1070, 21 October 1986.
35. House of Lords, col.317, 18 December 1986.
36. See Giles Radice, MP, Labour Shadow Spokesperson on Education, House of Commons, col. 1060, 21 October 1986; '...I don't believe *Jenny lives with Eric and Martin* should be for general use and nor does ILEA.'

8 Pushing Us Off the Pavement

1. E.E. Schattschneider, *The Semi-Sovereign People*, 1960, New York, p.71.
2. For a fuller discussion of my use of the word power, see 'Productive, Relational and Everywhere: Theorising Power and Resistance within Foucauldian Feminism', *Sociology*, 1984.
3. See generally Michèle Barrett, *The Politics of Truth*, Cambridge, 1991, pp. 29–30; Terry Eagleton, *Ideology: An Introduction*, London, 1991, pp.5, 18–21.
4. Louis Althusser, *Lenin and Philosophy and Other Essays*, London, 1971; see also Stuart Hall, 'Signification, Representation, Ideology: Althusser and the Post-Structuralist Debates', *Critical Studies in Mass Communication*, 2, 1985, pp.102, 109.
5. John Gyford et al., *The Changing Politics of Local Government*, London, 1989, pp.310–12.
6. Steve Leach, 'Strengthening Local Democracy', in John Stewart and Gerry Stoker (eds), *The Future of Local Government*, Basingstoke, 1989, p.103.
7. John Gyford et al., *The Changing Politics of Local Government*, op.cit., p.299.
8. Ibid.
9. G. Mather, 'Thatcherism and Local Government', in John Stewart and Gerry Stoker (eds), *The Future of Local Government*, op.cit., p.214.

10. The Earl of Halsbury, House of Lords, 18 December 1986, col.310.
11. Gary Kinsman, 'Men Loving Men: The Challenge of Gay Liberation', in M. Kauffman (ed.), *Beyond Patriarchy*, Toronto, 1987, p.105.
12. Marilyn Frye, *The Politics of Reality: Essays in Feminist Theory*, Trumansberg, 1983, p.135.

9 Towards a New Equilibrium

1. John Gyford et al., *The Changing Politics of Local Government*, London, 1989, p.280.
2. Quoted in D.S. King, 'Political Centralisation and State Interests in Britain', *Comparative Political Studies*, 21, 1989, p.198.
3. John Gyford et al., *The Changing Politics of Local Government*, op. cit., p.326.
4. G. Salaman, 'Organisations as Constructors of Social Reality', in G. Salaman and K. Thompson (eds), *Control and Ideology in Organisations*, Milton Keynes, 1980, ch.11.
5. Norman Flynn, 'The New Right and Social Policy', *Policy and Politics*, 17, 1989, p.103.
6. See E. McGarrell et al (1990) 'Obstacles to seemingly simple reform: A case study of bail reform', *Policy Studies Review*, 9, p.438, on the difficulties where implementation involves interagency development and communication.
7. Davina Cooper, 'The Future of Equalities Work', *Everywoman*, 71, 1991, p.16.

10 Decentring the Local State

1. See generally on this issue, Kathy Ferguson, *The Feminist Case Against Bureaucracy*, Philadelphia, 1984.
2. M. Lipsky, *Street Level Bureaucracy*, New York, 1980.
3. Ibid.
4. See Christine Buci-Glucksmann, *Gramsci and the State*, London, 1980, ch.3.

Appendixes

Appendix A: Lesbian and Gay Municipal Equality Structures, 1983 to 1987

Below is a list of some of the main authorities that developed lesbian and gay organisational structures between 1983 and 1987.

Authority	Committee Structure	No. of Officers	Unit Structure
Camden	Lesbian and Gay Committee ⅓ Co-optees (none in effect)	4	Lesbian and Gay Unit
GLC	Gay Working Party Sub-Groups Majority Co-optees	—	—
Haringey	Lesbian and Gay Committee (Reporting to Community Affairs Committee) Majority Co-optees	6	Lesbian and Gay Unit
Islington	Gay and Lesbian Advisory Working Party, then Gay and Lesbian Sub-Committee (Reporting to Policy and Resources Committee), then Lesbian and Gay Committee Co-optee numbers and representation variable	—	—

Authority	Committee Structure	No. of Officers	Unit Structure
Lambeth	Lesbian and Gay Working Party (Reporting to Policy and Resources Committee) Majority Co-optees	—	—
Nottingham	Gay and Lesbian Sub-Committee, Gay Men's Sub-Committee Lesbian Sub-Committee (Reporting to Equal Opportunities Committee) Majority Co-optees	2 job-shares 1 lesbian 1 gay man	Equal Opportunities Unit
Manchester	Lesbian Sub-Committee Gay Men's Sub-Committee (Reporting to Equal Opportunities Committee) Majority Co-optees	4 2 lesbians 2 gay men	Equal Opportunities Unit
Southampton	Standing Advisory Committee on Lesbian and Gay Rights (Reporting to Equal Opportunities Committee) Majority Co-optees	—	—

Appendix B: Interviews

Below is a list of people who were interviewed for this book and the positions then held during the period covered. The interviews were conducted between 1990 and 1993.

Manchester City Council

Paul Fairweather, Gay Men's Officer
Paul Hinshaw, Gay Men's Officer
John Nicholson, Labour Councillor, Member Gay Men's Sub-Committee
Chris Root, Lesbian Issues Officer
Marilyn Taylor, Labour Councillor, Member Equal Opportunities Committee
Nottingham City Council

Jo Fraser, Equal Opportunities Officer (Lesbian Issues)
Harry Joshua, Co-ordinator Equal Opportunities Unit
Richard McCance, Labour Councillor, Chair Gay and Lesbian Sub-Committee

Camden Borough Council

Emmy Doye, Co-optee Camden Women's Committee
Sandra Plummer, Labour Councillor, Chair Lesbian and Gay Committee
Jane Skeates, Lesbian and Gay Unit Officer

Haringey Borough Council

Ron Bell, Conservative Councillor, Member Lesbian and Gay Sub-Committee
Vince Gillespie, Labour Councillor, Chair Lesbian and Gay Sub-Committee, Member of Positive Images
Bernie Grant, Labour Councillor, Leader of Council
Bob Harris, Labour Councillor, Chair Education Committee, Member Lesbian and Gay Sub-Committee
Savi Hensman, Co-optee Lesbian and Gay Sub-Committee, community activist
Steve King, Labour Councillor, Deputy and (subsequently) Leader of Council
Soreh Levy, Lesbian and Gay Unit Officer (Policy)
Femi Otitoju, Lesbian and Gay Unit Officer (Training)

Islington Borough Council

Paul Barnett, Arts and Grants Officer
Robert Crossman, Labour Councillor, Chair Gay and Lesbian Sub-Committee
David Dawson, Co-optee Gay and Lesbian Sub-Committee
Stan Marshall, Borough Librarian

Lambeth Borough Council

Linda Bellos, Labour Councillor, Leader of Council
Esther Leeves, Labour Councillor, Member (later Chair) Lesbian and Gay
    Working Party
Graham Nicholas, Labour Councillor, Chair Lesbian and Gay Working Party
Rachel Webb, Labour Councillor, Member Lesbian and Gay Working Party

Others

Lynn Alderson, Head Leeds City Council Equal Opportunities Unit
Linda Arch, Member of Positive Images
Debby Epstein, Birmingham Labour Party
Patrick Hall, Chair Leeds NALGO Equal Opportunities Committee
Ellen Kelly, Edinburgh City Council Women's Unit
Ken Livingstone, Leader GLC
Anne Matthews, Leader Southwark Council
Margaret McGregor, Chair Edinburgh City Council Women's Committee
Jan Parker, ALA Lesbian and Gay Officer
Sheila Rushforth, Birmingham City Council Women's Officer
Anita Southwell, NALGO Activist
Peter Tatchell, Gay Activist

Bibliography

Adam, B. (1987) *The Rise of a Gay and Lesbian Movement*, Boston: Twayne.

Adams, M.L. (1989) 'There's no place like home: On the place of identity in feminist politics', *Feminist Review* 31:22–33.

Althusser, L. (1971) *Lenin and Philosophy and Other Essays*, London: New Left Books.

Altman, D. (1971) *Homosexual: Oppression and liberation*, Sydney: Angus and Robertson.

Altman, D. (1980) 'What changed in the seventies?' in Gay Left Collective (eds) *Homosexuality: Power and politics*, London: Allison and Busby.

Altman, D. (1989) 'AIDS and the reconceptualisation of homosexuality' in D. Altman et al. (eds) *Which Homosexuality?*, London: Gay Men's Press.

Amos, V. and Parmar, P. (1984) 'Challenging imperial feminism', *Feminist Review* 17:3–20.

Ang, I. (1991) *Desperately Seeking the Audience*, London: Routledge.

Association of Metropolitan Authorities (AMA), (1988) *The Organisation and Management of Equalities Policies*, London: AMA.

Baaden, J. (1991) 'Sells papers, ruins lives: Homophobia in the media' in T. Kaufmann and P. Lincoln (eds) *High Risk Lives: Lesbian and gay politics after the clause*, Bridport: Prism.

Ball, W. and Solomos, J. (eds) (1990) *Race and Local Politics*, Basingstoke: Macmillan.

Barrett, M. (1980) *Women's Oppression Today*, London: New Left Books.

Barrett, M. (1991) *The Politics of Truth*, Cambridge: Polity.

Barrett, S. and Fudge, C. (eds) (1981) *Policy and Action*, London: Methuen.

Barrett, S. and Fudge, C. (1981) 'Examining the policy-action relationship' in S. Barrett and C. Fudge (eds) *Policy and Action*, London: Methuen.

Barrett, S. and Hill, M. (1986) 'Policy, bargaining and structure in implementation theory' in M. Goldsmith (ed.) *New Research in Central-local Relations*, Aldershot: Gower.

Beetham, D. (1987) *Bureaucracy*, Milton Keynes: Open University Press.

Ben-Tovim, G. et al. (1986) *The Local Politics of Race*, Basingstoke: Macmillan.

Bhavnani, K. and Coulson, M. (1986) 'Transforming socialist-feminism: The challenge of racism', *Feminist Review* 23:81–92.

Birch, K. (1980) 'The politics of autonomy' in Gay Left Collective (eds)

Homosexuality: Power and politics, London: Allison and Busby.

Blanchford, G. (1981) 'Male dominance and the gay world' in K. Plummer (ed.) *The Making of the Modern Homosexual*, London: Hutchinson.

Blunkett, D. and Jackson, K. (1987) *Democracy in Crisis*, London: Hogarth.

Boddy, M. and Fudge, C. (eds) (1984) *Local Socialism?*, London: Macmillan.

Bondi, L. and Peake, L. (1988) 'Gender and the city: Urban politics revisited', in J. Little et al. (eds) *Women in Cities*, Basingstoke: Macmillan.

Bouchier, D. (1983) *The Feminist Challenge*, London: Macmillan.

Bridges, L. et al. (1987) *Legality and Local Politics*, Avebury: Aldershot.

Brittan, A. and Maynard, M. (1984) *Sexism, Racism and Oppression*, Oxford: Basil Blackwell.

Brownhill, S. and Halford, S. (1990) 'Understanding women's involvement in local politics', *Political Geography Quarterly* 7:396–414.

Buci-Glucksmann, C. (1980) *Gramsci and the State*, London: Lawrence and Wishart.

Burch, M. and Wood, B. (1983) *Public Policy in Britain*, Oxford: Martin Robertson.

Burrell, G. and Hearn, J. (1989) 'The sexuality of organization' in J. Hearn et al. (eds) *The Sexuality of Organization*, Los Angeles: Sage.

Butcher, H. et al. (eds) (1990) *Local Government and Thatcherism*, London: Routledge.

Butler, J. (1990) *Gender Trouble: Feminism and the subversion of identity*, New York: Routledge.

Button, S. (1984) *Women's Committees: A study of gender and local government policy formation* (SAUS Working Paper 45).

Campbell, B. (1987) 'A feminist sexual politics: Now you see it, now you don't' in Feminist Review (eds) *Sexuality: A reader*, London: Virago.

Cant, B. (1986) 'Outsiders and citizens', [unpublished].

Cant, B. (1988) 'Normal channels' in B. Cant and S. Hemmings (eds) *Radical Records: Thirty years of lesbian and gay history*, London: Routledge.

Cant, B. (1991) 'The limits of tolerance?' in T. Kaufmann and P. Lincoln (eds) *High Risk Lives: Lesbian and gay politics after the clause*, Bridport: Prism.

Cant, B. and S. Hemmings (eds) (1988) *Radical Records: Thirty years of lesbian and gay history*, London: Routledge.

Castells, M. (1977) *The Urban Question*, London: Edward Arnold.

Castells, M. (1983) *The City and the Grassroots*, London: Edward Arnold.

Chitty, C. (1989) *Towards a New Education System: The victory of the moral right?*, Sussex: Falmer Press.

Clark, G. and Dear, M. (1984) *State Apparatus: Structures and language of legitimacy*, London: Allen & Unwin.

Clark, W. (1987) 'The dyke, the feminist and the devil' in Feminist Review (eds) *Sexuality: A reader*, London: Virago.

Cockburn, C. (1977) *The Local State*, London: Pluto Press.

Cockburn, C. (1988) 'Masculinity, the left, and feminism' in R. Chapman and J. Rutherford (eds) *Male Order: Unwrapping masculinity*, London: Lawrence and Wishart.

Cohen, D. and Dyer, R. (1980) 'The politics of gay culture' in Gay Left Collective (eds) *Homosexuality: Power and politics*, London: Allison and Busby.

Cohen, S. (1972) *Folk Devils and Moral Panics: The creation of the mods and rockers*, London: Granada.

Cohen, S. and Young, J. (eds) (1973) *The Manufacture of News: Deviance, social problems and the mass media*, London: Constable.

Collins, P. (1990) *Black Feminist Thought*, Cambridge: Unwin Hyman.

Collins, R. (1986) 'Seeing is believing: The ideology of naturalism' in J. Corner (ed.) *Documentary and the Mass Media*, London: Edward Arnold.

Connell, R. (1987) *Gender and Power*, Cambridge: Polity.

Cooper, D. (1989) 'Positive images in Haringey: A struggle for identity' in C. Jones and P. Mahony (eds) *Learning our Lines*, London: Women's Press.

Cooper, D. (1991) 'The future of equal opportunities work', *Everywoman* 71:16-17.

Cooper, D. (1993) 'An engaged state: Sexuality, governance and the potential for change', *Journal of Law and Society*, 20, 3, 1993. Reprinted (with different conclusion) in Joe Bristow and Angie Wilson (eds) *Activating Theory*, London: Lawrence and Wishart.

Cooper, D. (1994) 'Productive, relational and everywhere: Conceptualising power and resistance within foucauldian feminism', *Sociology*, [forthcoming].

Cooper, D. (1995) *Power in Struggle*, Buckingham: Open University Press [forthcoming].

Cooper, D. and Herman, D. (1991) 'Getting the family "right": Legislating heterosexuality in Britain, 1986-1990', *Canadian Journal of Family Law* 10:41-78.

Costigan, R. and Thomas, P. (1990) *Promoting Homosexuality: Section 28 of the Local Government Act 1988*, Cardiff: Cardiff Law School.

Cox, A. et al. (1985) *Power in Capitalist Society*, Brighton: Wheatsheaf Books.

Coyle, A. (1989) 'The limits of change: Local government and equal opportunities for women', *Public Administration* 67:39-50.

Crewe, I. and Searing, D. (1988) 'Ideological change in the British conservative party', *American Political Science Review*, 82:361-84.

D'Emilio, J. (1983) 'Capitalism and gay identity' in A. Snitow et al. (eds) *Powers of Desire*, New York: Monthly Review Press.

Dale, R. (1989) *The State and Education Policy*, Milton Keynes: Open University Press.

David, M. (1986) 'Moral and maternal: The family in the right' in R. Levitas (ed.) *The Ideology of the New Right*, Cambridge: Polity.

Davis, M. (1992) *Sexual Politics, Gay Rights and the Labour Party 1967-91*, MSC Thesis [Birbeck College, Unpublished].

Dearlove, J. (1973) *The Politics of Policy in Local Government*, London: Cambridge University Press.

Derbyshire, P. (1980) 'Sects and sexuality: Trotskyism and the politics of homosexuality' in Gay Left Collective (eds) *Homosexuality: Power and politics*, London: Allison and Busby.

Dickey, J. (1987) 'Heterosexism and the lesbian image in the press' in K. Davies et al. (eds) *Out of Focus: Writings on women and the media*, London: Women's Press.

Dixon, J. (1988) 'Separatism: A look back in anger' in B. Cant and S. Hemmings (eds) *Radical Records: Thirty years of lesbian and gay history*, London: Routledge.

Dixon, J. et al. (1989) 'North London young lesbian group: Specialist work within the youth service' in C. Jones and P. Mahony (eds) *Learning Our Lines: Sexuality and social control in education*, London: Women's Press.

Dunleavy, P. (1980) *Urban Political Analysis*, London: Macmillan.

Dunleavy, P. (1981) *The Politics of Mass Housing in Britain, 1945-1975*, Oxford: Clarendon.

Dunleavy, P. (1984) 'The limits to local government' in M. Boddy and C. Fudge (eds) *Local Socialism?*, London: Macmillan.

Dunleavy, P. and O'Leary, B. (1987) *Theories of the State: The politics of liberal democracy*, Basingstoke: Macmillan.

Durant, R. and Diehl, P. (1989) 'Agendas, alternatives and public policy: Lessons from the U.S. foreign policy arena', *Journal of Public Policy* 9:179-205.

Durham, M. (1989) 'The Thatcher government and "the moral right"' *Parliamentary Affairs*, 42:58-71.

Durham, M. (1991) *Sex and Politics*, Basingstoke: Macmillan.

Dworkin, A. (1983) *Right-wing Women*, London: Women's Press.

Dye, T. (1984) *Understanding Public Policy*, Englewood Cliffs: Prentice-Hall.

Dyer, R. (1981) 'Getting over the rainbow: Identity and pleasure in gay cultural politics' in G. Bridges and R. Brunt (eds) *Silver Linings*, London: Lawrence and Wishart.

Eagleton, T. (1991) *Ideology: An introduction*, London: Verso.

Eatwell, R. and O'Sullivan, N. (eds) (1989) *The Nature of the Right*, London: Pinter.

Edelman, M. (1988) *Constructing the Political Spectacle*, Chicago: University of Chicago Press.

Edwards, J. (1988–1989) 'Local government women's committees', *Critical Social Policy* 24:50–64.

Eisenstein, Z. (1981) *The Radical Future of Liberal Feminism*, New York: Longman.

Eisenstein, Z. (1984) *Feminism and Sexual Equality*, New York: Monthly Review Press.

Eisenstein, Z. (1987) 'Liberalism, feminism and the Reagan state: The neoconservative assault on (sexual) equality' in R. Miliband (ed.) *Socialist Register*, London: Merlin.

Eisenstein, Z. (1988) *The Female Body and the Law*, Berkeley: University of California Press.

Elcock, H. (1981) 'Tradition and change in Labour Party politics', *Political Studies* 29:439–447.

Evans, D. T. (1989/90) 'Section 28: law, myth and paradox', *Critical Social Policy*, 27:73–95.

Evans, D. T. (1993) *Sexual Citizenship: The material construction of sexualities*, London: Routledge.

Feminist Review (eds) *Sexuality: A reader*, London: Virago.

Ferguson, A. et al. (1984) 'The feminist sexuality debates', *Signs* 11:106–125.

Ferguson, K. (1984) *The Feminist Case Against Bureaucracy*, Philadelphia: Temple University Press.

Ferguson, K. (1987) 'Work, text and act in discourses of organisation', *Women and Politics*, 7:1–21.

Findlay, S. (1987) 'Facing the state: The politics of the women's movement reconsidered' in H. Maroney and M. Luxton (eds) *Feminism and Political Economy*, Toronto: Methuen.

Findlay, S. (1988) 'Feminist struggles with the Canadian state', *Resources for Feminist Research* 17:5–9.

Fishkin, J. (1987) 'Liberty versus equal opportunity' in E. Paul et al. (eds) *Equal Opportunity*, Oxford: Basil Blackwell.

Fiske, J. (1987) 'British cultural studies and television' in R. Allen (ed.) *Channels of Discourse*, Chapel Hill: University of North Carolina Press.

Fiske, J. (1989) 'Moments of television: Neither the text nor the audience' in E. Seiter et al. (eds) *Remote Control*, London: Routledge.

Flannery, K. and Roelofs, S. (1984) 'Local government women's committees' in J. Holland (ed.) *Feminist Action*, London: Battle Axe.

Florig, D. (1986) 'The concept of equal opportunity in the analysis of social welfare policy', *Polity* 18:392–407.

Flynn, N. (1989) 'The new right and social policy', *Policy and Politics* 17:97–109.

Foote, J.S. (1990) *Television Access and Political Power*, New York: Praeger.

Foucault, M. (1984) *The History of Sexuality*, London: Penguin Books.

Fox Piven, F. (1984) 'Women and the state: Ideology, power and the welfare state', *Socialist Review* 14:11–19.

Franzway, S. et al. (1989) *Staking a Claim: Feminism, bureaucracy and the state*, Cambridge: Polity Press.

Frye, M. (1983) *The Politics of Reality: Essays in feminist theory*, Trumansberg: Crossing.

Fudge, C. (1981) 'Winning an election and gaining control: The formulation and implementation of a local political manifesto' in S. Barrett and C. Fudge (eds) *Policy and Action*, London: Methuen.

Galtung, J. and Ruge, M. (1981) 'Structuring and selecting news' in S. Cohen and J. Young (eds) *The Manufacture of News*, London: Constable.

Gay Left

Gay Left Collective (eds) (1980) *Homosexuality: Power and politics*, London: Allison and Busby.

Gilroy, P. (1990) 'The end of anti-racism' in W. Ball and J. Solomos (eds) *Race and Local Politics*, Basingstoke: Macmillan.

Gittins, D. (1985) *The Family in Question*, Basingstoke: Macmillan.

Glasgow University Media Group (1976) *Bad News*, London: Routledge and Kegan Paul.

Glasgow University Media Group (1980) *More Bad News*, London: Routledge and Kegan Paul.

Glasgow University Media Group (1982) *Really Bad News*, London: Writers and Readers.

Goldsmith, M. (1986) *New Research in Central-local Relations*, Aldershot: Gower.

Goldsmith, M. (1990) 'Local autonomy: Theory and practice' in D.S. King and J. Pierre (eds) *Challenges to Local Government*, London: Sage.

Goodwin, A. (1990) 'TV news: Striking the right balance' in A. Goodwin and G. Whannel (eds) *Understanding Television*, London: Routledge.

Gordon, I. and Whiteley, P. (1979) 'Social class and political attitudes: The case of Labour councillors', *Political Studies* 27:99–113.

Goss, L. (1989) 'Out of the mainstream: Sexual minorities and the mass media' in E. Seiter et al. (eds) *Remote Control*, London: Routledge.

Goss, S. (1984) 'Women's initiatives in local government' in M. Boddy and C. Fudge (eds) *Local Socialism?*, London: Macmillan.

Gottdiener, M. (1987) *The Decline of Urban Politics*, Newbury Park: Sage.

Greenwood, R. (1987) 'Managerial strategies in local government', *Public Administration* 65:295–312.

Greer, J. (1986-7) 'The political economy of the local state', *Politics and Society* 15:513–537.

Gross, B. (1987) 'Real equality of opportunity' in E. Paul (ed.) *Equal Opportunities*, Oxford: Basil Blackwell.

Gyford, J. (1985) *The Politics of Local Socialism*, London: George Allen & Unwin.

Gyford, J. et al. (1989) *The Changing Politics of Local Government*, London: Unwin Hyman.

Hajer, M. (1989) *City Politics: Hegemonic projects and discourse*, Avebury: Gower.

Hale, M. and Kelly, R.M. (1989) 'Gender, democracy and representative bureaucracies' in M. Hale and R.M. Kelly (eds) *Gender, Bureaucracy and Democracy: Careers and equal opportunities in the public sector*, Connecticut: Greenwood.

Halford, S. (1988) 'Women's initiatives in local government...where do they come from and where are they going?', *Policy and Politics* 16:251–9.

Halford, S. (1992) 'Feminist change in a patriarchal organisation: The experience of women's initiatives in local government and implications for feminist perspectives on state institutions', in M. Savage and A. Witz (eds) *Gender and Bureaucracy*, Oxford: Blackwell.

Hall, M. (1987) 'Private experiences in the public domain: Lesbians in organisations' in J. Hearn et al. (eds) *The Sexuality of Organisations*, London: Sage.

Hall, S. (1973a) 'A world at one with itself' in S. Cohen and J. Young (eds) *The Manufacture of News: Deviance, social problems and the mass media*, London: Constable.

Hall, S. (1973b) 'The determination of news photographs' in S. Cohen and J. Young (eds) *The Manufacture of News: Deviance, social problems and the mass media*, London: Constable.

Hall, S. (1985) 'Signification, representation, ideology: Althusser and the post-structuralist debates', *Critical Studies in Mass Communication* 2:91–114.

Hall, S. (1988) *The Hard Road to Renewal*, London: Verso.

Harne, L. (1988) 'From 1971: Reinventing the wheel' in A. Sebestyen (ed.) *'68 '78 '88: From women's liberation to feminism*, Bridport: Prism.

Harriss, K. (1989) 'New alliances: Socialist-feminism in the eighties', *Feminist Review* 31:34–54.

Hearn, J. (1987) *The Gender of Oppression: Men, masculinity and the critique of marxism*, Brighton: Wheatsheaf.

Hearn, J. and Parkin, W. (1987) *'Sex' at 'Work': The power and paradox of organisation sexuality*, Brighton: Wheatsheaf.

Hearn, J. et al. (eds) (1989) *The Sexuality of Organization*, Los Angeles: Sage.

Held, D. (1989) *Political Theory and the Modern State*, Cambridge: Polity.

Hemmings, S. (1980) 'Horrific practices: How lesbians were presented in the newspapers of 1978' in Gay Left Collective (eds) *Homosexuality: Power and politics*, London: Allison and Busby.

Herek, G. (1987) 'On heterosexual masculinity' in M. Kimmel (ed.) *Changing men*, London: Sage.

Herman, D. (1990) 'Are we family?: Lesbian rights and women's liberation', *Osgoode Hall Law Journal* 28:789–815.

Herman, D. (1993) 'Beyond the rights debate', *Social and Legal Studies*, 2, 25–43.

Herman, D. (1994) *Rights of Passage: Struggles for lesbian and gay legal equality*, Toronto: University of Toronto Press.

Hoggett, P. (1991) 'A new management in the public sector?', *Policy and Politics* 19:243–256.

Hogwood, B. and Gunn, L. (1984) *Policy Analysis for the Real World*, Oxford: Oxford University Press.

Holland, P. (1988) 'Still revolting' in A. Sebestyen (ed.) *'68 '78 '88: From women's liberation to feminism*, Bridport: Prism.

Holub, R. (1984) *Reception Theory*, New York: Methuen.

Hunt, A. (1985) 'The ideology of law: Advances and problems in recent applications of the concept of ideology to the analysis of law', *Law and Society Review* 19:11–37.

Hurtado, A. (1989) 'Relating to privilege', *Signs* 14:833–855.

Isaac, J. (1990) 'The new right and the moral society', *Parliamentary Affairs* 43:209–226.

Jackson, M. (1984) 'Sexology and the social construction of male sexuality' in L. Coveney et al. (eds) *The Sexuality Papers*, London: Hutchinson.

Jalbert, P. (1983) 'Some constructs for analysing news' in H. Davis and P. Walton (eds) *Language, Image, and Media*, Oxford: Basil Blackwell.

Jeffery-Poulter, S. (1991) *Peers, Queers and Commons*, London: Routledge.

Jeffreys, S. (1990) *Anti-climax*, London: Women's Press.

Jennings, R. (1977) *Education and Politics: Policy-making in local education authorities*, London: Batsford.

Jessop, B. (1982) *The Capitalist State*, Oxford: Martin Robertson.

Jessop, B. (1990) *State Theory*, Cambridge: Polity.

Jones, K. (1989) *Right Turn: The conservative revolution in education*, London: Hutchinson Radius.

Jones, C. and Mahoney, P. (eds) (1989) *Learning Our Lines: Sexuality and social control in education*, London: Women's Press.

Jorstad, E. (1987) *The New Christian Right, 1981–1988*, Lewiston: Edwin Mellen.

Kaufmann, T. and Lincoln, P. (eds) (1991) *High Risk Lives: Lesbian and gay politics after the clause*, Bridport: Prism.

Kavanagh, D. (1987) *Thatcherism and British Politics*, Oxford: Oxford University Press.

King, D. (1988) 'Multiple jeopardy, multiple consciousness: The context of Black feminist ideology', *Signs* 14:42–72.

King, D.S. (1989) 'Political centralisation and state interests in Britain', *Comparative Political Studies* 21:467–494.

King, D.S. and Pierre, J. (eds) (1990) *Challenges to Local Government*, London: Sage.

King, R. (1986) *The State in Modern Society*, Basingstoke: Macmillan.

Kinsman, G. (1987) 'Men loving men: The challenge of gay liberation' in M. Kaufman (ed.) *Beyond Patriarchy*, Toronto: Oxford University Press.

Kitching, G. (1983) *Re-thinking Socialism*, London: Methuen.

Kitzinger, C. (1987) *The Social Construction of Lesbianism*, London: Sage.

Klatch, R. (1987) *Women of the New Right*, Philadelphia: Temple University Press.

Kogan, D. and Kogan, M. (1983) *The Battle for the Labour Party*, London: Fontana.

Kress, G. (1983) 'Linguistic and ideological transformations in news reporting' in H. Davis and P. Walton (eds) *Language, Image and Media*, Oxford: Basil Blackwell.

Laffin, M. (1986) *Professionalism and Policy*, Aldershot: Gower.

Lansley, S. et al. (1989) *Councils in Conflict: The rise and fall of the municipal left*, Basingstoke: Macmillan.

Leach, S. (1989) 'Strengthening local democracy' in J. Stewart and G. Stoker (eds) *The Future of Local Government*, Basingstoke: Macmillan.

Levitas, R. (ed) (1986) *The Ideology of the New Right*, Cambridge: Polity Press.

Lewis, D. (1984) 'Conclusion: Improving implementation practice' in D. Lewis and H. Wallace (eds) *Policies into Practice*, London: Heinemann.

Lipsky, M. (1980) *Street Level Bureaucracy*, New York: Russell Sage Foundation.

Livingstone, S. (1990) 'Interpreting a television narrative: How different viewers see a story', *Journal of Communication* 40:72–85.

London Labour Briefing

London Gay Teenage Group. (1984) *Something to Tell You*, London: London Gay Teenage Group.

Lumsden, I. (1984) 'Sexuality and the state: The politics of 'normal' sexuality', *Atkinson Review of Canadian Studies* 1:3–9.

Macdonnell, D. (1986) *Theories of Discourse*, Oxford: Basil Blackwell.

Mackinnon, C. (1982) 'Feminism, marxism, method and the state: An agenda for theory', *Signs* 7:515–544.

Magnusson, W. (1985) 'Urban politics and the local state', *Studies in Political Economy* 19:111–42.

Maroney, H. (1988) 'Using Gramsci for women: Feminism and the Quebec state, 1960–1980', *Resources for Feminist Research* 17:26–30.

Marshall, B. (1989) 'Gays and Marxism' in S. Shepherd and M. Wallis (eds) *Coming on Strong*, London: Unwin Hyman.

Marshall, J. (1980) 'The politics of tea and sympathy' in Gay Left Collective (eds) *Homosexuality: Power and Politics*, London: Allison and Busby.

Marshall, J. (1981) 'Pansies, perverts and macho men: Changing conceptions of male homosexuality' in K. Plummer (ed.) *The Making of the Modern Homosexual*, London: Hutchinson.

Mason, D. (1990) 'Competing conceptions of "fairness" and the formulation and implementation of EOPs' in W. Ball and J. Solomos (eds) *Race and Local Politics*, Basingstoke: Macmillan.

Mather, G. (1989) 'Thatcherism and local government' in J. Stewart and G. Stoker (eds) *The Future of Local Government*, Basingstoke: Macmillan.

Maynard-Moody, S. et al. (1990) 'Street-wise social policy: Resolving the dilemma of street-level influence and successful implementation', *Western Political Quarterly* 43:833–47.

McCaskell, T. (1988) 'The bath raids and gay politics' in F. Cunningham et al. (eds) *Social Movements/Social Change: The political practice of organising*, Toronto: Between the Lines.

McGarrell, E. et al. (1990) 'Obstacles to seemingly simple reform: A case study of bail reform', *Policy Studies Review* 9:433–43.

McIntosh, M. (1978) 'The state and the oppression of women' in A. Kuhn and A. Wolpe (eds) *Feminism and Materialism*, London: Routledge and Kegan Paul.

Media Research Group. (1987) *Media Coverage of London Councils*, London: Goldmith's College.

Mercer, K. (1990) 'Welcome to the jungle: Identity and diversity in post-modern politics' in J. Rutherford (ed.) *Identity: Community, Culture, Difference*, London: Lawrence and Wishart.

Mercer, K. and Julien, I. (1988) 'Race, sexual politics and Black masculinity' in R. Chapman and J. Rutherford (eds) *Male Order: Unwrapping Masculinity*, London: Lawrence and Wishart.

Miliband, R. (1978) *Marxism and Politics*, Oxford: Oxford University Press.

Miliband, R. (1984) *Capitalist Democracy in Britain*, Oxford: Oxford University Press.

Moore, C. (1991) 'Reflections on the new local political economy: Resignation, resistance and reform', *Policy and Politics* 19:73–85.

Morgan, P. (1981) 'From battered wife to programme client: The state's shaping of social problems', *Kapitalistate*, 9:17–39.

Morley, D. (1983) 'Cultural transformations: The politics of resistance' in H. Davis and P. Walton (eds) *Language, Image and Media*, Oxford: Basil Blackwell.

Morley, D. (1986) *Family Television, Cultural Power and Domestic Leisure*, London: Comedia Publishing Group.

Morley, D. (1989) 'Changing paradigms in audience studies' in E. Seiter et al. (eds) *Remote Control*, London: Routledge.

Mort, F. (1980) 'Sexuality: Regulation and contestation' in Gay Left Collective (eds) *Homosexuality: Power and politics*, London: Allison and Busby.

Mort, F. (1985) 'Purity, feminism and the state: Sexuality and moral politics, 1880–1914' in M. Langan and B. Schwarz (eds) *Crisis in the British State*, London: Hutchinson.

Mouffe, C. (1981) 'Hegemony and ideology in Gramsci' in T. Bennett et al. (eds) *Culture, Ideology and Social Process*, London: Batsford.

Murdock, G. (1973) 'Political deviance: The press presentation of a militant mass demonstration' in S. Cohen and J. Young (eds) *The Manufacture of News: Deviance, social problems and the mass media*, London: Constable.

Nain, G. (1991) 'Black women, sexism and racism: Black or anti-racist feminism?', *Feminist Review* 37:1–22.

Nanton, P. and Fitzgerald, M. (1990) 'Race policies in local government: Boundaries or thresholds' in W. Ball and J. Solomos (eds) *Race and Local Politics*,

Basingstoke: Macmillan.

Nelson, A. (1990) 'Equal opportunities: Dilemmas, contradictions, white men and class', *Critical Social Policy* 28:25–42.

Newton, K. (1976) *Second City Politics*, Oxford: Oxford University Press.

Ng, R. et al. (1990) 'Community, class struggle and state formation' in R. Ng et al. (eds) *Community Organising and the State*, Toronto: Garamond Press.

Nickel, J. (1987) 'Equal opportunity in a pluralist society' in E. Paul et al. (eds) *Equal Opportunity*, Oxford: Basil Blackwell.

Nisbet, R. (1986) *Conservatism*, Milton Keynes: Open University Press.

O'Donovan, K. (1985) *Sexual Divisions in Law*, London: Weidenfeld and Nicolson.

O'Sullivan, N. (1989) 'The new right: The quest for a civil philosophy in Europe and America' in R. Eatwell and N. O'Sullivan (eds) *The Nature of the Right*, London: Pinter.

Onlywomen Press (eds) (1981) *Love Your Enemy?*, London: Onlywomen.

Otitoju, F. (1988) 'The should we, shouldn't we? debate' in B. Cant and S. Hemmings (eds) *Radical Records: Thirty years of lesbian and gay history*, London: Routledge.

Ousley, H. (1984) 'Local authority race initiatives' in M. Boddy and C. Fudge (eds) *Local Socialism?*, London: Macmillan.

Ousley, H. (1990) 'Resisting institutional change' in W. Ball and J. Solomos (eds) *Race and Local Politics*, Basingstoke: Macmillan.

Out

Parker, J. (1988) 'No going back' in B. Cant and S. Hemmings (eds) *Radical Records: Thirty years of lesbian and gay history*, London: Routledge.

Paul, E. (1987) *Equal Opportunity*, Oxford: Basil Blackwell.

Pearce, F. (1973) 'How to be immoral and ill, pathetic and dangerous, all at the same time: Mass media and the homosexual' in S. Cohen and J. Young (eds) *The Manufacture of News: Deviance, social problems and the mass media*, London: Constable.

Perrigo, S. (1986) 'Socialist-feminism and the Labour Party: Some experiences from Leeds', *Feminist Review* 23:101–8.

Petchesky, R. (1985) *Abortion and Women's Choice*, Boston: Northeastern University Press.

Pfeffer, J. (1981) *Power in Organisations*, London: Pitman.

Pierre, J. (1990) 'Assessing local autonomy' in D.S. King and J. Pierre (eds) *Challenges to Local Government*, London: Sage.

Plummer, K. (ed.) (1981) *The Making of the Modern Homosexual*, London: Hutchinson.

Plummer, K. (ed.) (1992) *Modern Homosexualities*, London: Routledge.

Poulantzas, N. (1973) *Political Power and Social Classes*, London: New Left Books.

Poulantzas, N. (1978) *State, Power, Socialism*, London: New Left Books.

Radway, J. (1987) *Reading the Romance*, London: Verso.

Randall, M. (1988) 'Feminism and the state: Questions for theory and practice', *Resources for Feminist Research* 17:10–16.

Randall, V. (1982) *Women and Politics*, London: Macmillan.

Randall, V. (1991) 'Feminism and political analysis', *Political Studies* 39:513–532.

Ranson, S. et al. (1986) 'Nationalising the government of education' in M. Goldsmith (ed.) *New Research in Central-local Relations*, Gower: Aldershot.

Rhodes, R. (1986) 'Power dependence: Theories of central-local relations' in M. Goldsmith (ed.) *New Research in Central-local Relations*, Gower: Aldershot.

Rich, A. (1981) *Compulsory Heterosexuality and Lesbian Existence*, London: Onlywoman.

Riddiough, C. (1981) 'Socialism, feminism and gay/lesbian liberation' in L. Sargent (ed.) *The Unhappy Marriage of Marxism and Feminism*, London: Pluto.

Roe, E. (1989) 'Narrative analysis for the policy analyst: A case study of the 1980–1982 medfly controversy in California', *Journal of Policy Analysis and Management*, 8:251–73.

Ross, B. (1988) 'Heterosexuals only need apply: The Secretary of State's regulation of lesbian existence', *Resources for Feminist Research* 17:35–38.

Rowbotham, S. (1989) *The Past is Before Us*, London: Pandora.

Saggar, S. (1991) 'The changing agenda of race issues in local government: The case of a London borough', *Political Studies* 39:100–21.

Salaman, G. (1980) 'Organisations as constructors of social reality' in G. Salaman and K. Thompson (eds) *Control and Ideology in Organisations*, Milton Keynes: Open University Press.

Saltzstein, G. (1985) 'Conceptualising bureaucratic responsiveness', *Administration and Society* 17:283–306.

Sanders, S. and Spraggs, S. (1989) 'Section 28 and education' in C. Jones and P. Mahoney (eds) *Learning our Lines: Sexuality and social control in education*, London: Women's Press.

Sanderson, T. (1988) 'Faltering from the closet', in B. Cant and S. Hemmings (eds), *Radical Records: Thirty years of lesbian and gay history*, London: Routledge.

Sargent, L. (ed.) (1981) *The Unhappy Marriage of Marxism and Feminism*, London: Pluto.

Saunders, P. (1979) *Urban Politics: A sociological interpretation*, Harmondsworth: Penguin.

Saunders, P. (1981a) *Social Theory and the Urban Question*, London: Hutchinson.

Saunders, P. (1981b) 'Community power, urban managerialism and the "local state"' in M. Harloe (ed.) *New Perspectives in Urban Change and Conflict*, London: Heinemann.

Saunders, P. (1984) 'Rethinking local politics' in M. Boddy and C. Fudge (eds) *Local Socialism?*, London: Macmillan.

Schattschneider, E. (1960) *The Semi-sovereign People*, New York: Holt, Rinehart and Winston.

Schreader, A. (1990) 'The state funded women's movement: A case of two political agendas' in R. Ng et al. (eds) *Community Organising and the State*, Toronto: Garamond Press.

Schwartz, N. (1984) 'Race and the allocation of public housing in Great Britain: The autonomy of the local state', *Comparative Politics* 16:205–22.

Segal, L. (1987) *Is the Future Female?*, London: Virago.

Seidel, G. (1988) 'Right-wing discourse and power: Exclusions and resistance' in G. Seidel (ed.) *The Nature of the Right: A feminist analysis of order patterns*, Philadelphia: John Benjamin's Publishing Co.

Seidel, G. and Gunther, R. (1988) '"Nation" and "family" in the British media reporting of the 'Falkland conflict' in G. Seidel (ed.) *The Nature of the Right: A feminist analysis of order patterns*, Philadelphia: John Benjamin's Publishing Company.

Seidler, V. (1989) *Rediscovering Masculinity*, London: Routledge.

Seidler, V. (1987) 'Reason, desire and male sexuality' in P. Caplan (ed.) *The Cultural Construction of Sexuality*, London: Tavistock.

Seiter, E. et al. (eds) (1989) *Remote Control*, London: Routledge.

Sellgren, J. (1987) 'Local economic development and local initiatives in the mid-1980s', *Local Government Studies* 13:51–68.

Seyd, P. (1987) *The Rise and Fall of the Labour Left*, Basingstoke: Macmillan.

Shapiro, M.J. et al. (1988) 'A discursive practices approach to collective decision-making', *International Studies Quarterly*, 32:397–419.

Shepherd, S. and Wallis, M. (eds) (1989) *Coming on Strong*, London: Unwin Hyman.

Shiers, J. (1988) 'One step to heaven?' in B. Cant and S. Hemmings (eds) *Radical Records: Thirty years of lesbian and gay history*, London: Routledge.

Shiers, J. (1980) 'Two steps forward, one step back' in Gay Left Collective (eds) *Homosexuality: Power and politics*, London: Allison and Busby.

Showstack Sassoon, A. (ed.) (1987) *Women and the State*, London: Hutchinson.

Smart, C. (1989) *Feminism and the Power of Law*, London: Routledge.

Smith, L. and Jones, D. (eds) (1981) *Deprivation, Participation, and Community Action*, London: Routledge and Kegan Paul.

Snitow, A. et al. (eds) (1983) *Powers of Desire*, New York: Monthly Review Press.

Solomos, J. (1989) 'Equal opportunities policies and racial inequality: The role of public policy', *Public Administration* 67:79–93.

Solomos, J. and Ball, W. (1990) 'New initiatives and the possibilities of reform' in W. Ball and J. Solomos (eds) *Race and Local Politics*, Basingstoke: Macmillan.

Spare Rib

Spry, C. (1991) 'Out of the box' in T. Kaufmann and P. Lincoln (eds) *High Risk Lives: Lesbian and gay politics after the clause*, Bridport: Prism.

Stewart, J. (1983) *Local Government: The conditions of local choice*, London: Allen and Unwin.

Stoker, G. (1989) 'Creating a local government for a post-fordist society: The Thatcherite project?' in G. Stoker and S. Leach (eds) *The Future of Local Government*, Basingstoke: Macmillan.

Stoker, G. (1988) *The Politics of Local Government*, Basingstoke: Macmillan.

Sumner, C. (1979) *Reading Ideologies*, London: Academic.

Sumner, L. (1987) 'Positive sexism' in E. Paul (ed.) *Equal Opportunities*, Oxford: Basil Blackwell.

Tatchell, P. (1983) *The Battle for Bermondsey*, London: Heretic Books.

Thompson, D. (1985) *Flaws in the Social Fabric: Homosexuals and society in Sydney*, London: George Allen and Unwin.

Thompson, J. (1984) *Studies in the Theory of Ideology*, Cambridge: Polity.

Thorneycroft, B. et al. (1988) 'The liberation of affection' in B. Cant and S. Hemmings (eds) *Radical Records: Thirty years of lesbian and gay history*, London: Routledge.

Tobin, A. (1990) 'Lesbianism and the Labour Party: The GLC experience', *Feminist Review* 34:56–66.

Vance, C. (1989) 'Social construction theory: Problems in the history of sexuality' in D. Altman et al. (eds) *Which Homosexuality?*, London: Gay Men's Press.

Wainwright, H. (1987) *Labour: A tale of two parties*, London: Hogarth.

Walby, S. (1990) *Theorising Patriarchy*, Oxford: Basil Blackwell.

Wallis, M. (1989) 'Gramsci the goalie: Reflections in the bath on gays, the Labour Party and socialism' in S. Shepherd and M. Wallis (eds) *Coming on Strong*, London: Unwin Hyman.

Watney, S. (1980) 'The ideology of GLF' in Gay Left Collective (eds) *Homosexuality: Power and politics*, London: Allison and Busby.

Watson, S. (1990) (ed.) *Playing the State: Australian feminist interventions*, London: Verso.

Weeks, J. (1977) *Coming Out*, London: Quartet Books.

Weeks, J. (1980) 'Capitalism and the organisation of sex' in Gay Left Collective (eds) *Homosexuality: Power and politics*, London: Allison and Busby.

Weeks, J. (1985) *Sexuality and its Discontents*, London: Routledge and Kegan Paul.

Weeks, J. (1989) 'Movements of affirmation: Sexual meanings and homosexual liberation' in K. Peiss and C. Simmon (eds) *Passion and Power: Sexuality in history*, Philadelphia: Temple University Press.

Whiteley, P. (1983) *The Labour Party in Crisis*, London: Methuen.

Wilson, E. with Weir, A. (1984) *Hidden Agendas*, London: Tavistock.

Withall, K. (1990) 'How not to tackle racism on TV', *Race and Class* 31:49–60.

Wolfe, J. (1991) 'State power and ideology in Britain: Mrs Thatcher's privatisation programme', *Political Studies* 39:237–52.

Wolman, H. and Goldsmith, M. (1990) 'Local autonomy as a meaningful concept', *Urban Affairs Quarterly* 26:3–27.

Wolpe, A. M. and Donald, J. (eds) (1983) *Is There Anyone Here From Education?*, London: Pluto Press.

Wright, E. O. (1978) *Class, Crisis and the State*, London: New Books.

Young, A. (1990) *Femininity in Dissent*, London: Routledge.

Young, K. (1990) 'Approaches to policy development in the field of equal opportunities' in W. Ball and J. Solomos (eds) *Race and Local Politics*, Basingstoke: Macmillan.

Young, K. and Connelly, N. (1984) 'Review of local authority policy after the Race Relations Act', *Local Government Studies* 10:13–25.

Index

211